THE NATURAL MYSTICS

THE NATURAL MYSTICS

Marley, Tosh, and Wailer

COLIN GRANT

W. W. NORTON & COMPANY
NEW YORK • LONDON

For information about permission to reproduce selections from this book,
write to Permissions, W. W. Norton & Company, Inc.,
500 Fifth Avenue, New York, NY 10110

For information about special discounts for bulk purchases, please contact
W. W. Norton Special Sales at specialsales@wwnorton.com or 800-233-4830

Manufacturing by Courier Westford
Production manager: Julia Druskin

Library of Congress Cataloging-in-Publication Data

Grant, Colin, 1961–
The natural mystics : Marley, Tosh, and Wailer / Colin Grant. — 1st American ed.
p. cm.
Includes bibliographical references and index.
ISBN 978-0-393-08117-6 (hardcover)
1. Reggae musicians—Jamaica—Biography. 2. Marley, Bob.
3. Tosh, Peter. 4. Wailer, Bunny. I. Title.
ML385.G78 2011
782.421646092'2—dc22
[B]
2011012323

W. W. Norton & Company, Inc.
500 Fifth Avenue, New York, N.Y. 10110
www.wwnorton.com

W. W. Norton & Company Ltd.
Castle House, 75/76 Wells Street, London W1T 3QT

1 2 3 4 5 6 7 8 9 0

For Jo

CONTENTS

PROLOGUE:
NO COUNTRY FOR OLD MEN

TWENTY-five thousand boisterous music lovers made their way to Jamaica's National Stadium in Kingston on Boxing Day, December 1990 for the Sting Festival, an event which the promoters described modestly as 'The Greatest One-Night Reggae Show on Earth'.

More than forty bands were booked to appear. The first was due to take to the stage at 6.15 p.m., but many in the crowd lingered on the outskirts hoping to catch a glimpse of the musical motorcade, especially the top acts billed as the 'Devastating Dozen', a mix of gold-toothed dancehall DJs and dreadlocked Rasta reggae stars – including Bunny Wailer, the last surviving member of the original Wailers.

The duo Ghost and Culture sparked guffaws, some taunts and good-natured banter when they rolled up to the stadium gates and emerged, chalk-faced, from a funeral casket on board a hearse. But even this stunt was outshone by the main attraction: the ragamuffin DJ Shabba Ranks. Fresh from negotiations for a million-dollar contract with CBS, 'Mr X-rated' himself arrived in a white presidential limousine, accompanied by four police outriders. To his many fans, some of whom had brought along pistols to be fired in a gun-salute, Shabba's grand entrance was not only befitting, but expected. In a few hours, armed with a microphone, he would thrust himself on stage and begin trading insults in a lyrical clash with Ninja Man, his rival for the title 'King of Jamaican Music'.[1]

Such a spectacle could not have been envisaged ten years previously at the time of Bob Marley's death from cancer. Together with Bunny

Wailer and Peter Tosh, Marley had formed the most influential reggae group of all time. Bunny Wailer struggled to come to terms with Marley's passing and, on at least one occasion, he'd had a vision that Bob Marley was still alive. He'd rushed to tell Peter Tosh the good news – that he'd seen Marley bathed in light on stage, surrounded by an adoring crowd. Tosh placed a hand on Wailer's shoulder and whispered, 'But Bob's dead. The Wailers are dead!'[2] Following the murder of Tosh in 1987, Bunny Wailer baulked at efforts to promote him as the new 'poet laureate for the oppressed'. Now he stood to the side and watched in dismay the elevation of dancehall stars who didn't 'sing in keys ... know chords or changes'. But more than this perceived lowering of musical standards, it was the DJs' embracing of the culture of 'slackness' – lewd and vulgar sexualised lyrics with a focus on 'punany' – that distressed Wailer. 'What they are bringing to the music can't work,' he told journalists. 'What the DJs are doing is destructive to themselves.' Bunny Wailer could do little to arrest the march of Jamaican culture towards a Utopia of slackness but *he* was not, and would never be, a 'punany' lyricist.[3]

The musical marathon rolled on through the night. But though the musicians kept the beat, they couldn't always keep to their allotted time. It wasn't until 5 a.m. that Bunny Wailer and his band, the Solomonics, were summoned from the green room. In front of the huge crowd, Wailer paused for the ritual he had assigned to himself over the last few years: lowering his gaze, he tried to conjure his dead compadres, Tosh and Marley, onto the stage with him. And then slowly, with a gentle quietness that was almost imperceptible at first, Bunny Wailer started to sing.

He was due to perform twenty-one songs. He started with a series of 'specials' which had not yet become reggae standards, and which, of course, bore little resemblance to the highly energised booming blast of dancehall. Later, the promoters would chide him for not being 'more sensitive to the needs of the audience, though not in a vulgar way'.[4] Elements in the auditorium were growing impatient over the tardiness of the advertised clash between the ghetto-fabulous, simulated sexual gymnastics of Shabba Ranks and the kamikaze-headscarfed Ninja Man, whose parody of gangster violence shone in the tiny Kalashnikov embellishment on his gold-capped tooth.

It took a little while for the first rumblings of discontent to reach the stage. Above the buzz and hubbub of the crowd, the occasional vaporous effusions of semi-drunken, spliffed-up wags; above the cries of cold-supper vendors, jerk-chicken men, grapenut and peanut hucksters and youths lugging crates of warm beer for sale, Bunny Wailer could discern an uglier sound. Not even to the most determined wishful thinker could belligerence be mistaken for ardour or veneration. But still there might be some small element of doubt and difficulty in divining the intent behind the growing cacophony. After all, Jamaican crowds were past masters of interaction and audience participation, both welcome and unwelcome. By Bunny Wailer's fourth song any lingering self-deception was no longer possible. The boorish elements, popping up randomly like explosive geysers, were increasingly rancorous and abusive.[5]

A medallion of the Lion of Judah adorned the fine and noble forehead of Bunny Wailer as a third eye; lovingly tended dreadlocks swept down his shoulders and back; and with his arms raised before him and hands cupped almost in prayer, he more closely resembled a mendicant than an international music star. He had begun the set in sublime communion with his fallen brothers, but his temper was disturbed by the discordant braying of a small section of the audience. The diminutive, 5-foot-3--inch star stopped singing. He began flapping his arms, gesturing to his band to put down their instruments. The jeering continued. Bunny Wailer came to the edge of the stage, his face ablaze with fury and rage. Did they not know his pedigree? Did they not feel privileged by his attendance? Shouldn't the elders of reggae (he was forty-three) be revered? Had he not helped put Jamaica on the map? Hadn't he toiled for years without recognition, made huge sacrifices? Had he not fashioned music to soothe the soul and raise the spirits? Well no more: 'I and I . . .' His litany of disbelief was interrupted.

The first bottle pierced the night air, whistled past his head and landed a few feet behind him. It acted as a release and a salvo of missiles followed, the air was thick with beer bottles, cans, rocks and stones. The dancers and band members ran for cover. For a while Bunny Wailer was immobilised. Then roadies rushed to shield him from the onslaught of yet more bottles and bricks, and ushered him from the stage.

The post-mortem began in earnest the following morning. 'Wailer Feels the Sting' screamed the *Gleaner* headline. Jamaica was 'faced with a calamity'[6] following a night which was a 'gross production in shame.'[7] In a country where the concept of respect was central to its culture, the feeling of dishonour and embarrassment was enormous. Tributes were paid to Bunny Wailer which read like obituaries. But the shock and trauma was so great that few articulated what was undeniably the case, that the bottling off stage of one of the giants of reggae marked a violent changing of the guard.

Just beneath the surface of the angry and frightened letter-writers to the *Gleaner* was the unspoken question: if reggae music had delighted and enthralled so many around the world, transformed a tiny island into a musical superpower, and given a platform to the Wailers, a trio of extraordinarily poetic and powerful natural mystics, then how could it, in the space of thirty years, rise and fall so spectacularly and end so brutally?

A cultural coup had taken place, and in decades to come the lament that 'the singers must come back' haunted the land. In the 1980s, the passing of Bob Marley and Peter Tosh had left a vacuum, and on 26 December 1990, the last remaining Wailer, the Caribbean's finest voice, had been rendered mute.

NEGRO AROUSED

TOSH, Marley and Livingston were all born in the 1940s, within a few years of each other, and during a period of extraordinary volatility in Jamaica. As the decade began, the colonial government was still reeling from the near island-wide strike which saw bloody and vicious clashes between police and protestors; from that calamity, two cousins, a shrewd barrister and a bellicose moneylender emerged to form a political alliance that ushered in universal suffrage for the black masses; soon after, the *Empire Windrush* set sail for England with its 492 passengers representing a 'Great Migration' to the Motherland; and the decade closed with Jamaicans poring over the sensational newspaper coverage of the hunt for Rhygin, the notorious two-gun killer.

There would be lasting ramifications from each of these events, but ultimately, the Frome Rebellion of April 1938 was the most bitter and defining moment of the era. Jamaica was still a colony of Britain, a part of its creaking empire. Its population of just over a million was mostly black – the descendants of the enslaved who had laboured under the driver's whip on the enormous sugar plantations of the eighteenth and nineteenth centuries. And though the island's economy was no longer wedded to one commodity, sugar was still hugely important. In 1938, Tate & Lyle had just opened a new sugar factory at Frome in the parish of Westmoreland. On 29 April, workers queuing for wages were aggrieved at the unexpectedly small amounts they received. The crowd grew belligerent and when a panicking estate manager fired a gun over their heads he sparked a storm of protest which, by its end, was to leave several dead and many more injured. Sugar estates were set ablaze, and once the flames died down, armed police approached them cautiously, as one might return to a battery of fireworks that had failed to explode and yet still might. Soldiers in tin hats advanced on protestors with bayonets fixed. In the ensuing months, the authorities careered from one emergency to the next in a perpetual state of flummox. Reason gave way to the kind of hysteria not seen on the island since the bloody slave revolts of the past. People cried out for a saviour. Thousands swarmed the harbour at Kingston on the rumour that Marcus Garvey, the exiled Black Nationalist leader, was on the high seas steaming back to help resolve the conflict. But Garvey never came.

In the 1920s and 30s the poor black population had yoked their fortunes to Garvey's; they had adored him for the magnificence of his oratory, pressed into the service of their cause and colour. Garvey, an enraged black hero, stood in opposition to the conspicuous 'greed and self-advancement of members of the [white and fair-skinned] Legislative Council' who governed Jamaica.[8] But, it might be argued that after he departed the scene, they found themselves just where they'd been *before* he arrived: at the very bottom of society. Garvey's presence, though, remained like Banquo's ghost, forever roaming the land. In Jamaica's pathological pigmentocracy, privileges continued to be dispensed relative to ever-decreasing degrees of blackness. Those who benefited did not disturb themselves with the plight of their darker-hued compatriots. 'Up until [Jamaicans] got universal adult suffrage in 1944, a black man could not be inspector of police,' recalled the journalist Vivian Durham. 'He couldn't go further than sergeant major. It would have been incredible to have a black man being a justice of the peace.' Perhaps understandably the black man cursed his lot and wished he'd been born white.[9] Frome exposed the tensions that polite society considered best left unexplored. The editors of the national newspaper, the *Gleaner*, put it succinctly out of bounds when they trumpeted: 'Colour questions are not permitted in these columns.' Even so, the paper had been happy in the past to place adverts where the unashamed premium placed on fair skin was apparent:

Wanted, twenty men and women to gather coconuts,
Creoles invited first of all,
If none available, then Coolies or Chinese.

Frome highlighted the gulf between the middle class and the great mass of black people: the chasm, for instance, between someone of Chris Blackwell's background and the three Wailers. The future record producer – a wealthy white Jamaican and descendant of the Crosse and Blackwell dynasty – was shipped to England, in order to attend Harrow, one of its grandest private schools; while Tosh, Marley and Livingston were, at best, destined for a fractured education at an elementary school.

Nothing was the same after Frome. The early lives of the young boys who would become the Wailers were defined by the fallout from that rebellion. But after the fires were dampened, the dead were buried and the smoke had cleared, there was little visual reminder of the conflagration, save for a work of art that perhaps signalled how things had changed: a statue called *Negro Aroused*.

Tosh and Marley were dead. Bunny Livingston had become a recluse, I was told. But, when he wasn't feeding his chickens or planting crops on his farm in the countryside, he might be found in Kingston. The record shops could be a reasonable place to start. Tuff Gong, named after the record label originally founded by the Wailers in the late 1960s, and which still sold old-school reggae, was the most likely venue. Inside it was dark and cavernous: the windows were permanently boarded up and there was hardly any stock. The shop seemed devoted to Bob Marley albums but there weren't very many of them; it was as if they were intended as decoration rather than for sale. There were no Bunny Wailer albums, and no sign of him. 'Check back with me in a couple of days,' said the man behind the counter. 'I know where he is right now, you know, but whether he will see you? Well . . .' He let the sentence trail off, allowing me to fill in the gaps. Dozens of people, not wanting to disappoint, said variations of the same thing.

Every day, during that first week of searching for the last remaining Wailer, I kept on passing a craggy and neglected statue which had a strangely alluring quality. One day I asked the taxi driver to stop.

My memory of *Negro Aroused* was of it stretching out to sea, down by Kingston Harbour. A sleek, solid, bare-chested black man – his head snapped back – gazes up towards the heavens. But for the gentleness of his pose, the scale of the sculpture, with its heavy muscular arms and torso, would evoke a Fascistic überman. Yesterday he was the degraded stereotype: a docile and truculent Jamaican peasant toiling on sugar estates like Frome; today he is a new man in control of his own destiny. But much more than simply savouring the broken bonds of his dependence, the subject of *Negro Aroused* is ecstatic. The artist, Edna Manley, had captured the psychic moment of his awakening to this dawn of possibility, to the realisation that he is free, and from this day forth will forever be free. 'I was trying to create a national vision,' Manley recalled when she reflected on the fervour and intensity of that time, in the late 1930s. 'It almost killed me.'[10]

The British public had shown only passing interest in Jamaica before 1938. Esther Chapman, an expat resident, spouted the commonly held view of this sleepy outpost of Empire when she characterised the Jamaican peasant as 'essentially a gay, light-hearted, emotional person, fatalistic in his attitude to life, and as a rule taking no thought for the morrow'. His main requirements, Chapman earnestly surmised, were 'food, shelter, bright and attractive clothing, a little spare money for rum or gambling, and the opportunity for easy love-making'.[11] The view of the Jamaican worker hadn't changed much from that assigned to him by Alexander Barclay, 100 years previously. Barclay lamented the exaggerated bleating of Negrophiles in the 'two-penny pamphlets on the oppression of the Negroes'. One had only to 'listen to [the Negro's] careless song, under the sunshine of a perpetual summer', to realise that there was no 'need of his commiseration'.

> Me sing all day, me sleep all night,
> me no have no care, my heart is light,
> me t'ink not what tomorrow bring,
> me happy so me sing.[12]

After 1938 such an idealised picture was more difficult to sustain. That summer marked a turning point in Jamaica's relationship with Britain and Empire. Its slumbering people, previously said to be as 'narcoleptic as sodden leather', had become enraged, and the strikes and demonstrations that broke out all over the island were now accompanied by a new sound – the first rebellious murmurings of Independence. The Pan-African activist George Padmore sent an urgent memorandum to the Colonial Office with a veiled but chilling warning which evoked the dark days of slave insurrections:

> In 1833 there was reason to apprehend a Universal Negro rebel-lion and Emancipation was granted from above to prevent the cataclysm from below, as had occurred in San Domingo. Similarly today it is not a question of rebellions if, but rebellions *unless*, democratic government is granted.[13]

The threat was clear: did the British want to see the island turn into another Haiti, and have to wade through blood, before finally waving goodbye? *Negro Aroused* was born out of a sense of fierce injustice and an urgent need to establish a separate non-colonial identity. Up until then artistic expression had been largely mimetic, mirroring the aesthetic sensibilities of the motherland, England. Manley recalled judging a local painting and drawing competition and was dumbfounded by the absence of recognisable Jamaicans: 'There was one little study or sketch of a Jamaican market scene, and, believe it or not, the market women under the scarlet bandanas had yellow hair, pink faces, and even blue eyes.'[14] Anglo-Saxon features were transposed onto Jamaican faces, and in sober watercolours the Jamaican 'bush' was transplanted to the English shires. But *Negro Aroused* turned its back on Albion and the Home Counties. It expressed perfectly a growing sentiment that Manley's husband, Norman (a future prime minister of Jamaica), later gave voice to when he wrote: 'The immediate past has attempted to destroy the influence of the glory of Africa, it has attempted to make us condemn and mistrust the vitality, the vigour, the rhythmic emotionalism that we get from our African ancestors and even worse it has imposed on us the Greek ideal of balanced beauty.'[15]

Negro Aroused restored an African harmony and standard of perfec-tion. Rising out of a man-sized plinth, it was designed to impress. At least that was how I remembered it from a decade before. Now, retracing my steps along the deserted waterfront, I couldn't find Manley's magnificent statue. The original seemed to have vanished and been replaced with this dismally grey copy, inferior in every way, mottled and scarified after too much exposure to the salty air blowing in from the sea. So, where was the original? The taxi driver seemed indifferent. But if he considered my frustration over the missing sculpture a tiny bit preposterous, he wasn't letting on. He suggested I try the people at the National Gallery, just a few blocks away. And to my unspoken anxiety about being stranded downtown afterwards with dusk approaching, he answered: 'I'm not going anywhere, man. Take your time.' I stepped out. The driver began immediately to recline his seat and arrange the interior as if he were bedding down for the night. He leant over and closed the car door, smiling without encouragement as I moved tentatively towards the glass entrance. I tried not to reflect on the fact that the engine (and no doubt the meter) were still running, and that the added, 'Take your time, man' was less an expression of friendliness, than the sound of a man with good reason to be pleased with himself.

It was just as deserted inside the gallery as it was in the nearby streets, so that my question: 'What's happened to *Negro Aroused*?' bounced off the walls, high ceilings and parquet floors. It was an enquiry perhaps worthy of a pompous viceroy or disappointed anthropologist. But no matter, the guard (there seemed no one else to ask) paid me the honour of repeating the question back to me, ever so slowly, with all the spin and shine taken off. Eventually, he commanded me to 'just wait' and went in search of a higher authority. Sooner than expected he returned with a curator. Her confidence was announced in the snap of her clothes – an elegant dress, cut from the kind of expensive material that encouraged the wearer to sashay. She had some bad news for me. But I had guessed the answer even before she began to speak: the ugly replica *was* the original.

I had thought of the guard as an old man who took pleasure and pride in his sharply creased uniform and patent leather shoes, polished to the point of distinction. I imagined his nickname to be 'Shine'. But looked at more closely, the walnut texture of his skin (an earlier life in the open before the rarefied air-conditioned sanctum of the gallery provided coolness and lasting shade) belied his true age, which was nearer to forty. Though he'd had a little 'schooling', the gallery guard could not have found employment in such an institution had he reached maturity in 1938. Back then it would have been beyond him. His curiosity would have been curtailed, and he reduced to pressing his face to the glass, peering in at the cultural artefacts (perhaps including a maquette of *Negro Aroused*) displayed – everyone knew – for the benefit of the glitterati alone. The sculpture had been purchased in 1937 for the Institute of Jamaica with money raised by public subscription. Such was the excitement among would-be patrons – as noted approvingly in the society pages of the *Gleaner* – that the subscription list had to be closed, as money flooded in well beyond the amount required. Earlier in the year, the fair-skinned Jamaican moneyed class, knocking back gin and tonic and rum punch, had toasted the unheralded success of, and attention given to, Edna Manley's exhibition in London. Secure in the validation of the metropolis, they'd subsequently leapt at the chance to promote and replicate its cultural ideals in the provinces. This, though, was no ironic celebration of ascendant Afrocentricity. The iconic status of the statue, as representing the rebellious Negro, had not, at this stage, been cemented in the upper-classes' public imagination: keen proponents of Jamaica's status quo might yet take comfort from the appearance in the *Gleaner*, alongside news of the statue's purchase, of a letter to the editor praising the continued loyalty of Jamaican servants.[16]

Seventy years later, everything had been turned upside down. Now the black gallery guard, looking back through the tinted glass at his previously excluded childhood self, did so from *within* the citadel. I was not swayed by his ignorance of the treasures under his keep. He called to mind Auden's

> *Of history, that never sleeps or dies,*
> *And, held one moment, burns the hand.*[17]

Manley's sculpture may not have been etched into the guard's psychological map, but history lies just beneath the surface of life in Jamaica; in the overheard snatches of an argument, a sentence that begins in the present, ends in the Morant Bay murders of 1865, having called in on Frome in 1938 and memorialised the euphoria of 1962's independence along the way.

Peter Tosh was born in the year of universal adult suffrage for Jamaicans. But the Jamaica of 1944 'beggared description', recalled Vivian Durham. It seemed reminiscent of 'Charles Dickens' England', a time when 'poverty wore rags and rascality wore robes ... there was a tremendous amount of infantile mortality [and] malnutrition'.[18] The fallout from Frome was still being felt. Times were hard and desperate tenant farmers in Clarendon spoke for many of their compatriots in 1938 when they appealed to the authorities 'in the name of God and British justice deliver us from starvation ... [for] if nothing can be done for us ... God knows what will become of us.'[19] The transmission of suffering may have been clear, the reception less so. The irritable Governor, Sir Edward Denham, considered such complaints the tiresome exaggerations of voices at the 'parish pump'. Drawing on his 'not inconsiderable experience' of the colony, Governor Denham reminded his superiors that the previous harvest had been 'a record banana year and excellent local food supplies with a good mango season, so that I don't think it can be said that conditions are worse than usual.'[20]

Tosh, Marley and Livingston were countryboys who escaped malnutrition. But they'd grown among people whose poverty forced them to improvise: banana leaves served as parasols; mango stones substituted for cricket balls; and it was common practice for redundant car tyres to be cut up and used as shoes (locals called them 'power shoes').

Of the three, Peter Tosh was perhaps the most adept at creating something from nothing. Born in the township of Grange Hill, Westmoreland, Tosh developed an early facility for music and an equal skill in fashioning instruments such as guitars from old tin cans. Only fragments of his, Marley's and Livingston's early lives have been pieced together. After all, the boys did not come from families with a tradition of diary-keeping or letter-writing, knowingly preserved as a down payment on the likelihood of future fame; they were bound for no glory other than that offered by the worship of God. None of the youths, or their parents, could be said to have led a life leavened by comforts. Rather, there was an expectation of unremitting toil. Crops such as yams, cassava and pimento fortified a life of subsistence, only tempered by seasonal adjustments to household finances afforded by occasional wage labour on the bigger farms or factories.

Tosh's father, James McIntosh, a part-time preacher, was just one of the Jamaican men who, two years after the Frome rebellion, a commission reported: 'drift about the island seeking casual opportunities of work'.[21] Tosh senior and the people of Westmoreland, though, were luckier than some of their compatriots. Regular employment could be found at the recently opened Frome estate factory of the West Indies Sugar Company, a subsidiary of the giant Tate & Lyle. The locals' proximity to the estate, however, did not necessarily guarantee first refusal on job opportunities. There was scarce time for James McIntosh and his neighbours to luxuriate in their good fortune; it wasn't long before rumours of the factory's enhanced pay and conditions spread round the parish pumps of every Jamaican town and village, precipitating a great rush of skilled and unskilled labour to Frome. Scores of men – stonemasons, carpenters and a host of others – descended on Westmoreland in such large numbers that managers at Frome settled on a policy of rotating the workers – one week on, one week off (without pay). Intermittent employment was bad enough; worse still were the conditions (especially the living quarters), which fell far short of expectations. Pictures in the *Gleaner* revealed gangs of tired men unwittingly snuggling up to the rats atop makeshift mattresses out in the open. All that was missing was the tiniest spark to set a torch to festering frustrations. It duly arrived on payday – Friday, 29 April 1938.

'Labourers gathered around the pay-table . . . fingering notes of small denomination, loose silver and copper coins,' reported the *Gleaner*. The wages were much lower than the men had allowed themselves to dream, and a great howl of dismay rolled around the room. Nothing in the imported estate managers' introductory booklets to Jamaica had prepared them for the effusions of anger and untranslatable dark oaths and curses that followed. A nervous clerk's equally nervous finger hovered over a trigger. A window was smashed. Then the inevitable happened: 'five shots rang out from the pay office, and bedlam broke loose'.[22] The disturbances quickly escalated from a few disgruntled and vociferous protests to over a thousand workers out on strike. A couple of months later, on 7 June, the *Gleaner* reported an escalation in confrontations, which included fatalities at Stettin near Albert Town, a riot at Wait-a-Bit, stoning of cars at Green Island, a beating of an overseer at Cedar Valley, and so on, and so forth.

In our family lore, the riots of 1938 were memorialised by my grandfather, Vivian Wellington Adams a police constable at the time. Over the years his account of the violence was reduced to just one incident – the strangled instructions of his commanding officer, Inspector Norman Drake: 'Shoot and shoot to kill.'[23] The particularities of the incident did not survive; only those chilling words. 'Old man Adams' never disclosed whether he was obedient to that direct command or not. He did, though, agree with the assessment of Lord Olivier, a former Governor of the island. Olivier was appalled by the over-reaction of the security forces. In a House of Lords debate, he castigated the colonial authorities for their fluster and flannel. 'The sending of troops to Mandeville' was, Olivier believed, 'the equivalent of calling upon the Life Guards of Tunbridge Wells to keep order during the hopping season'.[24]

Island-wide, the stratification of the police force mirrored Jamaican society: twenty-four white men, mostly imported from Britain, made up the officer cadre, supported by just over 1,000 black constables, corporals and sergeants. The explanation for this anomaly was simple. Inspector Herbert Thomas of the Jamaica Constabulary advanced the widely held assertion that 'men like their officers to be white.' Thomas saw little point in quibbling over the fact that the evolutionary advantage was tipped in the white man's favour, and held fast to a belief in the sanctity of the status quo. If black policemen 'were promoted to commissions there would be endless trouble about saluting – not to mention anything else – especially those whose complexions were of darker hue'.[25] Constable Adams could only advance in the force just as far as his colour would take him. In previous violent conflagrations divisions had been drawn along racial and class lines, with the old rallying call amongst the majority (outgunned) population sounding for revenge and for cleaving to your own: 'colour for colour: blood for blood'.

The rebellion of 1938 revived the age-old question of whether the Jamaican Constabulary could be relied on to use force to subdue their own. Come crunch-time would black policemen find their loyalties tested? Claude McKay, the former policeman turned poet, exposed the dilemma faced by the racially sensitised constable when he resigned his commission because of 'a most improper sympathy with wrong-doers.'[26] The authorities' nervousness dated back even further to the bloody Morant Bay disturbances of 1865. Every thirty years or so, the old anxiety returned.

In his autobiography, Inspector Herbert T. Thomas recalled the last major test of allegiance on 6 April 1902, in Montego Bay: 'a notable event, as setting at rest all the uncertainty which I had previously often heard expressed in various quarters as to whether our men would prove to their salt if they should ever be called upon to use their weapons against their kith and kin'. Thomas was proud 'to have had the honour of thus "blooding" the Jamaican Constabulary . . . they proved their loyalty to the hilt'.[27]

As at the turn of the century, so too on 29 April 1938 in Frome. 'There was a body of police, at a rough guess about sixty,' wrote Richard Hart, committing to his diary the events which were to cause the first big schism between the Constabulary and those in whose name they policed. 'They spread across the road and advanced in a solid line mercilessly wielding their batons. I saw a ragged bare-footed woman beaten till she fell to the ground . . . [Then] came four or five little army trucks manned by soldiers in tin helmets.'[28] In the first month of the disturbances crowds were fired on more than a dozen times; and on one occasion, several thousand demonstrators at Kingston's Victoria Parade were dispersed when a seaplane from the Royal Navy cruiser *Ajax* descended sharply and dived at the crowd firing blanks.[29]

The masses had come to hear the early trade-union leader whose defiant stance in the Rebellion had made him the people's hero. Alexander Bustamante was a name which resonated as much in the proud bosom of James McIntosh as in his son's. He was lionised by the great mass of peasant Jamaicans (including the parents of Tosh and Livingston and Marley's mother), whom the middle classes lampooned as the 'cow-tail and hoe-handle brigade'. Bustamante articulated a growing ambivalence towards the governing of Britain's Crown Colony. He considered Governor Denham a feather-hatted fuddy-duddy. 'God save the King, but Denham must go,' became his rallying cry. Known affectionately as 'Busta' and later as 'The Chief', the former moneylender spoke eloquently and passionately for the poor and disenfranchised. On the barricades he tore open his shirt, thrust his chest in front of the armed policemen and defiantly cried: 'Cowards! Shoot me, but leave these unfortunate hungry people alone!'[30]

Universal adult suffrage and Bustamante's contesting of a general election were still six years away but there were many, especially amongst the expat community, who feared an irreversible shift in the balance of power after 1938. 'Is the Negro with his hastily acquired top dressing of civilisation laid over a half-concealed mass of primitive instincts, upon whose superstition, uncontrolled sex-indulgence and rage, lying and thieving propensities there is scarcely any check to be put in line with the white man now that he has realised his power.'[31] So wrote the incensed wife of a British estate overseer to the prime minister, Neville Chamberlain, on 15 June 1938. Her underlying fear of the rising tide of colour was premature, but one which nevertheless came to pass. Frome highlighted the isolation of the races and classes. There were, of course, exceptions. For Norman Manley, one of the island's most celebrated barristers (who held no particular brief for the poor working man), the Frome Rebellion stirred hitherto unaroused feelings of a common cause with the Jamaican everyman.

Manley was galvanised into action when the clumsy authorities arrested his cousin, Alexander Bustamante. At the height of the disturbances, Bustamante and another labour activist, the flamboyant former soldier Sergeant William Grant, were arrested and charged with inciting people to unlawful assembly. They were sent to jail without bail and a state of emergency was declared by the governor. If Manley, the Rhodes Scholar, was admired for his intellect and professional ability, Bustamante was loved in a manner which defied reason. Critics were sceptical about Bustamante's transformation from a moneylender, who'd not hesitated to chase defaulters through the courts, to a passionate trade-union leader and champion of the poor. Few, though, could argue over his enormous talent to convey powerful emotions.

Bustamante's imprisonment was designed to muffle his dissenting voice and dampen the ardour of his growing band of followers. When Manley learnt of the arrest, he was consumed by a foreboding that the island would descend into even more terrible bloodshed and fire. He took to the streets and gauged the temper of the people, before embarking on a round of urgent negotiations. Norman Manley warned the colonial administrators that they might like to weigh the unproven benefits of continuing to jail Bustamante against the certainty that if he wasn't freed, Kingston would burn. Bustamante was released, and within a few years two popular political parties were founded: the Jamaica Labour Party (JLP) presided over by Bustamante, and the People's National Party (PNP) led by Manley.

Frome showed that the Negro had been aroused. But reflections on Bustamante, Manley and the tumultuous times that gave birth to Peter Tosh were not subjects shared between him and his father. Although Reverend James McIntosh presided over a small congregation (whose members included the youthful Alvera Coke who was made pregnant by him), he also answered to the description of the itinerant workers in constant search of gainful employment who 'avoid[ing] their natural and legal family responsibilities', roamed the island seeking work and 'having relationships with women whom they abandon, avoiding summonses of parish courts, refusing to establish homes and become dependable citizens'.[32] Even if pastor McIntosh objected to his characterisation as an identikit absent parent and 'menace to society', he could not have been said to be a dependabie father. Decades later, when approached on the matter, he, without blinking, professed ignorance of his progeny: 'I never really know he was my son. No, I couldn't really know because I never link with him.' McIntosh, ultimately, failed to find fault with himself because, as he freely admitted, 'I never know what the mother was doing. So I never know the position.'[33] Though abandoned by his father, Tosh was no ghost-child, 'born-to-die'. Peter Tosh endured, along with the young Bob Marley and a majority of his peers, an absence of (biological) fatherly input into his upbringing. Tosh once acknowledged that society classified him as illegitimate, but that knowledge did not make him 'lose faith' with himself. The stigma, in any event, was diminished by the fact that the majority of Jamaican children were born out of wedlock. In many instances the idea of fatherhood did not extend beyond the bodily act of procreation: men gave as much thought to their offspring as to a handkerchief they once used to blow their nose.

Abundant literature has testified to the role that slavery played in inculcating this lasting pattern of behaviour, with men and women kept apart in barracks and only brought together to mate and produce valuable creolised infant slaves for the future benefit of the plantation. No recognition or sanctity was given to marriage between the enslaved; women were subject to the pleasure of the slave master or overseer. 'Every estate on the island – every Negro household – was a common brothel; every female a prostitute; and every man a libertine,' wrote one nineteenth-century observer.[34]

Professor Frederick Hickling was animated by the subject. The lime-green and ochre walls of his office on the campus of the University of the West Indies and the plethora of elegant wooden African ornaments gave the room an air of coolness. Its design seemed fitting for calm scholarly inquiry, but the man before me was in a rage. Freddie Hickling was incensed. He was, apparently, personally affronted by my questions, at least by the framing of the enquiry as to the reasons for the preponderance of 'feckless fathers' in Jamaica. Didn't I know about slavery? Didn't I know my history? 'Absent fathers! Oh man!' I had unwittingly knocked a scab on a wound that had never healed. Only minutes into our interview, red spots of irritation began to break out over his face; he grew increasingly febrile. I feared he would convulse. Rage was not a characteristic I associated with professors of psychiatry, but even allowing for a degree of posturing, the passion was real. The enslaved men, kept in barracks, 'were allowed visiting rights,' Hickling hissed. 'They could visit, for the business of procreation . . . You see the same pattern with young men today, but the pathology was introduced in the eighteenth century'.[35]

The system evolved. Perhaps, with the passage of time, there was some softening of the brutality of life, and a degree of latitude given towards the establishment of more stable unions between the enslaved. Even so, an early historian of Jamaica, Edward Long, said much the same thing as Hickling about the unsteady attachment of men to wives who 'are only a sort of occasional concubines, or drudges, whose assistance the husband claims in the culture of his land, sale of his produce, and so on.'[36] It was apparent that Hickling drew as much on historical texts as medical papers and journals in his practice of psychiatry. 'Let's get the history right,' he bellowed. 'If we can't get the history right, we won't get the diagnosis right.'

In 'Red X', the audio diary that Peter Tosh recorded in preparation for an autobiography that was never published, he hardly spoke about his father, and when he did so, although what he said was scornful, it was without malice. When asked about his father's profession, he said: 'My father, James McIntosh, is a bad boy, a rascal. That's what him do for a living. He just go around and have a million-and-one children!'

Tosh analysed his own life, which he came to see as the governing template for much of the island's population.[37] Tosh, as noted, was not alone. Illegitimacy was the norm. In a 1938 survey, seven out of ten births recorded at the Kingston Jubilee Maternity Hospital were illegitimate. But among the poorer classes there was little stigma attached to birth outside of legal recognition. Great numbers of co-habiting

Jamaicans were 'married', in all but name. Such a state of affairs, though, did not obscure the fact of the shameless serial mating and loose, non-committal arrangements, in which upper- and middle-class critics divined the seeds of Jamaican society's major ills, and fidgeted over their remedy. In the aftermath of the Frome Rebellion, the governor's wife, Lady Huggins, was among the first to offer a prescription: the Mass Marriage Movement.[38] The ever-smiling Lady Huggins (a 'blonde bombshell' known as 'Molly' among the cocktail party set and famed for winning tennis tournaments) traced the root cause of childhood neglect and malnutrition rife in Jamaica to the 'distressingly high percentage of illegitimacy'. She was not content to confine herself to the role of a ubiquitous social butterfly flapping around the garden parties that she hosted at King's House; rather, she launched herself into a campaign to accent the virtues and benefits of marriage. Her committee was comprised of Amy Bailey and other concerned members of the Jamaica Federation of Women, who raised funds for gowns and wedding rings for prospective brides and grooms.

Ten couples took part in a mass wedding ceremony on 24 July 1940. Over the coming years, Lady Huggins was the guest of honour at countless others.[39] But men such as James McIntosh were not persuaded by the arguments of her benevolent organisation, launched a few years before the birth of his son. For him, and many other Jamaican men, responsibility ultimately rested with the mother – an attitude captured ably by George Lamming's novel *In the Castle of My Skin*. G, the protagonist, recognises he is the issue of a man 'who had only fathered the idea of me (and) left me the sole liability of my mother who really fathered me'.[40] But Tosh's young mother could not cope with the responsibilities of bringing up a son on her own. She recognised that help was needed, that 'one finger can't crack lice', as they say in Jamaica; and she *was* fortunate. Peter Tosh's maternal great-aunt and uncle assumed the role relinquished by his biological father. At the age of six, Tosh moved into the household of Uriah Campbell. The Campbells were a clannish people with various plots of family land dotted around Belmont as well as the neighbouring villages and towns in the parish. Tosh was to spend much of his childhood shuttlecocking between the district capital, Savanna-la-Mar – not much changed from the century-old description as 'all lagoon, morass and water'[41] – and Belmont, a small fishing village of dirt-red roads and simple huts made from wattle and daub or – if finances could be got – from concrete. Neither did the amenities differ markedly from his birthplace: the lagoon there needed to be cleaned more regularly if it was not to remain a menace to health, and if it was to relieve the strain of overuse on the recently upgraded well. Then there was the problem of transport. A decade after the first proposal, councillors were still debating how to make the roads safe for wheeled traffic.

The Campbells were noted fishermen and small-scale farmers. In the pages of the *Gleaner*, a Uriah Campbell from neighbouring Lucea was pictured with a prize catch, a ten-foot 'monster' Blue Marlin weighing 272lb. Working the land was never so spectacular, except in the disappointment of a failed or diseased crop. Even so the desire for land was great. British civil servants were often bemused by the peasant's 'almost fanatical desire to own and to be left alone in the possession of his land.'[42] A century on from Emancipation, the question of land settlement had not been resolved. Tilling one's own fields was more desirable than selling one's labour on the big estates. Though it was not always as profitable, it was free from the sting of humiliation that was still attached to cutting sugar cane or harvesting bananas on slave plantations.

An equitable redistribution of land had faltered right from the start of Emancipation, and deliberately so. It was not a proposition that was met with enthusiasm by the planters or the British government. Both feared the ruin of the former plantations if the workforce, no longer obliged to toil under the driver's whip, abandoned them. A Colonial Office circular of 30 January 1836 advocated hiking up the price for Crown Lands (the hundreds of thousands of acres forfeited to the Crown through unpaid taxes) to 'place them out of the reach of persons without capital'. The object, stated frankly in the circular, was not to deprive 'the Negro of every other resource for subsistence *but* merely to condense and keep together the population in such a manner that it may always contain a due proportion of labour'.[43]

To circumvent these restrictions the black man turned to the Baptist missionaries (fervent advocates of Emancipation). They, in turn, employed proxies to buy land for the newly freed. This, within the space of a few years, evolved into the Free Village Movement. Baptists such as William Knibb, who ran a mission in Savanna-la-Mar, encouraged the emancipated to found their own villages, based on a concept of individual and common ownership of the land for the good of their communities. Two hundred villages had been established by 1840. In addition, there were some enlightened planters who granted back-lands on their estates to ex-slaves or leased them at peppercorn rates. Notwithstanding these and other progressive acts, it was a source of much resentment that one hundred years later most of the land in Jamaica was still owned by a tiny elite. The land that was available to poorer members of society changed hands regularly. In February 1945, for instance, half a dozen properties owned by farmers in Belmont (including one of the Campbells') were sold at auction. They bought and sold their smallholdings but rarely had the chance to consolidate.

Not that expansion formed any part of the mindset of Peter Tosh's great-uncle, Uriah Campbell, for whom succour and enlightenment were to be found in the hymn's refrain: 'This world is not my resting place.' There was only one certainty: tenure of the land was temporary. Tosh was soon to discover that he had moved into a home of regimental religiosity; worship at the altar of the local church was compulsory. His unbroken attendance at the simple wooden temple, roofed over with corrugated zinc, every other night during the week and twice on Sundays belied his enthusiasm.

Even at such a tender age Tosh would have been inclined towards the cynical observation of a local journalist who wrote that church attendance owed 'more to sociability, a need for emotional uplift, mixed with a bit of entertainment ... and a good bit of superstitious awe, rather than any deep understanding or conviction'.[44] In his ninth year, Peter Tosh had already begun to hone a keen sense of indignation and disgust at the premium placed on fair skin that even emanated from the Church. Tosh was unashamedly black, but to be born so, he recalled from sermons, was to be 'born in sin and shaped in iniquity'. It was a point further rammed home when the congregation was asked to turn to the songbook, and cleared their throats before launching into 'Lord wash me and I shall be whiter than snow', a hymn which left Tosh feeling nauseous.

*

Lady Huggins had more luck with the man destined to become Bob Marley's father. Fifty-year-old Norval Sinclair Marley was a committed bachelor when he first started stepping out with seventeen-year-old Cedella Malcolm. Their brief, clandestine courtship was an unlikely one. She was poor, black and very much working class; he was white and middle-class. In Jamaican society there was usually no social bridge between the two groups. But then, 'Captain' Marley, as he preferred to be addressed, was something of an enigma. His olive skin might easily be explained as the product of an outdoor, sun-drenched life. There were whispers, though, that Marley was not of pure Anglo-Saxon stock, and that his dark complexion owed more to having been 'touched by the tar-brush'. Fully white, perhaps not; but socially white most definitely. He was said to have been a Quartermaster in the British West Indies Regiment, but as that unit had disbanded in 1921, there wasn't much call for supplies and uniforms. Norval Marley's service record shows that he was honourably discharged from the British army after the First World War: his rank was listed as corporal. What he did in the war is clear; what he did next is less so. He pops up in Nigeria as a policeman, and there is a sighting of him as a merchant seaman in South Africa. The narrative runs out in the 1930s and the thread is picked up again at the start of the 1940s, when he is appointed an estate manager on Crown lands in the Dry Harbour Mountains, where many of the Baptist Free Villages had been established. The Crown properties, remote back-lands on plateaux more than 2,000 feet above sea level, were renowned as places of contemplation and prayer. As overseer, Marley was to encourage peasants to purchase or lease plots of these unfancied lands for cultivation. The job was marked by long stretches of solitude, punctuated, in Norval Marley's case, by fleeting sexual assignations. Descriptions of Captain Marley – negotiating the estate on horseback with a stiff military ramrod back and all the while puffing on a barely-lit pipe – veered from charming to lecherous. But by the time he met Cedella in the spring of 1944, the 'Captain' had arrived at a critical point in his life. He could no longer stomp around the place like a young roustabout, whoring and gambling; he was tired.

In Captain Norval Marley, the Mass Marriage Movement was about to claim an early success – at least in Cedella Malcolm's account. When Cedella announced that she was pregnant, therefore, their liaison could no longer remain secret, she claimed that Marley suffered a sudden pang of propriety, and a few months later the two were married. The 'ceremony' was deliberately low-key; afterwards, along with their bridesmaids and the rest of the wedding party, they sipped punch and ate from a loaf of banquet bread. The morning after, it was apparent that the wedding, if not a fiction, was something of a charade. Somewhere between 'I do' and 'till death do us part' Norval Marley had misplaced his conviction. The newly wed overseer mounted his horse and fled St Ann's to the capital, unaccompanied by his wife, leaving her pregnant with a child who at least would not be born a bastard. If Norval Marley had married Cedella Malcolm, then he had acted against his better instincts and contrary to the wishes of his family, in whose eyes he had committed a 'racial disgrace'; the Marley clan had reportedly threatened to cut him off from his inheritance. Barely a few generations back, the idea of a white man marrying even a fair-skinned brown woman produced a shudder of horror in middle-class circles. Norval Marley was not related to the author of *Marly or a Planter's Life in Jamaica*, but as the anonymous writer of that nineteenth-century journal, a self-confessed 'Slave Driver [who] lay down the whip to take up the pen', observed: such a marriage 'if not expressly precluded by law, is so by custom'.[45] This applied, doubly so, to any union between a white man and a black woman. Captain Marley would have been laughed out of the tea-rooms and parlours. In abandoning his pregnant wife, Norval Marley reverted to type, to an older instinct (not just for survival), without fear of censure. He returned briefly to St Ann's to toast the birth of his son, Robert Nesta, but thereafter the trickle of letters from Norval to Cedella dried up altogether, and those from her to him were returned unopened.[46]

MY WIFE HAVING LEFT MY CARE AND PROTECTION, I AM NO LONGER RESPONSIBLE FOR HER

Such announcements appeared frequently in the pages of the island's newspapers, alongside the ledgers for births, deaths and marriages. Never mind that the claims were often an inversion of the truth. They articulated a sentiment that ensured that men who fell foul of the Maintenance and Bastardy Laws would not be prosecuted. A woman who legally pursued her baby's father was likely to be met by laconic officials, with better things to do with their time, wondering aloud why she was tormenting the poor fellow. Didn't the plaintiff understand that she was making unrealistic demands on her former bedmate? 'She must realise,' one reluctant father told researchers, 'it's not [just] one child I have to support.'[47]

Still, conscientious fathers were not unknown in the Jamaican countryside. Neville 'Bunny' Livingston (he later changed his name to Wailer) grew up in the same village – Nine Miles – as Robert Nesta Marley. They were neighbours. But Neville Livingston was born into a far more stable household. A majority of peasant famers grew pimento, coffee and bananas. But small-scale farming was always a lottery. In the choice of bananas the dice were perennially loaded against success and in favour of the dreaded Spotted Leaf and Panama disease. Livingston's father, Thaddeus, insured against disaster by enlarging his portfolio of work. Mostly, he plied his trade as a stonemason. But he seems to have had greater ambitions for himself and his family. Unusually, Thaddeus ('Toddy') branched out into retail, starting up a small business as a shopkeeper with designs on penetrating the lucrative grocery market, then largely the preserve of Chinese migrants.

Of the few hundred grocers' stores on the island, more than half were run by Chinese-Jamaicans. The Chinese grocery occupied an ambivalent space in Jamaican society. Out of one side of their mouths, Janus-faced customers would 'cuss bad words' over the Chinese proprietors' monopoly, and mock them for allegedly eating dogs; out of the other side of their mouths they would feign modesty and eternal gratitude ('skinning their teet' in Jamaican parlance), pleading for extended credit lines. H. G. De Lisser at the *Gleaner* expressed this attitude perfectly when he scratched his head over the confusion that somehow the Chinese grocer 'robs your oil and gives you a biscuit and you go away thinking you have got something for nothing'. Nonetheless, this Chinese ascendancy could pass unnoticed (or at least without comment) for long stretches, before some minor incident – refusal of credit or dispute over a purchase – roused sections of the population to rancour. Black rivals shed bitter tears (albeit of the crocodile variety) over alleged practices of unfair competition. But Toddy Livingston was not amongst those who signed a popular petition in 1940 arguing that further Chinese immigration be halted. The sale of fruit and vegetables enabled a reasonable return on investment but real money was to be made in liquor. Licences were at a premium and Toddy somehow managed to obtain one. Livingston was a hardworking storekeeper unafraid to match the long hours of his Chinese competitors.[48]

Halfway between Savannah-la-Mar and Nine Miles, I steered the hired car gingerly around Middle Quarters, looking for the non-existent sign to my destination. Middle Quarters seemed, at first, to consist of little more than an enormous roundabout, whose form did not follow function. After the third circumnavigation, it was apparent that few other cars had passed that way. Few ever did. I exited from the empty roundabout and pulled up beside a grocer's shack. Suddenly twenty or thirty women came rushing towards the car. All carried coloured Tupperware bowls filled with crayfish. Twenty bowls tried to breach the closing gap in the window, which seemed to wind itself up, though it must have been my finger on the button. The women formed such a press on the car that, even if I'd wanted to, I could not open the door. [Vendors such as these, selling one or two items of excess produce from meagre one-acre farms, are known as higglers in Jamaica.] Most were elderly, thin and loose-skinned. They took part in the ruckus reluctantly; an unspoken apology playing on their lips. Their good manners held, just about, even in their desperation. They called to mind the Jamaican migrants to the UK in the 1950s who confused the curmudgeonly local population, an official study noted, because their 'excessive politeness leads to suspicion and irritation'.[49] Theirs was the civility of those who have long been calumnied. It was an inversion of the lack of regard that they, and generations before them, had been shown by the 'buckra', the overseer or driver. 'Towards each other,' the historian James Mursell Phillippo observed of the newly emancipated Jamaicans, 'they manifest a politeness and respect sometimes approaching extravagance.'[50] Perhaps it is but a hop, skip and jump to today's 'respect' or 'nuff respec''. The higglers at the side of the car were kindred spirits to the country people who grounded Bob Marley, from whom he had received 'blessings' – the simple salutations of the morning. At the height of his fame, Marley would tell reporters that it was those 'blessings' that he most cherished, above almost anything else.[51] In times of plenty, the higglers might have exerted more restraint, but distress and the rare opportunity that I provided ruled out such an approach; they pleaded with me and argued among themselves, until it was apparent that none would make a sale – for now.

The excitement died down. The most seasoned of the women had quickly made the calculation that it was best not to expend all their energy; better luck might come with the next car. I emerged from the chilled interior of my vehicle. The higglers retreated as I advanced and presented myself to the proprietor of the shack. The cool drink, 'yes man, it cool,' the proprietor assured me, was sickly and warm. After a few swigs though, here in this strange no-man's-land, I heard, I unmistakably heard, the sound of someone calling my name.

Brother Williams had a warm and stentorian voice (the product of decades of delivering sermons). The voice was a perfect match for his nature: patrician and abundantly kind. The last time I'd seen him, ten years previously, Brother Williams had spoken from the platform at a Pentecostal church in Luton in southern England, and had folded the entire congregation into his enveloping kindliness. His generous and warm smile was a blessing.

In 1955, Brother Williams had watched boys risking their lives to dive for pennies thrown by tourists disembarking from ships at Kingston Harbour. That year, he'd made the decision to leave Jamaica, joining more than 7,000 others to begin a new life in the motherland, England. The decades passed. There followed a lifetime of fitting panels onto the non-stop procession of new cars on the production line of the shop-floor at Vauxhall Motors in Luton. Then one year the production line stopped – or he did – and he became one of the town's first returnees to Jamaica. He was something of a hero in our household. He'd gone back home. Where others had dreamt, Brother Williams had acted. Each week Jamaica's national paper, the *Gleaner*, had wended its way from the island to our home in Luton. All of the Jamaicans in town (probably in all of Britain) subscribed to it. The reverence for the *Gleaner* was akin to that normally reserved for the Bible. It aroused passions and settled disputes: it was concrete proof of the migrants' continued connection with Jamaica. Their eyes alighted dreamily on its back pages where adverts for the sale of property (simple line-drawn modernist impressions) and plots of land held out the promise of return. But the five-year plan was continually extended and the dream deferred – indefinitely.

Not so for Brother Williams. Fifty years later he had come full circle. But now there was money in his bank account and the added fiscal cushion of a pension from Vauxhall Motors. As delighted as I was to have happened upon him, at this most unlikely place, I also wondered just why Brother Williams was there. What *was* he doing at Middle Quarters? He paused before speaking and looked over his shoulder. Ten metres away, in the shade of an ackee tree, his wife stood beside a car. He beckoned to her but she didn't budge; she waved and smiled unconvincingly like a shy neighbour having to stop in the street when she'd hoped to pass unnoticed. Sister Williams gestured as if to say that she couldn't move, that she was guarding something. When I looked more closely I saw that there were clothes (suits and dresses) strewn across the bonnet of a car. 'Well,' Brother Williams explained, anticipating my question, 'Sister Williams has some clothes she would like to sell, so we bring them here . . . to do a little selling.' I didn't push for greater clarification. I could not process the sight and sounds. My brain went into a kind of spasm. Brother Williams's supposed rewards from a financially prudent life in England did not compute with this desperate roadside selling. A few minutes later I was back in my hire car, only half-listening to the complicated directions from Brother Williams as he tried simultaneously to discourage me from continuing on to Nine Miles on my own.

I was not so concerned for my safety as I drove away, tooting my horn beyond the point where they could still hear it. Rather, I worried that the next time I passed by Middle Quarters, Brother Williams and his wife would have joined the higglers, shoving to the front with a bowl of crayfish.

Migration had been a way out. It had been a chance to prosper. Brother Williams had been a pioneer in both directions, outwards and home. He'd gone over in the 1950s when the great migration of Caribbean people to the UK was still in its infancy. The first wave of 492 souls departed from the Jamaican capital Kingston for Tilbury in southern England in 1948 – three years after Bob Marley's birth. Tens of thousands would follow in subsequent years. But the scale of that migration from the island to the Motherland was always exceeded by the movement of peasants from the countryside to the towns and cities. This had led to criticism from time to time that 'too much or unsuitable education drives country boys from the land to the respect-able black-coated professions'. There was little danger of this being the outcome from the education that Tosh, Livingston and Marley were to receive. The latter two attended primary school at Stepney, one of the free villages founded in the aftermath of Emancipation. The Baptist minister, John Clark, who conducted a report on land settlement in the 1850s, described Stepney as 'a large picturesque village ... containing a temporary place of worship and a commodious schoolhouse'. By the time Livinsgton and Marley enrolled in school, a future education beyond the primary was not envisaged. Most secondary schools were fee-paying, and prohibitively expensive. One visiting sociologist warned, 'The bridge from the primary schools [to secondary] is narrow and insecure.'[52] He might have added: 'and rarely crossed'.

Along with sixty other pupils, Livingston and Marley shared a teacher at the Stepney All-Age School, a poorly funded institution with a reputa-tion for flogging. Corporal punishment brought the two boys together.

Toddy Livingston was renowned for whipping with bamboo canes, 'trained from young and bent at the end into the shape of a hook'. He was also adept at throwing out the cane like a fishing rod, catching children with the hooked end by the waist of their pants as they tried to run away. He kept a more vicious version, a 'scibblejack', for the roughnecks coming into his shop. The 'scibblejack' was a rod made from three canes plaited together. When wielded with force, it could cut into skin like a razor.

The headteacher at Stepney often requested canes from Bunny's father. Toddy would send them along with his son. But before placing them into the head's hands, Bunny Livingston passed them onto Bob Marley and other boys who were singled out regularly for punish-ment. They'd make barely visible incisions, cutting grooves into the joint of the cane, before approving their delivery to the headmaster The forceful flogger would be surprised and frustrated to find that the canes snapped when used.

The ratio of pupils to teacher was twice the national average, according to a previous census. And such schools with their catch-all age groups (from primary to the first years of secondary) meant classes included a range of ages and a wide spectrum of ability. A deficit of attention would not have been surprising in classrooms where the only divisions were those provided by their blackboards, and where doors and windows were always open. There were ample opportunities for disruption. Nonetheless, it was an improvement on the partial schooling on offer to the previous generation. The Jamaican Legislature had passed an Ordinance in 1945 making school attendance compulsory, between the ages of six and twelve, for children living within a two-mile radius of a school. But teachers had no pretensions to imparting anything other than a basic education. The pen of A. G. S. Coombs ran dry with sarcasm when he considered the merits of the system: 'A boy or girl after leaving elementary school, not finding himself in a position to go further is placed in the same category of the illiterate with only one difference: he or she can sign their names.'[53] Neither Livingston nor Marley appear to have been exceptional students. Marley's clumsy handwriting bore testimony to the rudimentary nature of his education, and the inability of his teacher to cope with such large numbers. He seems though to have made an early impression on Bunny Livingston. Two years younger, Livingston was drawn, in ways he did not yet understand, towards this classmate with a serious demeanour but an easy and disarming smile. Marley also attracted the attention of their teacher, Clarice Bushay, but she was wary lest it show. For there was at least one thing exceptional about the Stepney All-Age school: 'Because he was light-skin,' Bushay recalled about Marley, 'other children would become jealous of him getting so much of my time.'[54] It would have been unusual to find a pupil of Marley's complexion in such an impoverished institution. The brown middle classes tended to send their children to privately run establishments, and, though the habit of then dispatching them to secondary schools abroad had declined somewhat in recent decades, this was still the preferred option for families who could afford to do so.

At the time when Livingston and Marley were making the two-mile trek to school, to be exposed to the three r's (reading, writing and 'rithmetic), Chris Blackwell, a privileged teenage Jamaican fop, with ruddy cheeks and riotous hair – sent to England to be educated in the exclusive confines of Harrow School – had just about exhausted the patience of his headmaster. Blackwell was caught selling cigarettes and alcohol to his classmates. While it showed undeniable (if not commendable) business acumen, his actions could not be construed as gentlemanly behaviour, and clearly fell short of the standards expected at Harrow. 'It resulted in the school's first public caning in over 100 years,' wrote

Blackwell, '[and] was quite an ordeal.' Blackwell was expelled, or as he euphemistically put it, 'It was suggested that I might benefit from attending *another* school.'

Conduct unbecoming a gentleman was not, however, an impediment to entrepreneurship and in a few years Chris Blackwell's chutzpah and energy would serve him well as he transformed himself into one of Jamaica's first record promoters. In just over a decade he would become inextricably linked with the two boys from Nine Miles and the one from Savanna-la-Mar.

Tosh and Marley were also showing an early interest in making money, but in ways that met with general approval. Both recalled incidents of how their young selves enchanted locals with their rudimentary musicianship, singing hymns and folk songs; and converted a talent to amuse into hard currency. Tosh's mother was caught off guard and saw her son as if for the first time: 'I never know that he could play so quick until the schoolteacher told me that he could play the piano.' She revealed that from the age of four 'he used to sing and collect monies . . . those were shilling days, thruppence and shillings and people give it to him 'cause he could sing but them days he used to sing Christian songs'. Though it's unlikely that 'Lord wash me and I shall be whiter than snow' would have featured in his repertoire, Tosh sung his praises with gusto. To hear his sincere and lusty singing was heart-rending in one of such tender years, when daily the temptations mounted to lead the youths astray. Elders at the church were especially gratified that neither Tosh nor any of the local boys and girls showed signs of being infected by an alarming and burgeoning new craze: calypso.

The letters pages of all the island's newspapers burned with furious exchanges about the merits and evils of this Trinidadian import. The lewd lyrics were the cause of most vexation. But when prosecuted, calypso singers were apt to explain that if they didn't put a little bit of spice into the lyrics the music wouldn't sell. There were many Jamaicans who would rather that the music didn't even go on sale.

The calypsonians were foot soldiers of the Devil, bent on bringing Sodom and Gomorrah to Jamaica – or so their critics believed. No matter how dressed up in innuendo, calypsos like 'Night Food' and 'Rough Rider' were clearly paeans to fornication. Custodians of culture agonised over calypso's corrosive influence on the morality of the youth. Even so, calypso had its defenders. Edward Seaga (or more likely the subeditor at the *Gleaner*) mockingly wondered aloud in print: 'W'at dem call dis lewdness, Ah wander if it is so bad?' Seaga detected a strong whiff of hypocrisy among the outraged in their new-found commitment to social welfare. 'Children who sleep on or below the same bed in which their parents have intercourse . . . whose realism leaves nothing for the imagination,' were unlikely to be corrupted, wrote Seaga, by an artform that was amongst the 'wittiest of musical works'.

But God-fearing congregations in Nine Miles and Savanna-la-Mar would see their tongues cleft to their palates before giving voice to calypsonian lyrics – whether aural aphrodisiacs or obscene, copulative suggestions. At the church Bunny Livingston attended he remembered it as a 'clapping church', the kind where you were encouraged to 'read your Bible two times a day to drive vampire [the Devil] away'.[55]

'Vampires don't come out and bite your neck any more,' Tosh was to record of that period of his life. 'They cause something destructive to happen that blood will spill.' Tosh had in mind a terrible accident that occurred at the age of seven when, racing along a beach, he ran straight into some barbed wire, at head height: 'Two barbs, could be three or more, struck in my eyelid, right on the surface of my eyeball. I wiped blood from my eyes, I looked into mirror and I saw where my two eyelid was slit open, so wide I could see through them.' In Tosh's reasoning it was 'the first major pit of destruction that the devil dug before my feet'. The Devil had tried to blind him, literally and metaphorically, to the 'corruption, the filth, the shit, the destruction, the lies and hypocrisy and the order of the day'. The youthful Tosh was to share with Livingtson and Marley the conception that life was a constant duel between the good and evil abroad in the land. Accidents, illnesses and disasters didn't happen by chance. Lucifer's will both explained the shards of broken glass that pierced the bare countryboy feet of Bob Marley *and* why the wound wouldn't heal.

When Hurricane Charlie smashed through the island in 1951, knocking over peasant shacks, it was plain that God was not in the wind; Charlie blew the Devil's breath. And Peter Tosh was to find in the coming years that Satan, and his agents of destruction, would lay traps for him in ever-increasing numbers. Before the decade had ended, the young boy was bound for the pestilent slums of Kingston.

COLD GROUND FOR BED,
ROCK FOR PILLOW

'THE most dangerous things I ever heard or see in my life is when I find myself in Trench Town.'[56] Peter Tosh was not given to exaggeration. In 1956, heading for Kingston, he was uprooted from a life of solid rectitude, ill-suited to the fluidity of the capital. Countryfolk only ventured into the bigger towns when 'on missions they could not avoid', recalled Jervis Anderson, a contemporary of Tosh. With great hesitancy, they went there, 'to shop in clothing and hardware stores; to pay their taxes at government offices . . . and they no sooner completed their transactions than they began hurrying back home.'[57] In their conception, the Jamaican village was a virgin; west Kingston a pimp and Trench Town its whore. Tosh's mother did not want him to go 'up' to Kingston until he was 'saved'; until he was fully committed to the Lord and Christianity.

Undeniably, Trench Town was a hazardous zone, and a Trench Town postcode, if affordable, was not desirable. On a hot day – and there were many of them – the stench was overwhelming, as untreated sewage coursed along open trenches. While John Crows (vultures) gorged on the abundant piles of refuse and detritus downtown, the hummingbirds headed uptown, where, just a mile away, lanes were lined with the scent of jasmine and bushes of bougainvillaea. Set back from the roads, fringed by clusters of citrus trees, perfectly trimmed and sprinkled lawns swept up towards elegant whitewashed homes.

Birds might move freely between the two but there was an unofficial and largely self-regulated 'cordon sanitaire' separating uptown from downtown Kingston. In many of the smart middle- and upper-class houses watchmen were employed at night, and several guard dogs kept. These measures were largely precautionary, as the masses rarely travelled to the upper-class residential areas except to work as servants, butlers, drivers or gardeners. Years after his arrival in Trench Town Bob Marley still smarted from an early humiliating incident with the Jamaican constabulary. En route to a speculative meeting with a record producer in the exclusive Russell Heights district, the young and hopeful musician was stopped on his bicycle by police at an impromptu road-block on the borders of uptown. Marley was taunted for his naivety, and ordered to turn his bicycle around and ride on back to where he'd come from. Surely he understood that ghetto boys had no business in those parts of the city?[58]

The west-end slums were forbidding places, but Kingston was a city of extremes. Windowshoppers on Harbour Street had only to glance through the storefront displays to be exposed to the extent of the disparity in the lives of its population. For ladies of leisure, Nathan's Store advertised 'Dainty and cool but essentially practical' rayon-knitted cuff knee panties which came in cream or white, and which for a mere 4/6d would emerge 'from endless immersions in the washtub fresh for duty'.[59] Meanwhile, the domestic helpers, whose duty it was to wash the panties, earned 5/8d per week. As De Lisser observed, 'Almost anyone in Jamaica, with any pretension to respectability, invariably keeps a servant, and sometimes two, for wages are low.'[60]

Ranked among these well-to-do citizens of Kingston were conserva-tives who, confident of their progressive outlook, saw no profit in challenging a system that rewarded them. Although by the 1950s, Jamaica had a greater degree of self-rule, with Norman Manley as its Chief Minister, the island was still a colony, and, as Jervis Anderson remembered, 'progressive intellectuals were only a rumour.'[61] Looking backwards and bemoaning the present was a favoured pastime of the Anglophiles and Afro-Saxons on the island. In 1955, even as the island inched towards Independence, they excitedly prepared to celebrate the tercentenary of British rule in Jamaica. Taking a bow at the 'St Andrew Club Jamaica 300 Costume Ball' were characters assembled from the island's history. They included ladies dressed as the infamous poisoner, the White Witch of Rose Hall, and the fragrant nineteenth-century chronicler of social mores, Lady Nugent. Chief among the usual suspects in the men's camp was that agent of state-sponsored terror, Captain Morgan. Slaves in leg-irons did not feature. Nonetheless, there was some nervousness about the direction other parishes might take in drawing attention to the first two hundred years of Britain's brutish plunder of Jamaica as a sugar colony. Some councillors in Kingston considered it perverse to be celebrating what amounted to three hundred years of enemy occupation. Casting around for a distraction, the *Gleaner* was relieved to report on the Wolmer's Girls' School pageant, which 'introduced every community' without being 'offensive to anybody . . . not even castigating that eternal politician's whipping horse – the poor old English.' Though the paper worried that 'racial and fanatical chauvinism', might yet distort the rest of the celebrations, for now Wolmer's was to be cheered to the rafters for having 'rung the bell yet again'.[62]

The ticker tape, dried flowers, petals and bunting were just being cleared away when Peter Tosh set off from Savanna-la-Mar for Kingston. The festivities may have been over by the time he arrived but the success of the tercentenary celebrations had led to a boom in the island's tourism. A 1957 brochure for 'Jamaica Calypso Cruises' described the holiday destination as 'an isle of enchantment' – an appraisal endorsed by Ian Fleming the following year with the publication of *Dr No*. Readers revelled in the descriptions of exoticism and glamour, as they followed James Bond touching down at the island's main airport, folding himself into an Aston Martin and zooming along the 'cactus-fringed road towards the distant lights of Kingston' with 'the steady zing of the crickets, the rush of warm, scented air, the ceiling of stars, [and] the necklace of yellow lights shimmering across the harbour'.[63]

The view from Spanish Town Road, the route taken by Peter Tosh and countryfolk coming to the capital, was not so enticing, obscured as it often was by the smoke from the mountains of rubbish set alight on the outskirts, at Dunghill (later known as Dungle). Teams of squatters 'living on the Dungle' lay in wait for garbage carts and vied with the vultures for their contents. It was common practice, as noted in the 1964 novel *The Children of Sisyphus*, for the more enterprising garbage men to hold back certain items like the 'two pieces of cod-fish and a small bag of flour which had largely managed to evade the disinfectant', to barter with the squatters.[64] The road from the old capital (Spanish Town) to Kingston was a mere twelve miles, but would serve as useful preparation for what lay up ahead.

As a traveller drew progressively closer to Kingston, he might notice subtle shifts in social interaction, and his body begin to tense, along with the increasing levels of aggression and frustration in the people he encountered.

The sun was high and extremely hot. The hire car was cool, and my companion frowned every time I opened the window a crack. It was nearing 100 degrees outside. The final stretch of road was bordered by a never-ending line of rough, wooden huts selling fruit. My companion suggested that we stop for an orange or banana but I was reluctant to break the journey. At least, I argued, we could hold on until we found a reasonable-looking stall; the next one was bound to have a better selection – riper, more varied, more golden, not so bruised. But as we approached the city (and the countryside receded) the drop-off in the quality of the fruit on offer became more pronounced. I regretted not stopping earlier. Eventually, when it became clear that any further delay was futile, wishful thinking – the fruit would not improve from now on – we pulled up at the very next stall.

A large, well-fed woman sat beside the hut, barely protected from the sun; a rag rested on her lap which she occasionally took to wipe the sweat from her face. She looked up momentarily as the 'ding-ding-ding' of the opening car door sounded, and my passenger emerged and dashed to the shade of the stall, strangely like someone hurrying out of the rain. The woman at the shack held a knife in one hand which she used to cut into the thick skin of an orange; the peel dropped down in a kiss-curl as the knife went to work.

The stall was brim full of bananas, rows and rows of them; less a sign of prudent replenishing of stock than testament to the very few sales she had managed all day. The bananas were not in good shape; they were overripe and beginning to turn. My companion gingerly picked up a hand of bananas, and immediately, just through the force of gravity, the near-rotting fingers fell off. The stallholder looked on, remaining in her seat, all the while peeling the orange with the knife, but muttering now: 'She mash me bananas. Who tell she fi mash me bananas?' My fellow traveller, scanning the stall intensely, seemed unaware of what the woman was saying. She beckoned me out of the car, though as soon as I reached the hut she turned and whispered, 'I think they're all off. Don't think I'll bother.' She retraced her steps, hurrying out of the sun towards the car, and slid back into the passenger seat. The banana-seller shot up from the stool and, as I moved to get back into the car, she blocked my path.

'She mash my bananas.'

'Pardon?'

'She mash my bananas. Who tell she fi mash my bananas.'

'I'm sorry,' I said, 'but I think they're all rotten.' I opened the driver-side door. The woman held it by the edge.

'Them can't sell now . . . now she mash them . . . them can't sell.'

'She doesn't want any,' I said firmly. The heat was overpowering. I blinked away the sweat from my eyes, and made another effort to get back in but she wouldn't budge.

The woman suddenly screamed out: 'Call the police!'

'What?'

'Call the police!'

I looked along the empty road stretching on and on with no village or town in sight, and no police. 'Be my guest,' I suggested. 'Yes, go ahead.'

'You call them,' she shouted, 'on your phone!'

I explained – no longer hiding my irritation – that I didn't have a phone.

'Just because you is white,' she said, 't'ink you can treat people so.'

I didn't understand what she meant. I wasn't as dark as her. I hadn't spent all day in the punishing sun but I was, undeniably, black.

'Just because you is white . . .' She sliced off a bit of the orange and chewing angrily on it turned and appealed to the other stallholders.

I took the chance, while she was temporarily distracted, to jump into the car. But before I could shut the door, I felt something hit my neck. In the shock, I thought she had cut me. I turned the key in the ignition and we sped off. It was only after a few miles that I felt brave enough to stop and inspect the damage. The collar of my shirt was stained orange: she had spat out the orange at me.

Years later, leafing through the pages of *Ian Fleming Introduces Jamaica*, I began to see more clearly what should have been obvious from the start about the encounter with the banana-seller. The author of the Bond novels, which he composed during his annual winter retreat to Jamaica, believed that 'because colour was at one time so mixed up with class, the habit persists among the peasantry of thinking the boss, though he may be as dark as night, as a buckra (white man)'. The converse was also true, 'on a Jamaican farm, for example, one may hear a black headman complain loudly that he cannot cope with the lazy "niggers" in his gang, and be surprised to see that the "niggers" he refers to are in some cases almost white.'

Buses from the countryside pulled up at Kingston's Coronation Market, laden with too many people, livestock, a plethora of fruit and vegetables, and in 1956 a scrawny, lanky twelve-year-old Peter Tosh. He found shelter with his aunt, with whom he would spend the next few years, in the slum of Denham Town. When she died, Tosh moved in with a furniture-making uncle in Trench Town. There is no record of Peter Tosh attending school in Kingston; neither has the school records for Marley, who arrived the following year, been found. Coronation Market – a site of arrival and departure, and an intersection of migrants' desperate hopes and rude, painful awakenings – grabbed all the headlines with a riot that ensued from the arrest on 7 May 1959 of a bearded man, mistaken for a Rastafarian. Tear-gas bombs were used to disperse the crowd protesting on the detained man's behalf.

Rastafarians, strange, barefooted, raggedy 'beard men', appeared almost as an urban myth in the villages where Tosh, Livingston and Marley were raised. They were bogeymen, the marginal blackheart men who dwelt alongside the gullies, whom children were schooled to fear. After the police burnt to the ground the Rastafarian stronghold at Pinnacle, close to Spanish Town, its dispersed community was confined to Kingston and the surrounds. Those in west Kingston sported fearsome knotted dreadlocks; those in the east cultivated beards. Their nattily dressed leader, Leonard Howell, often seen surveying Pinnacle in a pinstriped suit riding on the back of his donkey, would not have countenanced otherwise. In Trench Town, the Rastas were only one example of an extraordinary cast of characters: shouting preachers of every denomination; Revivalists who, when the spirit took them, spoke in an unknown tongue; and pushcart vendors selling fried fish and vicious artificial-looking drinks, who competed with vagabond poets hawking their work, neatly typed on sheets. Yardboys, with time to spare, idled away the day. And sweet-backed saga (swagger) boys proffered their services to good-time girls.

Comical and ineffective car horns blared constantly. Untethered goats and pigs roamed nonchalantly around the busy streets. Everywhere music blared; from car radios, from steel loudspeakers perched on branches high up in trees, and from the dark, dank interiors of record shops. Throughout the day, buses belched out fumes and sufferers (as local people called themselves), giving Tosh the impression that Kingstonians were constantly on the move. Voluminous conversations appeared more dramatic than their content warranted, and everyone seemed on the verge of selling or closing some kind of deal. In time, they included the three youths who had 'come from country'.

Bunny Livingston helped out in his father's rum shop, putting a broom to good use, and squeezing lime juice to cut the grease when washing up glasses. When orders for Tosh's furniture-maker uncle slowed, he carried on a sideline selling syrup, with his nephew acting as an assistant. The syrup would be sold on to the 'snowball-men' whose stalls traded in the popular thirst-quenching 'snowballs' of shaved ice topped with syrup. Tosh also had a penchant for carving wooden utensils and even combs which might be sold for a few coins. For his part, Bob Marley ran errands all day – for food and medicines – fetching and carrying at the market and numerous drugstores, which stocked both prescribed medicines as well as 'below-the-counter', and the not-so-conventional remedies of faith healers and Obeah-men who practised sorcery. The Frome report from two decades earlier had highlighted the poor state of the nation's health. Notwithstanding cajoling health workers and hectoring newspaper columnists, there had not been significant improvements.

In 1958, Ian Fleming chose confidently to position three blind men in Kingston at the start of Dr No, for, as the narrator notes, 'they would not have been incongruous in Kingston, where there are many diseased people on the streets'. The incidence of infectious diseases was much higher in the ghettoes. If Peter Tosh woke early enough he would witness a strange procession: a scurrying line of women carrying small black plastic bags, know as 'scandal bags'. The opaque black bags obscured their contents but everyone knew they contained the 'scandal' of human waste products, to be discarded surreptitiously at the edge of the township or the river. The slum-dwellers were lucky to escape an outbreak of cholera. Tuberculosis and typhoid were rife. And though yellow fever was perennially lurking, polio was the greater threat, made worse by a popular fear of inoculation, lest they be 'cripple up and t'ing' as a side effect of the vaccine. As Bunny Livingston recalled, at the behest of their parents, children would duck into the warren of side streets at the approach of health workers armed with vials and syringes.

Kingstonians tended to favour the pharmacist over the doctor, and displayed a preference for sending away for potions, rather than visiting the local drugstore. The *Gleaner* carried adverts daily for such cures as 'Vi-tabs' which promised to restore manhood and vigour within twenty-four hours, and 'Dodd's Kidney Pills' which insured against recurring headaches.

Amongst this cornucopia of advertised remedies, a small headline appeared on 15 December 1955, which would have alarmed Bob Marley's estranged father, Norval, and had him reaching into the medicine cabinet for 'Dodd's Kidney Pills'. The headline simply stated: 'Inquiry Into Bigamy Charge', and went on to inform the public that a court hearing was set for the new year when Norval Marley would have to answer the charge that having contracted a marriage in 1944 with Cedella Marley, he went through another form of marriage with Lena Scott, almost a decade later.

Cedella had turned sleuth when alerted by a neighbour that her missing husband had been spotted living with another woman in Kingston. In her account, having steeled herself to confront the truth, Cedella had crept up to the address she'd been given and was startled when Lena Scott answered the door. After a few moments, Cedella recovered her composure sufficiently to make a veiled and tactful enquiry as to the whereabouts of Master Norval Marley, only to be shooed away by his new wife, as the lady of the house might dismiss an insignificant servant. Thereafter, Cedella resolved to settle the matter in court.

She presented herself, with her son in tow, at the Halfway Tree Court House on 17 February 1956. Cedella admitted that she had failed to register the birth of Robert Nesta, but was confident about the soundness of her claim that not only was Norval the father of her child but also her husband. The judge, though, was not convinced, and proved to be more sympathetic towards the defendant. The case against Norval was discharged quickly after hearing evidence from two doctors regarding his mental condition. Since Cedella had last seen him, Norval Sinclair Marley, now reported to be over seventy, had aged ten more years than was chronologically possible. His doctors testified that he was suffering from senile dementia, and was disorientated regarding time, person and place. He was said to be largely incoherent, irrational in his speech and suffering from various delusions. Though Norval Marley denied that he had married Cedella, in the medic's opinion he was incapable of understanding any court proceedings brought against him. And the judge ruled that, as his condition was deteriorating, there was little to be gained from sending him to Belle Vue psychiatric hospital. The bigamy proceedings were abandoned. Norval Marley died shortly after the court case, but any mourning from his 'first' wife and child was coloured by his disturbing denial of their legal status.

Their condition was not helped by the move to Kingston, where Cedella struggled to find work and would have had to compete with the army of prospective servants who placed adverts in the *Gleaner*, some unashamedly highlighting those features deemed most attractive.

Position Wanted,
Sensible middle-aged woman, almost white,
Seeks employment, linen keeper[65]

Fairness of skin might provide domestic candidates with the key to the front door of upper-class homes, but in the ghetto of Trench Town the opposite was often the case. In his early days there, Bob Marley was abused more than he would ever confess because of his light complexion. Ghetto dwellers were all 'sufferers' together, but at a time of hardening racial antipathy, there were some, wrote his mother, who vexed her spirit because 'them style Bob as a white man'.[66] This was particularly the case amongst the Nyabinghi branch of the Rastafarian cult in Kingston. Their hatred for the white oppressor (or his proxy) was visceral: a Nyabinghi session would open with the shout: 'death to the white man'. Theirs was an angry and exclusive club, based on a code of animus and a sliding scale of racial purity. Ultimately, Nyabinghi ceremonies were as much racial as spiritual sacraments. In shacks, where the air was thick with argument and marijuana, judgement was passed on those who sought to join, with the finality of the 'black ball' rolled out at a Victorian gentleman's club. Two Rastafarians might turn up for a meeting, one darker than the other, and the lighter-skinned man would be barred from entry and turned away.[67]

In the village of Nine Miles, his colour had little perceptible impact on Bob Marley, once the initial bubble of gossip about his origins had run out of oxygen. In Kingston, he ran a much greater risk of ridicule, but his fortunes were to improve with his association with the son of village neighbours, the Livingstons, who had also moved to Trench Town. Both Bob Marley and, to a lesser extent, Bunny Livingston answered to the description of 'force-ripe'. Jamaican youths toughened or matured beyond their years were 'force-ripe', through exposure to concerns and events from which parents might reasonably have shielded them. And though he was two years younger, Bunny Livingston saw himself somewhat as Bob Marley's protector, especially when Cedella and her son moved into Toddy Livingston's household. Cedella was offered work in his rum shop, and for the board of her and Bob she was obliged to perform a degree of housekeeping.

'Although these "housekeeper" arrangements, as they are called, may not be formed primarily for sexual reasons,' wrote the sociologist Edith Clarke, 'it is normal for the parties to have sexual relations and for children to be born.'[68] Thaddeus Livingston and Cedella Marley did not deviate from the norm. Where they did show innovation, however, was in the fact that Clarke's analysis referred to single or unmarried men living alone. Thaddeus's existing common-law wife was not, at first, privy to the terms Toddy would attach to their tenant's 'housekeeper' duties.

The Livingstons lived on Second Street, just a few blocks away from Peter Tosh. When Tosh recorded that in coming to Trench Town he was exposed to 'the most dangerous things I ever heard or see in my life', he had in mind events like the mob killing of a JLP activist who was battered and stabbed to death on 22 March 1958 on the corner of West Road where Tosh lived. That first political murder was an aberration, even for Trench Town. Nonetheless, it seemed to be symptomatic of a pathological inability among some slumdwellers to resolve conflicts save through aggression – verbal and physical.

'Few residents of Kingston would go unaccompanied to the slums [where] quarrels develop with lightning speed,' observed another contemporary researcher, Mary Proudfoot.[69] Trench Town dwellers lived cheek by jowl in sickening squalor. Shacks were thrown up by the latest wave of migrants or decamped squatters as soon as they arrived. Proudfoot itemised the materials most commonly used in their construction in chilling detail: the carcasses of rusting discarded cars; pieces of boarding; and sometimes just cardboard. When, on the last leg of his Caribbean tour in 1950, Patrick Leigh Fermor stopped off at Jamaica, he had the temerity to visit a Rastafarian encampment – marked by flagpoles fluttering the red, yellow and green tricolour flag of Abyssinia – to pay his respects to the 'abominable Negroes' of Dunhill (on the outskirts of Kingston), 'dressed in the most sordid rags'. The Rastafarians, he wrote gloomily, inhabited huts of about 'two yards square and constructed entirely of copies of the *Daily Gleaner* glued together.'[70] Even in the various Kingston slums, then, poverty was relative. 'I don't know if the ghetto is the same all over the world but in Jamaica there's nothing there . . . we're talking about the dirt and the dust,' recalled Leroy Sibbles, the effervescent lead singer of the Heptones, who lived there at the time. 'It's every man for himself.'

The reality of Trench Town was far removed from how things were meant to have been, and a libel upon the Utopian ideals of the planners who had proudly overseen its development as Kingston's newest and most modern township (then called Trench Pen) in the 1940s. Local councillors had acquired part of the estate at Trench Pen from the Trench family, Scottish planters whose presence on the island dated back to the 1700s. Over the years the Trenches had carved out their land and rented out sections of it; they were quintessential absentee landlords. But now in the 1930s they settled on selling a huge swathe, a square mile, to the council. The pens, kept usually as gardens for promenades and stockades for the livestock, would be cleared for human habitation.

The residential buildings (later known as 'government yards') started going up in 1942. They took seven years to complete, largely because of the careful attention given to materials for construction. Walls were made with a combination of brick aggregate and regular fired bricks. Handhewn bullet wood was used to construct the core frames; cedar for the windows and doors; and, finally, flat concrete tiles to line the roofs. The designs also specified that courtyards would be built to encourage communal contact and to create space for privacy and outside living. Even the gently sloping topography of Trench Pen was taken into account so that buildings varied subtly from street to street. The Fabian sympathisers who dreamt of Trench Town were inspired by

John Ruskin's vision of bringing the countryside to the city, of creating a townscape that was a 'clean and busy street within and the open country without, with a belt of beautiful garden and orchard round the walls.' Trench Town was a great achievement on a par with the model villages of Port Sunlight and Saltaire built in Victorian Britain.[71]

Philanthropy in Jamaica, though, came with a price. Some of the key advocates of the scheme owned businesses (brick-making and timber merchandise) which stood to gain from the local government contracts.[72] And from the outset the Housing Board showed a determination to preserve a semblance of the island's social hierarchy in the Utopian estate, and graded the deserving poor. There would be two types of building: 'cottages for persons of the artisan class, these being separate and distinct from tenements which should be occupied by individuals of the domestic type'. Over the years, the protracted building work ate into the funds assigned to the project. As no monies had been ring-fenced for a sewage system, Trench Town would have to do without, and resign itself to a future of 'scandal bags'. A single concrete trench filled with untreated sewage would serve the idyllic homes on the estate, and because the township was built in the shadow of the notorious open storm sewer of Sandy Gully, when the rains came foul water flooded the streets. Even so, more than 150 residential buildings were eventually erected, with the government yards stretching over six blocks. 'Argument done,' as they say in Jamaica. Well, not quite.

No sooner had the final brick been laid and the cladding applied than it was apparent that demand would massively outstrip the supply of accommodation. As each street was finished tenants would be joined by a never-ending stream of squatters. A survey conducted a year after completion revealed that almost 4,000 squatters had descended on and around the area of Trench Town. Ruskin's belt of beautiful gardens had become a scraggly ring of vicious-looking 'odious and a malodorous' cacti.[73] And councillors were soon competing in levels of outrage over the scandalous sight of 'men, hogs, crows, dogs and everything, mingling together in the rubbish and refuse thrown there from day to day'.[74] Furthermore, to discourage squatting the government refused to provide public amenities, a strategy which failed as a deterrent: squatters resorted to digging pit latrines and stealing water from fire hydrants.[75]

The environment had a brutalising effect on the slumdwellers, young and old. Mary Proudfoot noticed that youths mimicked the attitude of their elders: 'Even small children fight with knives and stones and pieces of broken glass,' she wrote. And the philanthropic priest, Hugh Sherlock, who took great interest in the welfare of youngsters, noted that half-naked boys as young as four years old had been co-opted into peddling 'weed' in the neighbourhood.[76]

As far back as 1938, the authorities recognised that something needed to be done to occupy the ghetto youth and steer them away from anti-social activities. On 28 February that year, the Secretary of State for the Colonies spelt out the special need for a boys' club in Kingston, to bring 'homeless and neglected boys who wander about the streets, particularly in the slum areas, under some supervision and guidance'. The proposed club would be located on the edge of Trench Town at Dunghill. Though acknowledging the urgency, the administration was reluctant to meet the costs, and even contemplated going cap in hand to the charitable Carnegie Corporation.[77]

The 'Boys Town' club on Collie Smith Drive, named after the gallant Jamaican cricketer whom thousands had mourned after he died in a car crash in 1959, went some way to answering the needs of idle youth. The club was associated with an All-Age school of the same name; it included a cricket pitch (a favourite haunt of Livingston) and football pitch which Bob Marley frequented regularly. Marley was always more passionate about football than cricket, but he can't have been anything other than thrilled when the great Frank Worrell, as a tribute to Collie Smith, padded up, and faced the local club the following year. Worrell was lionised. He played with an easy flair and panache – anything less would not have been acceptable in the Caribbean. In the absence of other heroic figures, cricketers became vessels for the adoration of the masses. Idolisation was not a given; it came with certain expectations. For more than any other group in society – musicians, priests or politicians – the cricketers' style mattered. Growing up in Trinidad, V. S. Naipaul noted the crowd's exultation as the batsman, displaying his bat as a peacock does its feathers, strutted to the crease. 'Unless the cricketer had heroic qualities, we did not want to see him, however valuable he might be,' wrote Naipaul, 'and that was why, of those stories of failure, that of the ruined cricketer was the most terrible.'[78]

That afternoon, sharing a pitch with Worrell was the closest the Boys Town boys ever came to cricketing glory. Looking back over the years, Locksley Cumrie, an alumnus of the club, made a mental roll call of past associates: 'A good number of my friends have died and none of them died a natural death. 90 per cent died by gun or machete.' Even so Cumrie concluded that 'without Boys Town club, it would have been worse.'[79]

The three boys, having recently arrived from the country, appear to have lived something of a feral existence at this phase of their lives. When Marley in a later song wrote: 'Cold ground was my bed last night/and rock was my pillow too', he drew on real-life experience for the lyrics. At various times, he had to fend for himself, almost a vagabond, 'cotching' (finding temporary accommodation) with friends or neighbours, forced to sleep on a pallet or a straw mat rolled out on the kitchen floor at night.

There is, however, much disparity between the accounts of the boys themselves and the remembrances of their parents or guardians. Fearing that her son might be subject to the bad influences that were ever present and almost unavoidable in the ghetto, Cedella wrote that she scrimped and saved for Bob's private education at Ebenezer School. Similarly, in a retrospective interview, Tosh's mother referred to the sacrifices she made to cultivate her son's musical talents; finding money to meet the considerable expense of paying for him to take weekly music lessons. The boys didn't quite see it that way. Tosh confided to his audio diary that his mother had all but abandoned him to the care of an aunt; and Marley, revealing a rare slip of rancour, spoke of growing up without supervision: 'Me grow stubborn you know. Me grow without mother and father. Me nuh have no parents for have no big influence 'pon me. Me just grow inna the ghetto with the youth. Stubborn, nah obey no one.'[80] Both accounts call to mind the exchange between Topsy and her inquisitor in *Uncle Tom's Cabin*. When asked about her upbringing, Tospy explains away the absence of parental input saying she was 'raised by a speculator' and, further, when pressed as to how she managed to reach adulthood, responds: 'Never was born . . . I s'pect I [just] growd.'[81]

Fictionalised versions of youths like Tosh, Marley and Livingston began to appear in the work of local writers. They ran barefoot through the books of Roger Mais, a savvy insider, who was among the first novelists to depict life in Kingston's west-end ghettoes. His *Brother Man*, written in 1954, seethes with melodrama and casual violence – from the women who brandish cutlasses ready to slash their lovers' cheeks, to the midnight cries of 'Murder! Murder!' in the deserted streets. And yet, at its centre is the saintly Rastafarian, Brother Man, who holds out the possibility of redemption even amid the squalor and pestilence. In researching his protagonist, Mais would have been spoilt for choice. Every street corner in Trench Town boasted a Brother Man – a singing one in the case of Joe Higgs, a righteous, beret-wearing Rastaman and natural-born teacher with an open countenance as wide as his grin; and a growly voiced intellectual in the shape of Mortimer Planno. Every utterance, no matter how commonplace, seemed pregnant with gravitas when Planno spoke. He also had the kind of fleshy, lumpy and swollen, unfinished gnarled face, like a rock covered in moss, so removed from prevailing perceptions of handsomeness that it intrigues. Within the decade, Planno would have cast a lasting spell over the three country boys. For now though, they were more interested in ways of sneaking into Kingston's open-air dances at Jubilee Tile Gardens or Chocomo Lawn, and more given to memorising the lyrics of popular American crooners such as Nat King Cole and Sam Cooke or the jumping jive of R&B cats like Fats Domino, than the enigmatic pronouncements of Rasta elders.

Fats Domino was so revered in Jamaica that, perhaps not surprisingly, he had a domino club named after him, as well as popular nightclub, the 'Fats Domino Beer Garden' – though there was to be no pit stop for Fats at the Beer Garden on his 1961 tour of Jamaica.[82] While working-class Jamaicans could hardly afford to patronise the uptown swanky nightclubs or the major theatres with tickets 'at popular prices' where his 'Royal Majesty of Music' wowed audiences in 1961, they might, for the price of a bottle of beer, storm the open-air dances where sound systems boomed throughout the weekend.

By the late 1950s, the sound systems had come to be dominated by half a dozen operators – DJs with a posse of supporters and fans whose allegiance was only guaranteed as far as the next record 'hit' home that night. The DJs turned the bass and volume up so high that, almost a mile away on Second Street, Marley and Livingston's window frames shook. 'You'd hear that booming sound all the way up the road,' remembered Viv Adams, 'but we weren't, as children, allowed to go ... The sound systems? ... There was always something a bit risqué about them ... They were a grown-up people thing, and some-times bad things happened. After all, the dancehall was very much a downtown thing, primal, elemental and explosive.'[83] For young boys whose musical exposure had, to date, been confined to the fervour of a resounding hymn in church, even the fringes of the dancehall must have felt extraordinarily intense. It was as if a sound that might be expected to fill a stadium was concentrated in someone's backyard.

The DJs' customised, handmade speakers were massive, the size of wardrobes; and were designed to pump out the biggest, baddest sounds. All the DJ needed was a patch of ground called a 'lawn', walled or fenced off with barbed wire (requiring payment on entry) at the back of a house or the side of a building, and a rack of wicked tunes to outdo his competitor. It was a vibrant and volatile world in which rival sound systems would hire 'bad men' to break up, or in some rare instances 'shoot-up' a competitor's equipment. They gave themselves fantastic monikers and outlandish outfits: Clement 'Sir Coxsone' Dodd and 'Duke' Reid ruled the world. Dodd was the epitome of cool restraint. His main rival, the flamboyant ex-policeman, 'gorgeous' Duke Reid was renowned for making his grand entrance to the dancehall 'flowing in ermine, a mighty gold crown on his head, a .45 in a cowboy holster ... and a cartridge belt across his chest'. In the wings there were a host of others waiting to take his crown.

Decades later, Lloyd Daley, who signed on as the 'Matador', still brimmed with satisfaction at the recollection of the night he drowned out Duke Reid's sound system with his own: 'It's not just the record, it's the sound – the weight I was dropping, the amount of bass ... A matador really is a bullfighter, and I would actually take my opponent as a bull.'[84] Of course, once testosterone levels had returned to a semblance of normality – the last single pulled from the deck and the empty bottles, now drained of beer, let fly into the crowd – the record would be the final arbiter of longevity. Long after ears stopped ringing, it was the lyrics or the riff of the music that echoed in punters' heads.

One or two record shops specialised in pre-release or imported records that were not yet in all the other shops. The trick for the master DJ was to find a record no one else knew about, scratch off the label so it couldn't be identified, and blast it to hell on the turntable because your rival was bound to have 'captured' it by the following weekend, or topped it with something better.

With this hunger for novelty, for the transient glory of exclusivity, the sound-system men began to look, not further afield, as might have been expected, but to the possibility of performers in their midst. In time, the DJs turned themselves into record producers with the accent on local versions of black American ballads, or on Jamaican songs coming out of a folk tradition, given an R&B twist.

Tosh, Livingston and Marley had arrived in the capital at a fortuitous time. Trench Town was a hothouse of musical expressiveness and burgeoning musical alliances. If Pocomania revellers did not jump up with doo-wop balladeers, nor Burru men jam to the beat of Kumina drummers, then they soon would.

Livingston and Marley were living in the same house; they hadn't yet met Tosh. As far as Bunny Livingston could recall, they first set sight on the enigmatic Tosh as he wandered round Trench Town singing 'Go Tell It on the Mountain'. Finally though, it was syrup that brought them together. Peter Tosh was peddling vats of condensed sugar-cane juice for his uncle when Joe Higgs ran into him. Higgs had been discovered by the Harvard-educated Edward Seaga, an early and unlikely music impresario who, in the previous two years, had lived amongst the Jamaican peasantry, deep in the countryside, conducting fieldwork in indigenous music.

With a simple recording machine he collected folk music and the ceremonies of religious cults (raw, rare, beguiling and hitherto unrecorded music which he later sold to Folkways Records). Seaga had moved deftly from the 'bush' into Kingston's fledgling recording industry. And with Higgs, one of his first signings, he had scored an early musical success with 'O Manny O'. Joe Higgs was barely out of his teens himself when he began to tutor Tosh, Marley, Livingston and many other Trench Town youth. He appears to have been something of an autodidact and born to teach. From his yard on Third Street, Joe Higgs gave regular lessons in harmony, framing, tone and pitch; he did so with no expectation of reward. And, rather than break charity with that noble idea of himself, having established this weekly, sometimes daily, precedent he stuck with it – even when his half-made, unofficial pupils left to achieve success on a much grander scale than he had ever managed. In the dirt yard outside his kitchen, Higgs presided over a collegiate and competitive world, peopled by young men and women who dreamt of musical glory – or more likely of its financial remuneration. With no false modesty Higgs often recounted how he'd been the catalyst behind the formation of the group destined to be the Wailers: 'I formed the Wailers and taught them voice consciousness. They weren't conscious of sound, harmony structure, proper timing and singing in key – or how to go about making a song until I taught them.' That recognition, the title 'Bob Marley's Teacher', in some small way compensated for the eclipse of his own musical ambitions that came thereafter.[85]

Higgs would also admit that their future success was far from guaranteed when they came knocking at his yard. The trio did not at first stand out among all the other candidates whose whopping, spontaneous and generous praise was offset by roiling arguments over whether a brethren had 't'ken a song off' another or 'stole him belongings', over future copyright and accusations of unattributed borrowings or outright theft. An early recorded artist, Owen Grey, was said to have had to flee Jamaica after he cut and wounded Clancy Eccles. The ratchet-wielding Grey had accused Eccles of stealing one of his songs and pirating it, and had exacted immediate and satisfying revenge.

Criticism was not always confined to this musical yard. The 'sticks could start coming' from any direction, remembered Anthony Doyley. Just by walking the streets of Trench Town, musicians exposed themselves to judgements from wizened grannies to youthful hoodlums: 'Say them boys would just finish rob somebody and ... they're having a drink an' a chat and Bob [Marley] would be walking down the road with his guitar and they would be saying things like, "Hoy deh! Say, you a musician, play us some song then, mek we hear you!" And if it's not good enough them would be start criticising it.'[86]

Such a verbal volley was more likely to be aimed at Peter Tosh at the start of 1961. Tosh, who was already more than six feet tall, towered over Marley and the diminutive Livingston, but there was yet another way in which he commanded even greater respect and attention: he possessed a guitar. Actually, it was on long-term loan from his church, but it was far superior to anything else the other two had to offer, and certainly a cut above Livingston's home-made effort, fashioned from a bamboo stick, an old, oversize sardine can and electrical wire stripped of its insulation.

Even in their early teens, music was more than a hobby, though family members still envisioned the youths embarking on a more practical trade. The census of 1960 revealed that almost 20 per cent of Kingston's potential labour force was unemployed. Although the *Jamaica Times* reported that 'industry is booming' and the *Gleaner* bubbled over with excitement at the prosperity which was bound to come from the great strides made in industry, particularly in tourism (from 1950 to 1960 the number of tourists visiting the north coast trebled from 70,000 to almost a quarter of a million), the prospects for boys such as Tosh and Marley who left school with few qualifications were dire.

The most likely avenues of hope lay in the profusion of small garages and mechanical workshops dotted around the capital. Jamaica had no car industry but it did have an extraordinary number of second-hand vehicles, and an army of mechanics determined to satisfy customers' desire to keep them on the road well past their life expectancy. As a consequence, there was a high demand for welders, and the families of both Tosh and Marley pushed them towards apprenticeships. The work was dirty and gruelling and filled both boys with loathing. 'Bob hated it,' recalled his mother, but each morning he would climb onto a bicycle lent to him by Bunny and make his way conscientiously to Millards Welders. For fifteen shillings a week he welded iron grilles, gates and curved ornamental work. But the job was dangerous: his mother recalls once, when he was working with the welding iron, 'a piece of metal flew off and got stuck right in the white of his eye, and he had to go to the hospital twice to have it taken out. It caused him terrible pain; it even hurt for him to cry.'[87]

Tosh was even more disenchanted with the apprenticeship. But then he was not given to anything, remembered his mother, which required a commitment to stick and stay. 'He didn't take life seriously,' she believed, even when there seemed little cause for gaiety. 'Peter was always running joke,' observed Wayne Jobson, the reggae DJ whose cousin Dickie was a director of Island Records.[88] Contrary to the way music journalists would later depict him, Tosh always possessed a great store of humour. His musical 'spars' (buddies) Marley and Livingston were said to be more sombre and serious.

Tosh might have displayed a jovial demeanour, but he was also prone to alarming swings in mood. Music was the only real constant. 'I was learning piano music at the age of ten,' Tosh confided to his diary. In his estimation he had covered five years' worth of piano work in nine months, until one day he heard an old farmer in the countryside playing a guitar: 'And it was a beauty to listen to the sound what the man get. That stop me think 'bout piano now.' Tosh sat down and watched the old man. As the hours passed and the light began to fade, he approached him with a suggestion: 'Me say lend me your guitar there man. So me start play the song what him just done play. And hear him say to me "Who teach you for play guitar?" Me say, "A you teach me, a right here so me learn."'[89] No one, apart from the farmer, had spotted his prodigious talent, but Tosh had glimpsed his own potential: 'If I only had the opportunity of having my own professional instrument, I would play the songs that angels sing.'

Though there was no formal arrangement between the boys, Peter Tosh's guitar accompaniment would prove vital to the success of the variety night competitions and auditions that the three vocalists hoped for. But there was always the threat that, when piqued, the prickly Tosh would prematurely bring a session to an end and take his guitar home with him. Tosh would later claim that, at least as far as the guitar was concerned, Marley had been *his* pupil. The trio, who would soon form the nucleus of a band, were equals, but Peter Tosh was first among them.

3

OPPORTUNITY KNOCKS

A sixty-seven-year-old man dressed immaculately in an evening suit strode to the front of the empty stage. Vere Johns inhabited his suit with the ease of a man who had done so, almost weekly, for the last twenty years. In front of the microphone, Johns spread out his arms and in his precise, elocutionist's voice welcomed the vast, cheering audience at the Palace Theatre to the first part of the evening billed as 'Opportunity Hour'. This was Jamaica's talent show extraordinaire, a nationwide event, with heats, quarter-finals and semi-finals before the eventual showdown between a handful of winning contestants. A veteran promoter, Vere Johns had presided over the show since his return to the island from the USA in the late 1930s.

The winners were drawn from a pool of performers who included singers and 'other acts' such as juvenile hula-hoopers, rhumba and belly-dancers sporting stage names like 'Madame Wasp' and 'Madame Sugar Hips'. The overall winners were guaranteed a £10 prize and, if they caught the attention of a scout or producer, the tantalising prospect of regular work in the entertainment industry. A lucky few might also be offered guest spots on Johns's radio show, *Opportunity Knocks* on RJR (Radio Jamaica and the Rediffusion Network).

The stars of tomorrow were only permitted one shot at fame on the variety show: opportunity knocked only once. There was, though, a popular ruse employed shamelessly to circumvent this restriction. Performers got on the right side of Vere Johns – literally, as the music maestro was blind in one eye. 'If he knew you by your voice, he tell you "No, you were there last week"'. If, like Barrington Spence, amid the ballyhoo and mayhem of the auditions for a place on the show, the canny candidate lined up 'on the blind side' of [Vere Johns] he might have a chance of going through undetected.[90]

'Opportunity Hour' ran to a very simple formula. Musical accompaniment was provided by the resident pianist and his orchestra, Johns was the host, and the audience was the judge. There was no 'clap-o-meter': the show's organisers merely took note of the volume of applause and enthusiasm of the audience, and rewarded the act which generated most excitement.

When Tosh, Marley and Livingston sang at one of their first outings at the Ward Theatre, the applause rolled round the aisles, and the screams, yelps and whistling crested with a shower of coins thrown onto the stage. 'Me look at some two and six-pence piece lick me head and all of them things,' Tosh recalled. 'So I stop sing and just go and pick them up . . . two pockets full! [But] before I come off stage, it was begged out. Every man in the audience come beg it back.'[91]

The local hero status usually lasted a little longer. 'Opportunity Hour' and its radio equivalent were popular entertainment, geared largely towards the labouring and artisan classes. A people's theatre, it created stars previously known to the audience as yardboys or seamstresses, now transformed into kings and queens for the day, week or month. The hour of opportunity ticked away in venues which doubled as cinemas. The talent show preceded the main billing of the night (usually a Hollywood movie) when the audience cheered and shouted out to their onscreen heroes – such as Burt Lancaster in *The Sweet Smell of Success* or Humphrey Bogart in *The Maltese Falcon* – with the same brim and force, wit and humour with which they championed the stage acts the hour before. This curious interaction between the crowd and the silver screen was common throughout the Caribbean. At about the same time in Trinidad, V. S. Naipaul was amused to note that when Lauren Bacall in *To Have and Have Not* told an admirer that she was born in Port of Spain, Trinidad, the audience erupted and shouted delightedly at the screen: 'You lie! You lie!'[92]

Kingston's uptown 'Myrtle Bank Crowd' was more demure; their pretension to metropolitan sophistication was catered for by a dozen nightclubs in the capital's corporate area. They snapped fingers to the jazz at the Colony Club at Crossroads and took to the floor at the Bournemouth Club or, as the sun dipped below the horizon, lounged at tables on verandas and listened to flickering, candlelit solos sung from a raft bobbing gently in the middle of the pool. And for those who considered even such entertainments a little too racy, refuge could always be found in the kind of upper-crust social gatherings satirised by John Figueroa in *Do You Appreciate Music?*, where a premium was placed on tertiary education. In the short story the narrator acknowledges the exclusivity of such societies: 'To have a degree distinguishes one in Kingston, so that the music appreciation gathering at Miss Kathlyn Kline's on Monday night was quite a distinguished gathering, for not one of the two men and eight women present did not have a degree.'

Obtaining a degree and subsequently gaining entry into such rarefied circles was always unlikely for the contestants at the Palace Theatre. Even so, Trench Town was not short of its own, home-grown intellectuals. The autodidact Joe Higgs, the district's unofficial music tutor, had excelled at 'Vere Johns's Opportunity Hour' in 1959.

But the fluctuating fortunes of Joe Higgs would prove a lasting lesson to those he mentored and other aspiring talents. For within months of his success at the variety show, Higgs, who sang with an ethereal beauty, was beaten brutally by the police for one simple reason: he was a Rastafarian.

The riot at Coronation Market in 1959 had resulted in much public ranting and raving over the 'Rasta problem'. As Jervis Anderson observed, many Jamaicans had a low opinion of the 'bearded cultists' and spoke of them almost as one would termites. From New York, where he'd relocated, Jervis Anderson counselled caution, if not a sympathetic understanding. Attempting to explain Rastas to his New York readership (later to be reprinted in the *Gleaner*), Anderson wrote with more amusement than disgust: Rastas were Jamaica's 'beat generation'. Granted, beatnik beards were not as scraggly, nor was their hair quite as unkempt, but they shared a suspicion of the virtues of state-sponsored employment; and both subscribed to ideals of 'peace and love'. Anderson concluded prophetically that the time would come 'when the fame of Jamaica's "beatniks" will spread abroad and the American [tourists'] first request in Jamaica will be "Show me a Rasta!"' Anderson's prayer that Jamaicans would eventually be just as proud of their 'bearded men' as they were of their rum, did not come to pass in the run-up to Independence. Rather, outraged citizens and the Jamaican Constabulary levelled fire at the Rastas.[93]

With a population sensitised to the negative connotations of Rastafari, even the egalitarian instincts of Vere Johns were tested. When the rhumba dancer Magarita Mahfood, whom he'd booked to appear at the Ward Theatre, turned up at the stage door with her backing band – Count Ossie and his Rasta Drummers – Vere Johns's cool professionalism deserted him: he panicked, like a cartoon character subject to trauma, jumping out of his skin. Taking the 'shimmying shaking bombshell' to one side, Johns whispered that what she proposed was impossible. But Mahfood, one of his most popular acts, would not go on without the Count Ossie band. In the compromise that was reached, the Rastas were allowed on stage but only if they remained right at the back and in the shadows, without illumination.[94] In some regard, the position of Rastas in Jamaican society mirrored that of African-Americans at the time. Like twinned particles subject to the laws of quantum mechanics, a provocation on one seemed to produce a response, and action, which would have an immediate and corresponding reaction in the other, even though it was several thousand miles away.

In the same year of Count Ossie's sidelining, in America the jazz-band leader Dave Brubeck was deemed guilty of an unforgivable faux pas when he had the gall to introduce Eugene Wright, a black bassist, into his otherwise all-white quartet. The band was booked to appear at an American campus one night in 1959, but the flustered college president complained that Brubeck's inclusion of Wright had compromised the integrity of the institution. '*You* can go on [stage],' he conceded reluctantly, 'but you have to put your bass player at the back, where he won't be too noticeable.'[95]

These custodians of culture would begin to feel the ground shifting beneath their feet more rapidly by the decade's end. In the USA, so-called 'race music' found its way across airwaves previously restricted to it, and into suburban homes in Wichita. Even more spectacularly, Count Ossie and his drummers would find themselves, in 1962, placed centre stage in front of Princess Margaret at the celebrations marking Jamaican independence, and Vere Johns would be among those cheering them on. The Jamaican writer and cultural historian Viv Adams recalls watching Count Ossie on the stage at the Palace Theatre as a ten year old, and the strange alluring quality to the drumming that made his heart melt.[96] Count Ossie and other Rasta drummers had honed their skills alongside another marginal set of the population called the Burru people, who ended up in the slums of Back-o-Wall, (an area whose name was

derived from the back wall of the local cemetery) and Dungle with the
Rastas. 'The Burru people were not a spiritual people, but they were
a drum-playin' people. They smoked weed and chanted,' recalled the
music promoter Herbie Miller. In Kingston, they 'scuffled', making a
living from hustling on the waterfront, and attracted the unwelcome
attention of the Jamaican Constabulary. 'Many times there was a Burru
session to celebrate someone getting released from prison . . . The Rasta
people had a natural affinity for these Burru men, but the Rasta are a
peace-and-love order; the Burru people were a bit more lawless. What
really united them was music.'[97]

That mesmerising appeal of the Rasta and Burru drummers was also
described by the Jamaican musicologist Verena Reckford. In her reminis-
cences of growing up in Spanish Town in the 1940s, she recalled ignoring
her mother's warning to beware the Burru, as, on her daily walk home
from school, she was drawn to their enchanting music. 'I passed peeping
through nail holes in the dirty zinc fence at the Burru men playing their
drums around a fire, singing and cursing "bad words" all the time. To
my child's soul, Burru music was the sweetest music ever heard. I could
not resist it. If the drums were momentarily silent when I was passing
by, I would "dally" hoping for them to start again.'[98]

Burru men and Rasta drummers were still more likely to be found
around campfires than on the bill at the Palace Theatre, but the
longevity of Vere Johns's 'Opportunity Hour' bore testament to the life-
transforming expectations of the huge numbers of their compatriots
who jammed the entrances at auditions. Vere Johns's wasn't the only
show in town. Chris Blackwell recalled that there were mini versions
of 'Opportunity Hour'. One such was presided over by Horace Forbes,
though his shows differed in one small detail: there was always a
contestant who was allowed to return for repeated second chances
at stardom – Horace Forbes himself. 'Forbes was really a singer that
nobody wanted to listen to,' says Blackwell, with more compassion than
malice. 'The only way he could sing was to be a promoter, and then
he'd get up and do his own bit of the set, during which people would
boo and throw stones.' But Forbes did inadvertently give a platform
to one or two future stars. Chris Blackwell went on to record a Forbes
contestant called Wilfred Edwards whose 'Your Eyes are Dreaming' was
an instant success. Though Blackwell now considers it 'a rather lame
attempt at American blues, or R&B', he acknowledges that such was

the thirst for Jamaicans to have and to hold something local, of their very own, that 'it didn't sound that lame at the time'.[99]

The limited outlets for performers did not discourage but rather fuelled competition, and led to musical experimentation. Perhaps it was not so evident in the acts of R&B mimicry at the Palace Theatre, or the saccharine and sanitised calypsos that greeted guests checking in at the foyers of the major hotels. Innovation, when it came, was mostly inspired by the fecund creativity of the downtown dancehalls.

Dancehall promoters did not adhere to carefully crafted business plans; they acted instinctively, taking note of local singers' quickening popularity among the music-loving masses. Almost overnight, promoters like Clement Dodd at Studio One, with more chutzpah than experience, turned themselves into record producers. But, remembered Chris Blackwell, at first 'the recordings didn't come out quite right. The accent was on the wrong beat, so to speak; the musicians of Jamaica just played it different.' From this Jamaican twist to R&B a novel sound evolved: ska.

Jamaican manufacturing has long been handicapped by its limited local production, as evident in its 'screwdriver' industries – where the parts are made elsewhere and then assembled on the island. The music industry was no different. In the 1950s Jamaica's popular music needs were served by America; they existed largely on offcuts of what was then referred to as 'race-music'. Intermediaries like Blackwell trafficked in imports, flying regularly to New Orleans or New York and returning laden with records whose labels, as noted previously, would be scratched off. Local production removed that dependency, but the first faltering steps were confined to flimsy acetate recordings destined to last only as long as the DJ could keep his edge on his competitors. By the time the novelty had worn off and the crowds no longer thronged the lawns, the acetates had worn out anyway. But it wasn't just that ska was a local version of the familiar R&B; its vibrancy was unique and infectious. 'Anytime you hear the music, you have to move,' recalled Tosh.

Jamaica, then as now, was known as the 'loudest island in the world'. And the simple studios, boasting one- or two-track mixing desks, somehow captured the energy and excitement of the performers. Blackwell felt the competition keenly: 'When the sound-system guys started making records themselves their records sold better than mine ... They didn't sound as clean and as neat but the sound was raw, raucous, exciting and happening. Very soon their records just took over and mine didn't sell so much.' The queues for auditions at Vere Johns' Palace Theatre were soon matched by the long lines of hopefuls waiting in the courtyard for their chance of stardom at Studio One. But if the sound-system men found themselves as accidental record producers, then so too did a handful of proprietors of Chinese grocery stores.

The happenstance of Leslie Kong's transformation might have sounded apocryphal had it not been almost conventional. One night an unheralded youth (who would later answer to the stage name Jimmy Cliff) walked through the door at Beverly's, a restaurant and ice-cream parlour which Kong ran with his brothers. Cliff made an unusual proposition. Had they ever considered branching out into Jamaica's exciting new recording industry? Before the Kongs could throw out the teenage prankster, Cliff broke into song. He had composed a kind of musical love-letter to Beverly's, which he was convinced they could use as a sure-fire entrée into the recording business. 'I sang the song "Dearest Beverly". The two other Chinese brothers, they laughed,' recalled Cliff, 'but the other one [Leslie], he said, "Oh, I think he has the best voice I've heard in Jamaica."' The guffaws gave way to sober reflection, and, within a few months – Abracadabra! Beverly's record label was born.[100]

In 1962, another youth, Robert Nesta Marley, made the pilgrimage to Beverly's, armed with a tune called 'Judge Not', which he'd composed and previously tried out at Vere Johns's talent show. Word had spread quickly about the latest opportunities on offer at Beverly's. Singers showed up all the time. Never mind that the effete Chinese-Jamaican grocer seemed to take greater pleasure in rejection than acceptance. After an impromptu audition in the street, Marley scurried along behind Kong to the Federal Recording Studios. The studio and resident session musicians were hired by the hour. Marley's plaintive debut was committed to acetate. And having signed a contract, 'releasing' the copyright to Beverly Records, Marley skipped out of the studio with £20 in his back pocket, a handsome sum – more money than a welder could earn in a year.

Sizeably more was on offer when Kong sanctioned the twenty-five-year-old Blackwell, who'd ventured to London and turned himself into a record importer, to distribute 'Judge Not' and a few other titles around the growing Caribbean ex-pat communities in the UK. After being squeezed out of the Jamaican music scene by rivals such as Kong and Clement

Dodd, Blackwell had seized upon the idea of targeting a niche market, one that he believed would be profitable and relatively untapped: expats in London. Chris Blackwell was finding that his unusual upbringing enabled him to negotiate communities that were sometimes polar opposites. By his own admission, he led a charmed existence and something of a double life. By night, a regular on the chic Bohemian social circuit, he scoffed vol-au-vents and knocked back cocktails with old Harrovians and other posh pals. By day, he crammed his tiny Mini Cooper with imported Jamaican records, slid into the driving seat, breathed in, slammed the door shut and zipped around the capital in search of customers. Now that he was no threat at home, the Jamaican producers were happy to align themselves with their compatriot abroad. With their commissions, Blackwell was able to wrest the ex-pat market away from Emile Shallet's Blue Beat label for the simple reason that 'Shallet wasn't liked'. As Blackwell noted, 'He wasn't exactly a crook. It's just that the record business was a bit dodgy in those days.'

Notwithstanding Blackwell's injection of rigour into mercantile morals, there is no evidence that royalties destined for Marley lined the pockets of anyone other than Leslie Kong. Even so, the lump sum Marley was able to take away was a noticeable improvement on whatever he might have obtained from Clement 'Sir Coxsone' Dodd. Black producers, such as Dodd, found it expedient to advance ideas of colour loyalty when signing performers to their labels and securing the rights to a song; but they sometimes also found it expedient not to pay, or at least not at a rate which the musicians deemed commensurate with the song's potential to 'hit' home in the charts.

The musicians' dilemma was exemplified by Derrick Morgan. Morgan, who was recording for Dodd at this time, wavered over the wisdom of paying more attention to the pull of his heart than the logic of his head. Finally, allegiance to race gave way to expedience. 'I really wanted to go back to Leslie [Kong] – he treated us better as a promoter, pay us better.'[101]

That equation was not so simply drawn by many of Morgan's contemporaries. Some singers refused absolutely to record for Chinese-Jamaicans. This principled stance seems to have been based on a set of quaint, old-fashioned virtues: envy and enmity. A more generous assessment might be that sections of the black masses, from which the singers were drawn, were simply bemused by what the Chinese had achieved in a relatively short space of time, and saw no sense in adding to it.

In 1962, the Chinese presence in Jamaica was estimated to be around 10,000 (less than 1 per cent of the population), yet their impact, after only one century on the island, was enormous.[102] They had become embedded in Jamaican society, and though their achievements were accepted grudgingly by a majority, significant others continued to compare them to a graft that would never take to the host. One angry letter-writer on the 'Alien Question' fulminated in the pages of the *Gleaner*:

> Let every Chinese pack his bag and baggage and depart to China; the Island would miss them, for only twelve months. But let the Afro-Jamaicans do likewise to their ancestral home, what would be the position? I make bold to say the backbone and wealth of the entire country would be utterly destroyed. Jamaica would be a wilderness.[103]

The first set of 300 Chinese immigrants from Hong Kong to Jamaica had arrived on board the *Epsom* in August 1854, after 108 days at sea. They were contracted as indentured labourers to work on sugar, coffee and pimento estates. Another 100 migrants set down at Falmouth on the north coast a few months later on board the brig *Vampire* – the sickly survivors of a 1,000-strong workforce sent to build the Panama Railroad. They were disappointed with what they found. Labouring on the estates in Jamaica neither suited their temperament nor their expectations. All were keen, explained their interpreter, to be afforded 'the opportunity for exercising their characteristic industry in accordance with their previous habits.'[104] Within two generations the Chinese-Jamaicans had transformed their standing from poorly paid workers to a group who ran a bulwark of Jamaican businesses – bakeries, grocery stores, betting shops, haberdasheries – and now record shops and record companies. Success brought them wealth and attracted resentment.

The traffic of prejudice was not, according to the drummer Leroy 'Horsemouth' Wallace, all one way. He recounted a disturbing incident when on tour with a predominantly Chinese-Jamaican band, Byron Lee and the Dragonaires: 'I was travelling with Byron Lee's band one time, Kes Chim and them was talking about "blacks from the ghetto", and I didn't like that. I figure I didn't fit in and I wait 'til they reach

Ochi Rios, [and] just opt out, give them back their shirts for the band uniform.'[105]

No doubt a lot of heat surrounded the domain assumptions each group held about the other. But it is undeniably the case that at key moments of friction in Jamaica, up to and beyond the 1960s, the Chinese population suffered at the hands of their irate compatriots. A virulent strain of anti-Chinese sentiment seemed to infect the population every thirty years. The British response often exacerbated their difficulties. At the height of the Frome Rebellion, when Chinese-Jamaican shop windows were being smashed and their stores looted, the Foreign Office assured the Chinese Ambassador that all necessary steps would be taken 'to protect [Chinese-Jamaicans] from riotous elements'.[106] Yet almost in the same breath the Governor advised that: 'Having regard to the unemployment position in Jamaica, and to the fact there are now in the colony a sufficient number of Chinese,' the Colonial government had voted to impose further restrictions. 'For the activity in which they are normally engaged, all alien Chinese, including children, should be debarred from entering the island after the 1st June, 1940.'[107]

This habit of creating a Chinese scapegoat also ran high in the veins of some record producers. Prince Buster's ribald jesting on vinyl that by signing with a Chinese producer, Derrick Morgan had shown himself to be a 'Blackhead Chinaman', sounded more sinister than comic.

There was a strong element of gamesmanship at play in such outbursts. When ska, the precursor of reggae, took off from mento (traditional Jamaican music) like a second-stage rocket, producers suddenly woke up to its fantastic potential for huge returns on minimal investment – providing you could land that elusive hit. The nascent record industry was competitive and picaroon. Prowling the streets of Trench Town, agents for the record labels would 'arrest' and 'capture' a budding star for their camp. Producers were like eager dancers at the high-school prom, unashamedly cutting in when they spied a pretty girl. 'Don't go down to no Duke,' pleaded Prince Buster, intercepting a young up-and-coming singer, Bobby Aitken, on his way to a rehearsal with a rival. 'Meet me at Federal on Tuesday,' he whispered, slipping Aitken £8 as further inducement.[108]

Peter Tosh drew little distinction between the producers. 'All of them is "pirate". All the producers are "pirate"'. Some, he conceded, were considerate, had 'a little heart' but most 'have no heart at all, no feelings. Worse if you black.' Even so, if fledgling performers presented themselves before the 'pirates' deemed them ready, they might not be granted another audition for several months, or even years.

In 1962, the three countryboys teamed up with Junior Braithwaite and two girls, Beverly Kelso and Cherry Green, to form a group, calling themselves the Teenagers. Tosh worried over the shifting line-up and whether the strength of his and Livingston's harmonies was compromised by the additional members. 'Them time there me did so much involve in harmony that we two sing harmony better than when five or four use to sing', Tosh recalled, 'because them kind of immature and . . . it [was] too technical. If you no born with it inside o' you man, no one can teach you.'

Tosh's was not a view shared by Joe Higgs, who was inclined towards the school of thought that saw genius as the product of 1 per cent inspiration, 99 per cent perspiration. And though Joe Higgs's sessions started before sunrise, there was never a shortage of youths willing to sign up for the commitment and discipline that was a prerequisite for joining. They included a singer known as 'Pipe'. 'Because our bellies were so empty,' he remembered, 'the rumbling of them would keep us up all night, so we had nothing more to do at that time.'

Actually, Higgs did not set aside a special time for rehearsals. An announcement could come at any hour from 1 o'clock in the morning through to 5 o'clock, just as the dancehalls were closing and the lines of revellers were beginning to form in front of the cold-supper huts. Sometimes Higgs took his musical apprentices to Back-o-Wall, the slum area and Rasta settlement. Back-o-Wall was thought to possess musical vibes which were particularly strong. All through the night the Burru men could be heard chanting and beating their drums, a hypnotic sound which would only begin to trail off as dawn broke.

Higgs's sessions often finished with a refreshing dip at a stretch of beach referred to by the locals as 'Hot and Cold' because of the varying temperatures of the water, caused by its proximity to an electrical power generator. And if money was available and he was particularly pleased with the way things had gone at a rehearsal, he might treat them to a snack at one of the cold-supper shacks. Sanghu's gambling house was always the favourite. Sanghu was 'pure entertainment'. Somehow he managed to act as banker at the dice table, cook, and sell food and herb, all at the same time. Old Sanghu was a veritable 'all night service man'. In the early hours, with the gamblers long departed, the musical youths would turn up to find Sanghu fast asleep. But you'd only have to rap on his door, recalled Livingston, 'and it must have been like an explosion going off in his head'. Sanghu would sit bolt upright, barely opening his eyes, and mutter, "Wha' you want?" He'd shuffle over to the stall, serve you your order and go on right back to sleep.' If on the rare occasion they couldn't rouse him, then the youths would head for Ma Chi Chi's stall for a celebratory swig of her famous sour-sop juice. 'You'd have to hit the bottom with an almighty thwack,' because the drink was so pleasingly thick. Despite the sour-sop, Sanghu had the edge over Ma Chi Chi, because Sanghu also sold ganja. The Teenagers recalled that, as well as to music technique, their mentor was the first to introduce his young charges – Tosh, Livingston and Marley – to the secret pleasures of this illicit but common drug.

Ganja (the Hindi word for cannabis) had been cultivated in Jamaica by indentured Indians brought to the island on five-year contracts to work after the emancipated slaves downed tools and refused to toil in the despised plantations. The first wave of Indians (derogatorily referred to as 'coolies') had arrived in 1845, but it was not until some fifty years later that the authorities awoke with some alarm to the 'ganja mania' in their midst; it was in danger of sweeping through the island. 'We have seen a coolie gardener – by nature a quiet, retiring man – behaving like a raving maniac while under the influence of the weed,' wrote the vexed editor of the *Gleaner* in 1913, 'and it is a well-known fact that a large percentage of the murders committed by imported coolies has been directly attributable to the excessive use of ganja.' The *Gleaner* was determined to raise the alarm because it well understood that the 'perturbation of mind [produced] in certain circles' by the revelation that the nefarious ganja-smoking 'habit is becoming acquired by natives in ... appreciable numbers'. [109]

By 1960, cannabis was used widely in Jamaican society, but a distinction was drawn between its various methods of consumption. Quietly acceptable was the practice of brewing teas, especially in rural areas, for its medicinal properties, or making poultices for open wounds or to protect the anterior fontanelles of babies; even blending cannabis with rum to concoct a tonic was barely remarked upon. But the *smoking* of ganja was outlawed. Conviction for possession resulted in a mandatory one-year sentence. And though ganja was associated in the layman's eyes 'with insanity', a lawyer's defence that cannabis had made his client 'mad' was unlikely to find favour with the judge. Over time, fantasies of machete-wielding 'coolie' gardeners were supplanted by terrifying fears that on every corner lurked a ganja-crazed and potentially murderous criminal – a formerly amiable and inoffensive 'sufferer' whose moral anchor had been untethered by the inhalation of cannabis smoke. Such a rationale especially took root following the killing spree by followers of the cultist Claudius Henry and the subsequent execution of his Rasta, ganja-fuelled son, for murder and treason on 28 March 1961.

When, shortly after, a team of researchers carried out a study into the 'acute effects of ganja' some volunteers bridled at the suggestion that they and other cannabis smokers constituted a close homogenous group, that there was not so much as a cigarette paper between them. The difference, one volunteer argued, could be measured in the numbers of spliffs. Athough not ashamed of his habit, he stressed that his intake was limited to two or three a week because 'if you smoke it too much it spoils you. You become like a Rasta man, ignorant and violent.'[110]

Tosh, Marley and Livingston were just about to embark on what would become a habit of a lifetime, whose stigma and illegality contributed to its allure. On top of which was its undeniable potency. Among manual workers, the team of researchers found widespread acceptance of the prevailing wisdom that taking the drug energised and enhanced productivity. Their tests, however, showed the opposite to be the case: the volunteers had fooled themselves, and 'their perception of increased output [was] a significant factor in bolstering their motivation to work'.[111]

Nothing would alter the perception that Trench Town, despite its enormous appeal, was anything more than an empire of dirt; nor that it was a place you ever escaped from without the benefit of God or pharmacology. Few residents would have begrudged the trio's early experimentation, nor Higgs's role in it. All the youth were destined for some kind of contact with ganja before long. It was inevitable.

Livingston, along with his adolescent friends, quickly developed a 'head for ganja'. He believed it made for greater clarity and channeling of his thoughts, allowing for such contemplation until all his daily concerns fell away. It even dampened his appetite and took the edge off his hunger. Years later, reflecting on the power of ganja, Bunny

Livingston maintained the conviction that it heightened his appreciation of music. 'Even when hungry and we burn spliff, we were filled enough to go through with whatever we were doing ... The song came out more! We had more feelings of actually experiencing the song we're singing about.'[112] Bob Marley was equally enthralled. He was especially impressed by the drug's ability to enhance creativity – a sincere belief which he held throughout his life. Marley later wrote that his experimentation coincided with a greater appreciation for jazz. 'After a while I smoke some ganja, some herb, and then I understood jazz. I tried to get into the mood where the moon is blue and understand the feelings expressed.' Around about the same time, albeit 3,000 miles away, Paul McCartney was taking his first puff. And that same rush of heightened sensory perception filled the young Beatle's mind with such awe that he ordered his tour manager to write down everything he said – though there's no record of the subsequent gobbledegook ever being rendered in song. For the Jamaican trio smoking weed would become something more than recreation. The first illicit 'draw' of 'herb' in the ghetto of Trench Town marked a step away from a short-lived adolescence towards a stage in 'manship'. It coincided with a growing confidence in their musical abilities, an end to their unofficial apprenticeship.

The sound of the Teenagers was coming together. In Higgs' yard their harmonies were tightening until one day during a rendition of 'Tears on My Pillow' Livingston cried out: 'A it dis' (This is it!) – their mastery of the song highlighted that they were finally ready.

Joe Higgs had groomed them to the point where they could now go before Clement Dodd for an audition at Studio One. Either nerves or superstition prevented Higgs from accompanying his charges on this hoped-for final leg. In the end, a Rasta drummer known as Secco (who was acquainted with Dodd), took them to the audition at the studio. Higgs stayed put in Trench Town and waited anxiously for their report. In the yard at Studio One, underneath the mango tree (where all the auditions were held) the Teenagers sang three songs – 'I Don't Need Your Love', 'How Many Times' and 'Straight and Narrow Way', but they hardly seemed to register with Clement Dodd. Each one failed to move the studio boss. The band returned to Trench Town, more bemused than crestfallen over their failure. Joe Higgs exploded when he heard their news. Why had they not sung 'Simmer Down'? He ordered them to return to Studio One. Clement 'Sir Coxsone' Dodd, it seemed, was mostly looking for sound-system songs; he had at least three sound-system outfits running at any one time on the island. Of their small repertoire the only Teenagers' song that came close to fitting that bill was 'Simmer Down' but Marley, especially, wasn't too enthused by it. He thought the song sounded like a nursery rhyme. He was truculent but then Peter started to sing and the others joined in. Clement Dodd interrupted after one verse. 'OK,' he said: 'that's the one!'

The group was contracted to Dodd's label in 1963. The details – a five-year contract and a guarantee of £20 for each side of a record – were not generous. But that slight twinge of disappointment soon gave way to an overwhelming feeling of elation. The Trench Town youths were on their way.

4

TROUBLE IN MIND

FOR several minutes the vampire knelt on Peter Tosh's chest. There was little he could do about it. His panic was not lessened by the creature's uneasy familiarity. As usual, the vampire had waited until he'd just fallen asleep. Now Tosh was most definitely awake but could not move. His brain failed to fire the smallest nerve ending, even to cause a finger to flex. But he could discern the creature, shrouded in a grey storm of shifting dots. His eyes must be open. However, blinking no longer seemed possible. The vampire bared its fangs, and slowly, like a skilled and determined lover, began to bear down on the vulnerable neck of the young Tosh. When he was eventually able to rouse himself, he was relieved to find that not only was his neck unmolested, but that he was still alive.

These visitations of nightly terror, which had plagued Tosh since his early teens, are not uncommon. Medical practitioners describe them as sometimes forming part of the background to 'sleep paralysis'. At several instances in his life, Peter Tosh suffered from bouts of this alarming condition, where a person starts to wake from sleep, is semi-conscious, and yet cannot move. In Tosh's fecund imagination the undiagnosed condition was interpreted as the handiwork of the Devil, and the paralysis, in particular, a presage to his premature encounter with the Grim Reaper. At such times Tosh would force himself back to full consciousness, summoning a battery of expletives with which to batter Satan. Tosh recorded in his audio diary one terrifying incident which recalled all of the others:

I was attacked by evil forces, spiritual evil forces. That cause my mouth to cease from function. Cause my hands and legs to cease from moving. It's only my mind that was in function . . . and I was on the brink of what you call death. At that moment it caused me to make some inner communication [with] the Creator that dwells within man . . . I begin to ask him this question: 'What must I do?' I say, 'What must I do, just lie down and dead so, just get up tomorrow morning and I'm dead?' And my spirit say just say, 'Move your Bombaclaat!' Him say, 'Don't hesitate, you're on the countdown.' It's like I heard three, two, and when one go I say: 'Move your Bombaclaat!' Immediately every spell was released.

Bombaclaat – one of the foulest 'five-pound' words in the Jamaican lexicon (uttering it was an offence subject to a £5 fine) – broke the spell, 'released them vampires'. Tosh put his salvation down to his 'spiritual communication' for without it, he said, you were destined 'to go to heaven with your big toes tied'.

Had he consulted a physician over his condition, Peter Tosh would no doubt have rejected the rational explanation. Outside of Jamaica, Tosh's description of predatory vampires might have seemed fanciful, but like so many of his compatriots, he believed unreservedly in the traffic of spirits between this world and the next. That spirit could be a vampire, Satan or a 'duppy' – a ghost. 'It's not the soul that makes the duppy,' wrote the anthropologist Martha Beckwith, 'for the soul goes to heaven; and it's not the body, for we know that goes away into the ground; but it's the shadow.'[113] This shadowy apparition was the one that believers, such as Tosh, most feared. Jamaicans understood that if they failed to bury a deceased loved one (or not so loved one) correctly, then the vexed spirit of the corpse – the duppy – would escape the coffin and take up residence in the home of his tormentors to exact revenge. This pervasive doctrine is still ever present on the island.

On a tour of Jamaica in the 1930s, the African-American novelist and folklorist Zora Neale Hurston was thrilled to report the peculiar protocol at funerals of nailing to the coffin the cuff of the deceased's shirt sleeves as well as the heel of his socks. By this precaution, wrote Hurston, the relatives felt safe because, 'now the duppy was nailed hand and foot'.[114]

Tosh wasn't so lucky. Countless friends and acquaintances testified to his habit of looking over their shoulder as they spoke, whispering distractedly that they mustn't turn around because they'd just been joined by guests who were uninvited and unseen. His close friend Evah Gordon remembered, 'Peter was a man who was always speaking about ghosts. You want a story from Peter … Back up on a normal day; Peter fills you with ghost stories.'[115]

The anecdotes might be entertaining in the telling but when the laughter abated, it was always apparent that Tosh found the visitations terrifying – especially if they occurred at night. In Jamaica, a small industry had been built up around the ability of certain gifted individuals – 'foyeyed' (four-eyed), in possession of special powers to detect duppies – to remove their curse.[116] But Tosh was neither inclined to seek out 'foyeyed' nor conventional medical practitioners.

Stress is thought to be one of the triggers of sleep paralysis. Curiously, the excitement surrounding the signing of a record deal at Studio One, and the proximity of some kind of success heightened rather than reduced the stress. Writing on the social structure of the Caribbean, Dr M. G. Smith observed that enforced economic subservience had acted 'to rivet on [the blacks] for so many generations the fetters of social inferiority, within which there was always consciousness of status and a desire to maximise it when this became relatively possible'.[117] Signing for Studio One was not the swift and sudden transformative moment that the youths had dreamt about. Perhaps they might eat more regularly now and afford a better pair of shoes, but when they looked about them nothing much else had changed. For example, if a degree of social mobility might be measured by bathing facilities, and the Jamaican bather's progress from the hip-bath through to the galvanised tub and concrete terrace bath or tank, before settling into the dignity of the bathroom, then in 1963, Tosh and Marley were still bending over to clean themselves at the standpipe.

Marley's vagabond existence continued. He was not yet reduced to seeking accommodation at 'penny lodgings', where you paid half a penny to stand up and a penny for the luxury of lying down for the night, but he was not far off it.

The sixteen-year-old's housing difficulties had been bequeathed to him by his mother. Robert Nesta Marley was a fatherless child forced to remain in the home of another woman whose husband, Toddy Livingston, had lain with Marley's mother. Cedella had become pregnant.

The forthcoming birth produced tensions in the Livingston household. There was no vicarious pleasure on the part of Bunny Livingston's mother. The nine months were a gestation of resentment.

When her waters broke in 1963, notwithstanding the difficulties the birth would bring, Cedella's expectation of a momentary reprise from the gloom – of a snippet of joy – was crushed by her overwhelming feeling of resentment for Jamaica's rigid class system. In her telling, the mother-to-be had made her way to the University Hospital only to be refused entry when the staff ascertained that she was from Trench Town. A black-and-white snapshot from that period captures the splendid isolation of Cedella's nuclear family: Bob Marley appears placidly in a Sunday-best blazer beside his unsmiling mother who cradles the newborn baby, Claudette 'Pearl'. He could be forgiven for looking forlorn, as they were about to be separated. A few months after the birth of her daughter, Cedella boarded a plane for Delaware and a new life in the USA, promising that she would 'send' for her son once she was established.[118] It would be three long years before she could do so, and in the meantime Bob Marley would find himself attracted to a young single mother, Rita Anderson, whose plight was reminiscent of that of Marley and his mother the decade before, and with whom he would form a lasting attachment.

Anderson's expressive face was marked by a permanently thoughtful brow, yet one that was offset by an easy and infectious smile. She was petite and nimble, despite a gait which exposed a tendency to 'walk and roll' because of her knock knees – a feature that Bob Marley found especially endearing. Their intimacy was born of a practical need. Bob Marley felt increasingly uncomfortable in Toddy Livingston's household; he had been humiliated and cast as a servant-boy, running endless errands in lieu of paying rent or adding to the family's coffers. More and more he was absenting himself from the Livingstons', but he moved from semi-detached to fully detached without the surety of alternative accommodation. Anderson pleaded (not always successfully) with an aunt with whom she lived with that the homeless Marley occasionally be allowed to sleep over. She paints a picture of him climbing through half-opened windows once her relatives were asleep, and climbing back out again before they rose.[119]

Marley was spooked by the precariousness of his position and seemed to pass the days in an unending state of anxiety that intensified at night. In her memoir, Rita Anderson recalled an early encounter on one of their first nights together, when her future husband had been petrified by the presence of a black cat lingering by the bedroom door. As Bob Marley dipped in and out of sleep, the cat appeared to speak to him. And though it was a language Marley struggled to comprehend, he could not resist the thought that, as the door squeaked shut, he was now at the mercy of a shape-shifting duppy, a malignant evil force intent on stealing his shadow.

Every Jamaican knew that supernatural forces, abroad in the land, appeared in the form of plants or animals. The unusual crying of animals filled people with foreboding. A howling dog, lowing cow or mewing cat were all suspected to be manifestations of the spirit world. A cat could easily be a duppy in disguise, and 'the quietly ruminating cow' was worthy of investigation, for the cow was looked upon 'not merely as a type of silent wise man, but as one who keeps the secrets of the duppy world.'[120] The sighting of the 'rolling calf' (a levitating calf with luminous eyes) struck fear into the beholder. Marley's head had been filled with such stories since his childhood in the rural Jamaican hinterland, where tales of duppies, mangled whispers in the wine-dark night of other-worldly visitations, and a swelling cacophony of superstitious beliefs substituted for the kind of modern entertainment available in the towns and cities.

Marley's grandfather, Omeriah Malcolm, was a renowned Myal-man, whom locals believed possessed healing powers, primarily through a knowledge of bush medicines and herbs. Myalism was an African atavism whose half-life had exceeded the centuries of the Atlantic slave trade and survived on the sugar plantations. At its heart was an ecstatic ritualistic dance, designed to conjure and make manifest the invisible. It proved, contended the historian G. W. Bridges, that 'the blood of pagan Africa still flowed thick and darkly in the veins [of the enslaved]'. In the shallow thinking of the island's British colonial masters, Myalism was associated disturbingly with a kind of sorcery known as Obeah, with fetishist oaths, drawn blood, grave dirt and deadly potions. Reports of Myalism (mostly depicted as a contagious disease) flooded the newspapers in early nineteenth-century Jamaica; Samuel Sharpe (the black spiritual leader held responsible and executed for a rebellion on the island just prior to Emancipation) was said to have been a Myal-Baptist. Believing there to be a link between Myalism and insurrection, the British authorities outlawed the cult.

The practice, though, was cast in the minds of large numbers of the populace in a more favourable light. Myal-men, often called 'Angel-men', were said to be able to counteract the debilitating spells of the Obeah-men, to 'take off the duppy' and free shadows stolen by the Obeah. As decades passed it became clearer that Myalism had also acted as a kind of stalking horse for a much more infectious fundamental Christian and millennial movement: Revivalism. Reverend Duncan Stewart gave a vivid first-hand account of this revival of the manifestation of the Holy Ghost, which had once gripped the quaking apostles on Christ's arrest. On his return to Jamaica in 1860 (thereafter known on the island as 'the Time of the Sixty'), the reverend witnessed great crowds falling prone to the ground, 'made subject of extraordinary conviction of sin', speaking in an unknown tongue (just like the apostles) and successfully crying out for mercy, for the Lord had 'emphatically girded them with gladness'. Stewart was overwhelmed by the scenes of excitement and the stamina of the sinners, for 'men, women and children continued to weep and wail . . . with little intermission for nearly a week'.[121]

Those who fell under the influence of Revivalism drank from the same cup consumed by the Myalists. And to the incensed and uninitiated, Myalism, Revivalism and its later incarnation Pocomania were all interchangeable 'orgies of dancing as well as disgusting and degrading gesticulation'. And to the disapproving letter-writers in the *Gleaner* Revivalism, like its cousin Myalism, stressed spiritual possession and sought this through unrestrained dancing and drumming. To those who wrote in a fit of fury to the newspaper's letter pages it was a pollution of sight and sound that was 'making Hades of our thoroughfares when everybody else is in bed'.[122] Decades later these vexed authors still tossed and turned in their beds at night at the not-too-distant memory of Alexander Bedward, the most famous Revivalist of them all. 'Shod in wooden sandals, a night shirt over his customary rags' at the head of an army of 3,000 black folk, Bedward led the faithful to Hope River where those seeking salvation were baptised, dipped fully in the 'healing stream', and emerged to the chants of the huge crowd singing 'weird and metamorphosed hymns'.[123] If Alexander Bedward alarmed the authorities with his apocalyptic vision, then their discomfort peaked with the strange announcement that he would be ascending to heaven on 31 December

1921, and that the faithful were welcome to join him on the celestial voyage. Thousands proceeded to the yard at Bedward's church, having divested themselves of their worldly possessions that were no longer required. They began to climb the trees, as instructed. At the appointed hour, they leapt, but instead of soaring towards the firmament, they came crashing down like chicks from the nest. The newspapers could barely contain their mirth: 'Bedward Stick to the Earth' mocked the headline in the *Gleaner*.

Bedward's subsequent audience – this time with the courts – led to his incarceration at Bellevue, an asylum for the insane. The great Revivalist's demise may have been the outcome desired by the authorities, but the 'sufferers' thirst for salvation, and for some kind of balm for the vagaries of their brutal lives – answered by men such as Bedward – did not diminish.

In the 1940s, 50s and 60s, Bedwardism, on a smaller scale, surfaced in the balm yards and sealing grounds of the Revivalists in Trench Town, and in numerous other slums and impoverished villages throughout the country. And perhaps more discreetly and modestly, the man himself reappeared in the shape of the 'captains' or 'shepherds' of this cultish religion, in men like Toddy Livingston.

At his balm yard in Trench Town, 'Captain' Toddy Livingston's plaited bamboo cane underwent a transformation; from the actual to the symbolic; from a rod of correction to a shepherd's crook – a totem of comfort and guidance. Toddy's duty of care, though, did not extend to the boy left behind by his lover. But even if Bob Marley had not been estranged from the Livingston household, it's unlikely that he'd have searched for succour from Toddy's ministry. While fear of an Obeah curse could be paralysing, neither Marley nor Tosh at this stage of their young lives believed relief or remedy might be found in the swirl of emotions commonly sweeping through the balm yards of the Revivalists. And further, for savvy street youths to surrender openly to such beliefs was beyond embarrassment.

Bunny Livingston, too, was cynical about the spiritual benefits of Revivalism, even though he'd grown up drinking in the atmosphere of Revival meetings – the unbridled dancing and exalted drumming and singing. As the son of a local 'shepherd' he had a front seat for all of the drama, rites and rituals. He was drawn especially to the drumming (he'd been beating drums, 'talking' with them, from the age of four), but later confessed that the real lure of church was more mundane:

he loved attending primarily because 'there was always a lot of eating going on . . . from daylight to daylight.'[124]

For every cynic there were dozens, perhaps hundreds, of credulous Jamaicans prepared to surrender themselves (and the contents of their wallets) to the power of the healers who, through potions or sympathetic magic, might rid them of their complaints. Obeah ran through Jamaican society like water: its influence was hard to resist. But the sceptical teenagers must have pondered the harsh lessons drawn from their peers, from men like the exemplary trombonist, Don Drummond, who seemed to succumb to the old adage that the best way to resist temptation was to give in to it.

Drummond, one of the founders of the Skatalites (the premier ska band on the island) was also one of the key session musicians whom Coxsone Dodd employed to accompany his fledgling acts. Drummond was a stellar trombone player whose haunting signature sound, a burr-like string of notes – yearning, wistful, melancholic yet sensuous – was honed after more than a decade of near non-stop playing in big bands – the swing and jazz 'road' bands which toured the island in the 1950s. Don Drummond and the Skatalites were among the first to achieve a kind of mass island-wide following. Previously, for such bands, the hotel ballroom had demarcated the limits of their renown. Before the Skatalites there had been few local celebrities to compete with the glamour of visiting African-American stars such as Louis Armstrong and Sarah Vaughan. Like shipwrecked people daring to hope for rescue, Jamaicans kept a close lookout for their heralded appearance from the sky or sea. There was something more than straightforward enthusiasm in the newspaper coverage of the Americans' arrival: there was gratitude.

Occasionally, though, these stars encouraged the islanders to turn around the telescope so that it was facing in. At her 1956 concert at the Glass Bucket Club, Sarah Vaughan was backed by the Jamaican All-Stars, a jazz band which included a fourteen-year-old Don Drummond, who, Vaughan told the press, figured among the top half-dozen trombonists she'd ever played with.

Don Drummond was only a few years older than the Teenagers

(who soon changed their name to the Wailin' Wailers), but he seemed almost to belong to another generation: he was the personification of fame and cool; the kind of performer Tosh, Marley and Livingston could only dream of becoming. A graduate of the Alpha Boys School (a halfway house between a reform school and an orphanage that had earned a reputation for turning out highly competent musicians), Drummond was venerated both for his musical skill and his idiosyncrasy. The direction taken by Jamaica's home-grown musical compositions into ska (no longer in deference to R&B imports) was not universally approved by the country's critics. Some still mourned the passing of the bossa nova, foxtrot and mambo from the cabarets and clubs. The *Gleaner*'s palate was far from satisfied by the new musical menu which was 'liable to be oompha-oompha-oompha from beginning to end' but for the 'embroidery of Don Drummond's slurring offbeat swing ... [which had] opened new horizons for what appeared to be a tomb without a view'. Drummond was said to be so far ahead of his contemporaries that many were intimidated by his presence on stage. Bunny Livingston's abiding memory was of the man with a chamois-cloth in hand forever lovingly wiping down and cleaning his trombone. He was nattily dressed to the point of distinction – at least as far as his wages would allow. For, as one's eyes travelled down from his elegant necktie, ticking off each concession to a handsome dress sense, it was evident that the money ran out at his feet. Livingston recalled the poignant pity of his 'thin crepe shoes'.

The Wailin' Wailers were proud and excited by their affiliation with Don Drummond and the Skatalites, whose playing gave verve to the unfettered virginal clarity of their first recordings on tracks like 'Simmer Down'. In recording sessions, such was his exuberance that his trombone gatecrashed songs written for other instruments. Livingston chuckled at the memory of one session when, 'Drummond just wouldn't let go of "Go Jimmy Go", even though he wasn't supposed to play the intro.' Tosh, Marley and Livingston's admiration of Drummond was complicated by reflections on the confounding actuality of his life. Their young minds struggled to make sense of it all. The discomfort and chaos of Drummond's world was an inversion of the clean and assured sound of his trombone-playing and the rigour of his musical achievement. He was inundated with requests to play on recording sessions. And yet, although arguably the most talented musician of his generation, Drummond could barely afford his own trombone: it was borrowed.

The tales of Drummond's eccentricity were legion. More than once he was reported to have been spotted wandering barefoot around Kingston mumbling to himself and, when the opportunity arose, casually spitting at white people. On another occasion, he appeared on stage and even before blowing a note, unzipped his flies and started urinating on the audience. Some of these stories were, no doubt, apocryphal, but it is clear that at times Don Drummond was not sufficiently anchored to the structures of everyday life. There's evidence that he too was unsettled by his own bizarre behaviour; whether of his own volition or forcibly, he was admitted to the acute wards of Bellevue, the island's main psychiatric hospital, on several occasions.

Each time Drummond was discharged into the care of his girlfriend, Anita 'Margarita' Mahfood. They shared a one-room apartment in the east of Kingston, and a passionate but tempestuous relationship. Wife or girlfriend beating was a common pastime in Jamaica. Though Drummond was not a renowned beater, early on in their affair he showed signs that even a minor provocation could result in a flash of unexpected violence: irritated by a niggling disagreement that distracted him from a composition he was working on, Drummond lashed out suddenly and stabbed Mahfood with a fountain pen.[125] To their neighbours they appeared an odd but dazzling couple. Mahfood flitted between poles of emotion: from rushing to the veranda and screaming 'Murder!' in the midst of every row, to keeping a close watch over her man, dispensing his medication like a conscientious mother to a sickly child.

Drummond was diagnosed as suffering from manic depression. Though he was a prolific composer (he wrote several hundred songs) oftentimes he was withdrawn: reduced to grunts or a string of monosyllables whose meaning was near impossible to decode. After a while friends started calling him Don 'Cosmic' – the title of his first solo album. By contrast, 'Margarita' Mahfood, usually billed on stage as 'the Arabian Figure-of-Eight Dancer', was an extrovert, a cocktail of delight. Men, especially, were intoxicated and seduced by the meticulous absorption of her dance. The shimmering rhumba queen was a latter-day Salome with a host of unrequited but salivating suitors. Bunny Livingston offered a frank analysis of her charms: 'If she started dancing, man, you couldn't help your hood from jumping up!' Mahfood's erotic performances were especially popular on the club and cabaret circuit. As Livingston alluded, she had an overpowering effect both on the experienced voyeur and on the fantasising, sexually naive youth: 'If you just look at her for a moment and then shut your eyes, you get cock-stand.' But Livingston drew a sympathetic line between Mahfood's professional flirtation and the whispered allegations of her promiscuity: 'Whatever game she was playing, she always came home to Don.'

In the early hours of 2 January 1965, Mahfood finished her third and final cabaret performance of the night at the Havana Club, and, expertly rebuffing the usual offer from a speculative punter to share one last cocktail 'for the road', slunk back to the apartment. She need not have bothered tiptoeing into the bedroom because Drummond was very much awake; he was also agitated and aggrieved. He'd miscalculated his medication, taken too many tablets and slept through the afternoon, evening and night. By the time he woke, he'd already missed an important gig at the Bournemouth Club with the Skatalites.[126]

Drummond returned to bed. Mahfood removed her make-up, washed and joined him. After a few minutes, though she didn't know why, she was disturbed by a vague feeling of anxiety, a nameless dread. Mahfood pulled back the covers, and was perplexed to see that there was something wrapped in a cloth which Drummond was gripping between his toes. As her eyes adjusted to the dark, the object slowly revealed itself to her: it was a knife. She sat bolt upright and leapt from the bed. Drummond asked her what was wrong: 'You don't want to sleep? Go an' sleep nuh, mon. Ain't you just come in?' Mahfood was dumbfounded: 'I cyan't sleep!' she shouted. 'Not [when] you have a knife wrap in a chamois between your feet!'

Neighbours later reported overhearing snatches of the bizarre conversation through the thin partitions separating the apartments. Drummond – his voice unnervingly calm – tried to reassure his girlfriend that she was mistaken: the knife was in his trouser-pocket which was hanging from the door. But Mahfood, sounding increasingly alarmed, insisted that the knife was in a chamois between his feet. Their quarrelling dragged on and, according to the neighbours, culminated in the familiar screams of 'Murder!' from Mahfood.

About an hour later, Don Drummond turned up at the local police station and told the bemused constable on duty: 'A woman in the yard stab herself with a knife and I would like the police to come and see her.' Two officers accompanied him to the apartment, and discovered the corpse of Anita Mahfood lying across the bed with a knife stuck in her chest. Drummond offered further details about this most unusual 'suicide', but the next day the newspaper headlines reported a more likely explanation: RHUMBA DANCER STABBED TO DEATH: TROM-BONIST ON MURDER CHARGE.

Drummond was depicted as a 'ghetto fanatic' who had traded 'his horn for a knife'. At his trial, more than a year later, counsel for the defence argued that to imprison Drummond would be to deprive the country of one of its greatest musical ambassadors, and that a great and unrealisable debt was owed to the twenty-two-year-old trom-bonist. But if Don Drummond was held up as the gold-standard of Jamaican musicianship, he was also the premier example of how the mental balance of a sensitive soul might go awry in Kingston. Among the crowds of excited armchair psychologists jostling in the gallery at the courtroom, it was popularly surmised that, almost inevitably, something had sheared in Drummond's mind. In failing to cope with ghetto-living conditions that were an unceasing storm of stress: in brooding on the unjust disparity between his musical achievement and financial success; in smoking copious amounts of cannabis; and in dabbling with Obeah, Don Drummond had been selected for madness. Don 'Cosmic' Drummond may have been considered the finest trom-bonist of his generation but, if the Wailin' Wailers stopped to consider the narrative of their hero's life, it served as a terrifying model of the potential pitfalls that lay ahead for them. And as far as it impacted on their own musical aspirations, the story of Don Drummond both elevated and undermined.

On 26 July 1966, Drummond was found 'guilty but insane' and sent to Bellevue where he would be incarcerated indefinitely.[127]

Professor Frederick Hickling has a theory about Drummond: the trom-bonist would not have seen himself as suffering from mental illness, but rather that someone was working Obeah on him.

The practise of Obeah as sorcery had been outlawed by the British in 1760; it was still illegal. The British had feared it held a greater influ-

ence over the slave population than the driver's whip. It was claimed
that an Obeah-man's skill with poison lay behind many unexplained
deaths among the slave population on plantations. Obeah-men were
denounced, and when uncovered would be arrested and expelled from
the colony. The authorities had also responded to the many tales of
dread, of the psychological terror of the Obeah-man, whom a neighbour would employ to 'set on', to put a vengeful curse on an enemy,
or even to concoct a poison for them.

In the 1930s, the anthropologist Joseph J. Williams observed the
stultifying effect on those who believed themselves cursed by an Obeah:
'They no sooner find Obi set for them near the door of their homes
or in the path which leads to it, than they give themselves up for lost,'
wrote Williams. 'No recourse is left but to the superior skill of some
more eminent Obeah-man of the neighbourhood who may counteract the
magical operation of the other.' I asked Hickling if it was still possible
to find Obeah-men in Jamaica and he rolled his eyes at my naivety.
True, Obeah-men (except in the rare instances of their criminal conviction) did not appear on the census or in the telephone directory; it was
not a title readily owned. As far as Professor Hickling was concerned
the Obeah-man and the healer were often one and the same. He could
be a force for good or evil. Some, he warned, were only half-educated,
and those steeped in malignant practices were the most dangerous. A
half-educated Obeah-man was 'someone who know all about poison,
but don't bother come to him for the antidote. He won't know it.'

Few in Jamaica spoke openly about Obeah, but Hickling found me
a guide who agreed to take me to St Thomas, a remote district on the
outskirts of the capital, where I might learn more.

Steve the guide, a big man with pronounced freckles and hooded eyes,
was more than an enthusiast, yet he was not a convert. He'd been
'privileged' to live among the villagers of the remote community; few
outsiders were ever welcomed. My pilgrimage was validation of the
obsessive research that had, he quickly admitted, tested his commitment
to his wife. I imagined the inverse of that might also be true.

The St Thomas district, in the east of the country, was known locally
to be a 'duppy' area with powerful Obeah-men. Other Jamaicans, Steve

explained, didn't mix with people from the area 'for fear they would set Obeah on you'. We were headed for the heart of St Thomas for an audience with Brother D, a man renowned for his supernatural power.

Our driver – not a St Thomas man – was silent and twitchy. He drove very, very slowly as if he was constantly considering turning back. At one point we had to ford a stream. He switched off the engine and shook his head. I felt he'd been hoping for such an excuse and only the promise from me of further, substantial remuneration convinced him to carry on. Even so he was not thrilled: some other nervousness troubled him. Every few minutes he was seized with an abdominal pain which caused him to double up, but he would not be drawn on what ailed him.

From the stream onwards, the road was an unmade dirt track. Passing a sulphurous pond, we veered left up a path that had virtually been reclaimed by the bush. Steve called it 'Science Corner'. 'Science' was the colloquial word for Obeah, and 'Scientists' were Obeah-men. We had entered a microclimate of heightened electrical activity: the air was heavy. Steve wore an 'I told you so' expression of triumph. A mile or so later, we emerged into a clearing: the road had run out. To drive any further would have taken us over the edge of a cliff.

I was surprised that the road had not led to a makeshift shack, like so many we'd seen perched precariously on the hillsides, yet knotted into some kind of permanence by the overgrown foliage encasing them. Instead, the driver pulled up outside a simple little church. A single red flag on a bamboo pole snapped in the wind – 'a spirit messenger', said Steve. The church was home to Brother D and a small but loyal village congregation. It was a rough-looking structure with exposed breeze-block walls and a galvanised tin roof which creaked and groaned and flapped at the edges, giving the impression that it was about to fly off. A generous assessment would have put its dimensions at 100 feet by 20 feet. Inside, the church was dominated by a huge wooden altar. Underneath was a basin filled with water. Duppies, Steve assured me, didn't like water. Beside the basin, two machetes were folded together, crossed as if they were a pair of giant scissors.

The altar was decorated in oranges, lemons – 'food for the duppies'. Steve had slipped into guide mode, anticipating each query, though he did not elaborate on my sarcastic aside, spelling out the contradiction of fruit to sustain the duppies and water to drive them away. Dotted around the altar were tiny bottles of a clear liquid that I couldn't name. The back wall shelves, from floor to ceiling, were crammed with hundreds of dusty, unopened bottles of Heineken lager and cream soda – 'totems for the healing ceremony'. A few villagers sat quietly in a row, as if awaiting their turn at confession or the doctor's surgery. They all shuffled along by one seat when the woman closest to Brother D eventually peeled away from him. Her eyes held tears that had never been expressed. Tugging at a child who seemed more sluggish than recalcitrant, she brushed past me, determined neither to take notice, nor to be acknowledged.

Brother D (the 'D' was for Daniel) acknowledged that he had the gift of healing but rejected the description of Obeah. 'Who tell you dat foolishness?' He chuckled dismissively at the suggestion, but was not entirely convincing. He preferred the term 'faith healer'. People revered him *but*, he conceded, they were also afraid of him. Brother D had been the preacher at the church for more than forty years. He was seventy-four. His skin was dark and tough from continual exposure to the sun. The aura of mystery around him was heightened by cataracts clouding his eyes and his slow elemental speech. He did not look at me but stared straight ahead as we spoke.

As a preacher and healer, Brother D's primary tools were fasting, prayer and olive oil. When I asked him what kind of people he helped, he looked past me to the door from which the mother and child had just exited: 'People with head trouble, madness like, insane.' The sluggish schoolgirl had jealous friends who'd been instructed to pluck a hair from her head to give it to an Obeah. This was a common request, to extract something of the target which an Obeah might later use – hair, a sample of urine or faeces – burnt faeces, for instance, would produce unbearable stomach cramps in the victim. Subsequent to the unnoticed hair-plucking the girl had been seen 'walking up and down, turning fool and talking stupidness'. Brother D was almost inaudible. He lowered his voice even further – confiding in me the incredulous realisation: 'Some people don't believe in superstitiousness, you know . . . I have an idea that evil can trouble the person.'

Healers were often said to have been called to the profession after suffering their own mental-health problems. And as a ten-year-old, Brother D's teachers had been so disturbed by him, believing him to be 'a madman', that they excluded him from the school. 'Little did the teacher know that I wasn't a madman but that it was the spirit.' Soon after, the boy had become a wayside preacher, and everything that he prophesised came to pass. Voices spoke to him. 'Suppose anyone going to chop up somebody,' Brother D cited a common example. 'The voice say, "bloodshed, bloodshed, bloodshed", you just hear that, "go tomorrow to Morant Bay, spin round three times and blow the warning right there".' Brother D would act as the voice commanded and alert the potential victim about the danger coming his or her way. And woe betides the fool who did not heed the warning.

The driver, I noticed, had been eavesdropping on the conversation. When it came time to leave, he begged a few minutes' audience with Brother D. On the long drive back, he seemed happier, less discomforted. Brother D had confirmed his suspicions. An ex-girlfriend had been to an Obeah-man with some of the driver's faeces. He and the toilet had been strangers ever since. 'One week now since I get relief,' he said angrily. But the trip to St Thomas had been fortuitous. Brother D had provided a remedy and some sensible words of counsel: 'You can't hold onto your shit: you have to let it go.'

Psychiatrists talk about the power of suggestion, but almost everyone I spoke to in Jamaica thereafter hinted that they had had some dealing with Obeah – even graduates with science degrees. When I raised this point in a subsequent interview with Professor Hickling, he exploded with laughter. Obeah wasn't regulated but, as far as Hickling was concerned, there was little difference between the conventional practice of psychiatry and the Obeah tradition. Long before Don Drummond had put himself into the care of the psychiatrists, he'd sought a consultation with an Obeah-man, he reminded me. Jamaica's population of more than two million was served by just two psychiatric hospitals. Something had to make up for the inevitable shortfall in care. The professor saw his work and that of the healers as complementary. Hickling fixed me with his intelligent eyes. A thought had just come to him. 'You know,' he said, 'I'm probably the biggest Obeah-man in Jamaica.'

In later years, when Bunny Livingston reflected on the plight of Don Drummond, he traced the roots of the trombonist's mental collapse to

Brentford Road, the headquarters (actually there were no other quarters) of Studio One. Livingston pointed a long, accusing finger in the face of Clement Dodd whom he suggested bore much of the moral responsibility for Drummond's decline. By then, Bunny Livingston's estimation of the record producer had soured and curdled; he had spent years of acrimonious reasoning that held Dodd to be culpable of tipping the scales of Drummond's delicate mental state. Livingston believed that Dodd had short-changed Drummond, just as he was intent on doing to the Wailin' Wailers at the start of their musical career. But in 1963, such thoughts only drifted gently across the mind of Livingston, like snow that did not settle. At that time, he was more generous and appreciative of the opportunity that Dodd had given them.

Studio One had no marketing department, no domestic and international sales team, and no accounts department. Studio One was Clement 'Sir Coxsone' Dodd. The Wailin' Wailers recognised that Dodd was not proceeding according to an industry-standard handbook. There were no guidelines for producers. Dodd was feeling his way in the dark. He found a seamstress and kitted out Tosh, Marley and Livingston in gold lamé suits; he recruited a photographer and had them pose for publicity shots worthy of the Drifters or the Temptations, and finally he pushed them in front of a microphone and bid them sing. All three relished the chance. They would assemble round a single mic, Marley in the middle, Tosh and Livingston at his sides, up close and their faces almost touching. The configuration best suited the balance of their voices rather than denoting the centrality of Marley. Their original music coach, Joe Higgs, was still a constant presence in their lives, accompanying them to Studio One.

'Joe [Higgs] was always in the studio, standing there – the teacher with his [metaphorical] whip,' Tosh recalled. 'You don't fool around. He's listening to see whether anyone misses the harmony.' Higgs wanted to stick around long enough to see the Wailin' Wailers mature and to perfect their harmonies. Though highly regarded by the Trench Town youth, Higgs wasn't always made to feel comfortable by Dodd: his self-appointed role as a go-between, voicing their grievances, was especially unwelcome. Once, when he had the temerity to question the amount of payment, Dodd answered with a flurry of fists to his face, and Higgs wound up in casualty.

The fastidious Dodd was a fine-boned, trim and tidy individual, not usually given to open displays of emotion. 'Downbeat' – the name he gave to his sound system – might also perfectly describe his manner. The contrast with some of the more flamboyant producers and sound-system men appeared all the more stark when Dodd made an effort to bridge the gap. Not for him the jewelled rings on every finger, flowing ermine cloak and belt of bullets of his rival, Duke Reid. No, the height of Dodd's extravagance is captured in an early photograph of the producer surrounded by a posse of supporters, sporting a cardboard crown.

Clement Dodd was aware of his good fortune, acknowledging that in signing groups like the Wailin' Wailers he was adding to his stable of gold-throated stars whose singing captured the zeitgeist of the moment. In that first flush of creativity at Studio One, with crudely padded walls and a simple mixing desk, the sound appeared magical. Years later, when more money began to roll in, Dodd was reluctant to upgrade the studio, fearing he might somehow lose *the* sound. Like an alchemist who had discovered the art of converting base metal into gold, Dodd was determined to keep the secret to himself, though his role as studio producer, recalled Livingston, was comprised of little more than 'sit beside the machine and turn the knobs, balance etc., coming on through the one little system in a one-track portable'. Dodd developed a ritual which he kept to each night. At the end of a recording session, he would pack up the equipment – microphones and mixing desk – because 'him 'fraid some man t'ief everyt'ing . . . so him pack it up every night and carry it home to him yard'. He wasn't just taking away the technical equipment; he was sequestering the formula.

In temperament, Dodd was close to the lottery winner who tells no one of his success, lives in the same house and quietly queues each Friday with his fellow workers for his wages from the factory job he has never given up.

Clement Dodd always gave the impression that money was tight and, according to Bunny Livingston, he was schooled in the art of appearing to be much more generous than he actually was: 'Instead of paying in pound notes, Coxsone paid in five-shilling paper – so you got a lot.' The band received a bundle of notes, giving the illusion of more wealth than its actual value. 'Coxsone was a master of psychology; although he was also seriously paranoid . . . It was monkey money, a gangster's bankroll.'[128]

Like most other producers in Jamaica, Clement Dodd substituted perks for royalties. 'In a studio you might get bun and soda pop, maybe one or two ice milks,' and Bunny Livingston still remembers the look of parental disappointment which furrowed Dodd's brow when such acts of patronage did not meet with the expected level of gratitude.

Studio One was a cottage industry and, outside of contractual obligations, Dodd seems to have run operations there informally, through grace and favour. He even took a paternalistic interest in Marley's welfare, allowing the itinerant and sometime homeless youngster to sleep in one of the back rooms at the studio at the close of play. The Wailin' Wailers may have felt patronised and treated as 'likkle youth', but largely they still were an adolescent band (ranging in age from sixteen to nineteen), who often responded to Dodd as a father-figure – whose conservatism one respected and whose blushes one spared. After rehearsals the group regularly retreated to an old, decrepit van that had been abandoned under a mango tree at the end of the yard. It was hot and sweaty inside but they valued it as a place where they could smoke marijuana without detection. Mr Dodd did not approve of ganja-smoking. But even so, if the sweet and sickly fumes found a way to his noble nostrils, he would feign ignorance and convince himself that nothing improper was going on.

The limits of his tolerance did not extend beyond this temporary myopia. Dodd's idiosyncratic approach to business was not open to discussion. Finally, in Clement Dodd's make-up, there was something of the Catholic code of deferring pleasure when it came to releasing records. The master tape would be locked away, and no one, save for Dodd the producer, was privy to the date of its intended release. Studio One musicians were divided as to whether this strategy was a mark of Dodd's genius – of supreme confidence – or its polar opposite: either Dodd knew intuitively when to bring out a record for it to have maximum impact, or he hadn't a clue. The Wailin' Wailers first record, 'Simmer Down', was a case in point – a song which they performed for him in the 1963 audition took Dodd more than a year to release. When he did so, it shot up the charts and went straight to number one.

5

NUFF RESPEC'

AT the Palace Theatre's Christmas Show in 1964, a notorious 'rude boy' graced the audience with his presence. Big Junior was still basking from the glory of his starring role as one of the blind Calypsonians in the Bond film *Dr No*. The description 'rude boy' was a perfect fit for Big Junior, as he showed no great respect for anybody other than Big Junior himself. He was a huge fellow and the devilment side of his character was finely developed. Ordinarily, if Bunny Livingston was in a drinking establishment and he saw Big Junior walk through the door, he would make a mental note to himself to 'spend only a minimal time', finish off his drink quickly and head out before the trouble began. Livingston and the Wailin' Wailers had only just taken to the stage when he spied Big Junior grinning, with a girl on each arm, in the front row.

Since recording 'Simmer Down', the band had spent the last few months polishing their stage routine. On Hellshire Beach, in the cool evening air, they perfected their performance, and worked on their all-important showmanship. The routine was, observed Livingston, 'pure gymnastics, the kind of flicking, splits and snap falls' that would have been worthy of James Brown. Now in late December they were ready. Accompanied by the Skatalites, the Wailin' Wailers appeared on stage in sharp shiny suits, black shirts with polka dots and patent leather shoes.

Halfway through the first number, Marley bent down on one knee, then the second knee, just in time for Livingston to roll over his back, and land with a flourish doing the splits. Both now tucked their hands under their knees and hunched over. Tosh stood over them imperiously, and began to bounce them like rubber balls. Finally, they popped up and finished the song with diamond smiles. The crowd was electrified. 'When we hit the stage, it was fire . . . People leapt out of the sky and rushed to the front.'[129]

But suddenly all the lights went off and the music cut out abruptly. After only a few seconds, the resident wags started jesting and verbally jousting with the house manager. The crowd became restless. They didn't realise that the power cut was an island-wide interruption, and when the electricity didn't immediately return, the mood turned ugly. People began to curse and make rude gestures. Almost inevitably, Big Junior's uncharacteristic good nature, stretched beyond its normal limits, snapped back into place; he defaulted to the easy familiarity of his 'rude boy' stance.

The fracas escalated with his intervention, as Big Junior started ripping up chairs and smashing them – of course with a certain flair. For a rude boy everything had to be done with style, even violence. The cinema had provided the model. As with John Wayne, then so too with Big Junior. He'd delicately brush a crumb from your cheek before breaking a chair over your head. For a while the Wailin' Wailers wavered, not knowing what they should do. 'Mek we leave the stage,' whispered Livingston, 'at least until everything come back on.' In the darkness, the band felt their way to the back of the stage, and immediately a shower of bottles flying through the auditorium towards the stage began 'crashing, crashing like tiny explosions'. The Wailin' Wailers kept backing away until they found a place of safety. 'Bwoi, we ended up in a little toilet,' recalled Livingston, jammed in with a girl group called the Soulettes. The disturbance went on for an hour – an uninterrupted hail of crashing bottles.

The group could still hear the screams from the auditorium. Amid the chaos, opportunistic thieves went to work: 'As a guy lights a paper and he sees your chain, the paper is out and the chain is gone, your bracelet gone, your wallet gone . . . If you had a good hat 'pon your head, it's gone.' Especially if the hat was a trilby – then it was definitely gone; the true rude boy valued his wardrobe above all else.

The Jamaican middle class had witnessed with dismay the rise of the irreverent rude boy. They were perplexed and fearful of him. Where had he come from? The answer was relatively straightforward. To fashion a rude boy you could take your pick from any one of the thousands of west Kingston's unemployed youths (70 per cent had no work), who, in the reverie of his shapeless day, imagined himself a celluloid gangster – Edward G. Robinson, Jimmy Cagney or George Raft. He might be identified by his knife. The soldier had his rifle; the rude boy had his ratchet knife; often he already sported a scar, courtesy of a rival, the so-called 'telephone scar' which ran from ear to chin. The ratchet knife was outlawed. When challenged by the police, the rude boy might claim the blade was used to peel oranges, but the trilby on his head blew his cover. The made-to-measure silk trousers finishing above the ankle, the red diamond socks and safe, 'don't-fuck-with-me' Clarks shoes put his identity beyond doubt.

As of now the rude boy belonged to no gang. His reputation rested on his individuality and ability to suggest menace. Whether on the street corner, the dancehall, theatre or cinema, he commanded respect. Viv Adams recalled how typically the crowd, waiting in line outside the Rialto, gave a wide birth to the lone movie-loving rude boy at the front of the queue, who played with his ratchet knife, flicking it repetitively, slicing the air around him.[130]

Some even styled the Wailin' Wailers, particularly Tosh and Marley, as rude boys – a description given some credence by their temporary dalliance with a new name for the band, 'the Wailin' Rude Boys', and by tales of Marley's vicious temper. On one occasion, alleged Jimmy Riley of the Uniques, Bob Marley became so embroiled in a violent argument with them after the Uniques outperformed the Wailers at an event called the 'Battle of the Bands', that 'he draw his knife and create a scene'.[131] Notwithstanding apocryphal exaggerations, the anecdote underlines the fierceness of the competition among bands, and the desperate dreams of beating the ghetto odds to emerge from the festering squalor of Trench Town.

For his part, Tosh seems to have sown the seeds for his later reputation as a militant hard-man during this period. The DJ Wayne Jobson, though, believes it to have been a mask, a front to enable him to negotiate the mean streets and make his way in the every-man-for-himself, picaroon world of Trench Town.

In contrast to his spars, Bunny Livingston's violence was all the more threatening for never having to be expressed. The youngest member of the band could walk most places without fear of molestation, courtesy

Trench Town, imagined as a gold standard in social housing, had become by the late 1950s and 60s, when Tosh, Marley and Livingston moved in, a ghetto known as 'The Rock'

Marcus Garvey: vilified by
some, deified by others,
and eventually proclaimed
Jamaica's first national hero

Alexander Bustamente
(in centre with bow tie) with
allies and supporters in 1938.
Bustamente was a hero of
the Frome Rebellion and the
island's first prime minister

Negro Aroused, Kingston Harbour. Edna Manley's über black man
freed from the shackles of his colonial past

Livingston, Marley and
Tosh as the Teenagers,
prototype R&B crooners
who adored Curtis Mayfield

The Mystic Revelation of
Rastafari – formed by the
inimitable master drummer,
Count Ossie, who performed
for royalty: Princess Margaret
and the Rhumba Queen,
Margarita Mahfood

The Teenagers with Rita Marley. Tosh, the most proficient guitarist considered himself Marley's teacher

Clement 'Sir Coxsone' Dodd, the producer of Studio One, with Bob Marley. Dodd thought of himself as a father figure to the teenager

Vere Johns presides over the talent contest show 'Opportunity Hour'. Johns stands at the microphone with a range of hopeful contestants on either side

Don 'Cosmic' Drummond (inset with his trombone) was the creative centre of the Skatalites who backed the first efforts of Tosh, Marley and Livingston on 'Simmer Down'

Joe Higgs wearing the beret that rarely left his head. Higgs was the first and lasting mentor of the three Trench Town youth

Leslie Kong, ice-cream vendor,
restaurateur and record producer
of *The Best of the Wailers*

The mercurial, maverick
Lee 'Scratch' Perry, producer
of some of the finest tracks
ever recorded by the Wailers

Chris Blackwell,
a Jamaican patriot,
reggae connoisseur
and founder of
Island Records

On a state visit to Jamaica in 1966, Emperor Haile Selassie disembarks from his plane only after the Rasta elder Mortimo Planno has persuaded the masses to clear a path for H.I.M.

Rasta elder Mortimo Planno, who introduced Tosh, Livingston and especially Marley to the Rastafari religion

of his father's reputation and the street credits Toddy had acquired from toughs like Babu Man. 'Babu Man had a little Indian in him,' recalled Livingston, 'he was a half-Indian guy or might have been quarter Indian. A rough guy, he don't steal or anything like that but if you mess around with Babu Man you're dead!' Bunny Livingston's father, who still ran a rum shop in west Kingston, was revered by the most frightening 'rude boys' because he was 'the bigger bad guy for those little bad guys like Babu Man'. Babu Man's largesse extended to Tosh and Marley, offering them unofficial protection. His only requirement was payment in song. 'Believe me, if Babu Man would request a song, you'd sing it.'

Men like Babu Man were a bonus in the partisan environment of west Kingston, where neutrality was not a position that could be adopted readily. Calling themselves the Wailin' Rude Boys suggested a straightforward alignment, and even though the band dropped 'rude boys' to become 'Wailers', the name change did not herald a shift in direction. The years 1964 and 1965 spawned several 'rude boy' (rudie) songs from a host of bands, most notably on the part of the Wailers' 'Simmer Down', 'Rude Boy Ska' and 'Hooligan' – the last an ironic and unflattering song inspired by the Christmas riot at the Palace Theatre.

It came as no surprise that the James Bond novels, with all their stylish violence, were penned by Ian Fleming as he wintered in Jamaica. Bond, as Desmond Dekker spelt out in his hit song, '007', was an archetypal rude boy. 'Shaken not stirred?' A rude boy wouldn't have his Martini served any other way.

'Rude boys' and 'rude boy' bands constituted a club of mutual attraction and fascination. But though 'rude boy' songs chronicled their outlandish crimes and misdemeanours, they also drew attention to the punitive consequences. 'Rude boy gone to jail' warned Marley, in a song which he confided to Esther Anderson (a later girlfriend) was inspired by his own arrest and time spent in police cells.[132] But if the Wailers embraced the rebellious attitude of the rude boy, then it was primarily because the term was often used pejoratively to describe anyone from the west Kingston ghettoes. Bunny Livingston empathised with those so-called rude boys who 'carry on bad', believing the only way to exist was to snatch, 'cause there was nothing for the ghetto people to survive legitimately'. After all, some Trench Town 'sufferers' were desperate enough to 'box food out of hogg's mouth' (steal from a pig's pen).[133]

One unexpected consequence of the preponderance of 'rude boy'

songs was that they began to appeal to the vanity of the roughest protagonists. Tracks like 'Cry Tough' and '007' became their anthems. Buzzbee
was a top-ranking rude boy whose quality of menace was unmatched.
'He travel with gun and knife,' remembered the singer Derrick Morgan,
'and he would use anything [to hand] to cut you.' Buzzbee would enter
a dancehall, flinging empty bottles in the air without thought of where
they might land. When he approached Derrick Morgan one day with
a request for his story to be rendered in song, the lyricist understood
that he'd been made an offer he could not refuse. Buzzbee told him:
'I want you to make one [song] off me. I just want you to boost me,
and I want it by Friday.' The result was 'Tougher than Tough'. The
night Morgan played the track for him at a bar, Buzzbee was extremely
agitated. 'When the song reached [the line] "strong like lion, we are
iron",' Buzzbee flung two full beer bottles against the wall, and shouted:
'We are iron'. It was a signal, fortunately, that Buzzbee loved the song.
'But he didn't love it for long,' recalled Morgan, 'because he lose his
life the following day.'[134]

If 'rude boy' was largely an attitude, then the term, in Bunny Livingston's estimation, could not strictly be applied just to outlaws and
gangsters. Joe Williams or 'Papa Joe' was the rudest of the 'rude boys,'
maintained the youngest Wailer. 'Papa Joe' was a policeman but 'not
like Wyatt Earp'; he would not announce himself with guns blaring;
he'd prefer to sneak up on offenders and take them unawares. 'He
would catch you in your bed snoring or on top of your girl making
out one last time. You'd feel a cold piece of steel on your head-back,
and chilling words like "Don't even move, just come."'

Joe Williams travelled in style in an open-topped jeep, patrolling with
his posse, passing through the streets in 'slow-motion' late at night.
Williams would stop the jeep and ask a suspect where he was going
and where he lived. Invariably, the terrified youth would mumble some
made-up address. Then Williams would move over and 'pat the seat and
ask if the youth wouldn't mind showing him where exactly he lived'.
'Papa Joe' affected to be in the best of moods, laughing and chatting
with the youth, until the address turned out to be wrong and the youth
confessed to a mysterious bout of amnesia. Whereupon Williams would
'offer [him] a cell in the police station for the night'.

'One night at the Palace Theatre "Papa Joe" lined up and searched
everyone in the theatre, *every* single one.' Steel-helmeted, rifle-wielding

policemen fanned out and carried out his orders. Even the Wailers were searched. 'People started swallowing their spliffs. The police confiscated hundreds of ratchet knives, and one or two knuckledusters. There were gun butts to the head; spliffs dropped from lips.'

Tales of violence, of police 'n thieves expressed in song, resonated in the ghettoes of Kingston, but elsewhere Jamaicans – especially the middle class – still showed an overwhelming preference for imported love ballads. Figures from the national broadcasting stations reveal the biggest-selling songs from 1963 still catered to middle-class sensibilities – songs as enticing as a warm bubble bath, with titles such as 'Whatchagonna Do About It?' by Doris Troy and 'Come Softly' by Jimmy James.[135]

The attraction of ska music was largely lost on this section of society, until the saccharine success of fourteen-year-old Millie Small's 'My Boy Lollipop'. Chris Blackwell had recognised Millie Small's talent and the infectious quality, the bonhomie, of her voice and flew her to London for the recording. 'My Boy Lollipop' marked a pivotal moment in the evolution of Jamaican culture. Not only was it a huge international hit, filling the coffers of Chris Blackwell's London-based Island Records; but back home in Jamaica, among the record-buying middle classes, it uncoupled the freight of negative associations they had attached to ska. The lyrics of 'My Boy Lollipop' may not have stood much analysis, but its unambiguous financial success prompted speculators and other businessmen to take a punt on ska artists.

The band leader and promoter Byron Lee saw himself as a conduit for the music between uptown and downtown. His own band, the Drago-naires, was a regular feature on the uptown nightclub and luxury hotel circuit. But he'd been lured down to the ghetto's dirt-floor dancehalls by the hot syncopated beat of ska, venturing to places the Myrtle Bank crowd shuddered at the thought of setting foot in. If Byron Lee was a voyeuristic dilettante as his critics maintained, then he was increasingly a committed and professional one. A few years earlier, Lee's excite-ment had spilt over into a business deal with the politician Edward Seaga, purchasing his West Indies Record Label, to record the surefire hits of bands like the Maytals (whose popularity then exceeded that of the Wailers). 'Nobody uptown knew what the [ska] music was about, they couldn't relate to it,' Lee remembered. 'We were responsible for moving the music from west Kingston to the upper and middle class who could afford to buy records.'[136]

Byron Lee was also the moving force behind the 1960s documentary film simply called 'Ska', which sought to further capture the thrill of the music for a foreign audience. 'Now everybody can do the ska,' intones the oh-so-hep compère at the Sombrero Club, 'it's the new dance you can't resist.' The cool cognoscente with a toothy smile goes on to instruct viewers (with the aid of pairs of volunteers) in the four basic steps of the ska dance: 'Bow your head, swing your arms, shake your hips, and do a dip.' Such niceties were far removed from some of the slum yards where partners danced as if having sex with their clothes on. 'The woman will lean up against a tree, a sound box or a fence,' observed one social worker, 'and the man will in rhythm to the music literally rub into her.'[137] The Sombrero Club offered downtown's risqué pleasures in a safe uptown environment. There was little danger of a shock to middle-class sensibilities, as revellers at the Sombrero Club and similar establishments were offered an attenuated version of ska. The treatment of the ribald 'Sammy Dead Oh' was a perfect example. Sammy was still dead at the end of the song 'Sammy Dead Oh' but it wasn't the 'grudgeful naygar' (maliciously envious black man) that had caused his death, rather the more innocuous and anodyne 'they'.

Lee dismissed the carping in his headlong embrace of ska. He was adamant that only after radio stations became aware of this middle-class enthusiasm would they pick up on the music, and pack away their prejudices. For much of 1964, the ska-inflected records that the uptown crowd were buying in ever-increasing numbers included 'Simmer Down'. The Wailers' song competed gallantly with the Drifters' 'Under the Boardwalk', trading places with that tune in the charts for many months. In doing so, the teenage band's ascent, though unremarked upon by the newspapers, attracted attention in the yards of Trench Town and other ghettoes. 'First people say: "Who dem youth?" New group with new song a-come,' remembered Livingston. '"Simmer Down" took a while to catch on, but after a time the Wailers couldn't walk nowhere, people start point you out now "one a them there", you know. So you couldn't hide 'cause that song one of the biggest things at that time.'[138]

The joy of the head-spinning public approval was second only to the thrill of hearing their first recorded song pumping out from RJR, blasting out across the airwaves and picked up at the dancehalls, or more intimately on the Philips gramophone that Livingston's mother had installed in the cabinet in their new home (on Rousseau Road, a tier or two above Trench Town). But if the teenagers looked for some recognition of their remarkable achievement in the national newspapers, they searched in vain. Outside of the regular listings of the hit parade there were few sightings of the Wailers in print. Perhaps it's not surprising, as the *Gleaner* was staffed to the rafters with those who prayed daily for the deliverance from the 'tyranny of the sound system'. And then one day, the *Gleaner* broke with tradition. Reporting on a murder trial at a time when respectable folk were recoiling at every new rude boy outrage, the *Gleaner* drew its readers' attention to an alarming and highly significant detail. The alleged murderer was said to have dozed under a mango tree, listening to the Wailers' 'Rude Boy Ska', as he contemplated the crime he was about to commit.[139]

The 'rude boy' had been clearly sighted by 1964, but many believed he'd had a previous incarnation some twenty years earlier. 'Rude boy' escapades dominated newspaper headlines in ways not seen since 1948. That year Jamaicans followed the daring and murderous exploits of Rhygin – the notorious 'two-gun killer' – reported in the *Gleaner* in chilling detail. Ivanhoe 'Rhygin' Martin, who single-handedly terrorised the island for several months, was the original 'rude boy'.

Jamaicans caught their first glimpse of Rhygin as a fourteen-year-old youth. His initial offence was a 'wounding' in a vicious attack that earned him twelve strokes of the tamarind switch. Another wounding two years later led to a 20-shilling fine. He then served six months in jail for larceny. There he became an avid reader of 'true detective stories' and acquired the nickname 'Captain Midnight'. In 1946 he was put on trial for burglary, having broken into a dressmaking parlour and stolen dress material valued at £50 and, more seriously, for possession of a revolver without a permit. Martin conducted his own defence, irritating the judge with his exceedingly long melodramatic pauses, was found guilty, and sentenced to a year's imprisonment. A similar offence shortly after his release led to a five-year sentence at the General Penitentiary. He escaped from jail on 30 April 1948 and 'started his mad rush down the road to doom'.

On 30 August, armed police (some disguised as women) lay in wait for 'Rhygin' at the Carib Hotel. Brandishing revolvers which bore the inscription 'Defender', Rhygin shot his way out of the ambush, killing a policeman. Rhygin then wrote to the *Gleaner*, warning he would take his revenge on those who had betrayed him. The next day, in line with the Jamaican custom of 'if you can't catch kweshi catch 'im shirt', he murdered the girlfriend of the man he believed had informed on him. Another associate died at the hands of the desperado three days later. On 5 September the police offered a £200 reward for Rhygin's capture, and put out a description to aid the public:

> Aged twenty-nine. 5 foot 3 inches. May be wearing high heels – 'Duke' heels they are known as in Kingston's West End underground – making him 5 ft 5 inches. Medium build, colour black, hair and eyes black, several front teeth missing in upper jaw but may be wearing false teeth, all plain or with one or two teeth of gold. Often wears polarised sunglasses with a narrow bridge. Has a habit of looking backwards every few steps, and spitting after a few words he speaks. Approach with caution. He is dangerous. He is armed.

Rhygin's diabolical deeds sowed panic in Jamaican society. There were several reported sightings of the gunman. A courageous barmaid in western Kingston made a bid to turn him in when a man answering to Rhygin's description entered the bar and ordered a 'Porto Pruno' wine – a drink which the barmaid/sleuth had heard Rhygin was fond of. As the suspect lifted his second glass, she broke a bottle (of water) over his head. But the next's day's headline: 'No, Not "Rhygin"' told of her error.

A manhunt was launched but Rhygin avoided capture for more than a month. Eventually, after a white-knuckle journey to a small island at Lime Cay, and down to his last dozen bullets, he was tracked by officers of the Jamaican Constabulary armed with rifles and tear gas. The police let loose their arsenal and he died on the sand. 'Rhygin carried out his last vainglorious boast that he would not be taken alive,' reported the papers. 'Cornered at long last, he fought like a rat in a trap and like a rat he died.'[140]

The slain outlaw had achieved such a level of notoriety by his end that thousands lined the route from the waterfront as his corpse was escorted to the 'dead house' (morgue). The 'slaying and manhunt' had exposed some uncomfortable truths about Jamaica. Rhygin was not universally despised. Indeed, there were many in Kingston's ghettoes who had helped him to avoid capture and celebrated his duel with the police: for them Rhygin was a bad 'nayga' – something of a star-boy like Humphrey Bogart, Alan Ladd and all those celluloid bad white 'naygas'.

It was no accident when, in the late 1960s, the makers of the film *The Harder They Come* chose the name Rhygin for their anti-hero. Rhygin, played by the singer Jimmy Cliff, underwent a cinematic transformation to become a naive but talented countryboy who comes to Kingston seeking his fortune as a singer. Disillusion creeps in fairly early on when he's exploited by unscrupulous record producers. A few wrong turns and he metamorphoses into a rude boy embroiled in vice, violence and corruption and, just like his real-life counterpart, descends into a dark and nihilistic world on a murderous spree.

Thirty years on, Trevor Rhone, the co-author of the screenplay, enthused over the bold imaginative leap that he and the director, Perry Henzell, had taken in ensuring that the film captured the language of the streets. Just how bold can be judged by the distributors who, nervous about the thickness of the patois, took the precaution of adding subtitles to the film. Rhone was an elegant seventy-something when I interviewed him, a man whose laconic manner disappeared as his memories dropped through the layers of the past, like one trapdoor after another. His rich, stage-crafted voice was a perfect pitch for his enthusiasm. Rhone maintained a level of high drama and humour throughout our conversation. 'The first thing you, young man, should know is that Jamaica was never the same after the screening. *The Harder They Come* marked an irrevocable change in society, and a seismic shift in the people's perception of themselves.'[141] Rhone argued that, for the very first time, instead of Hollywood stars, Jamaicans were now seeing their own local heroes as giants projected onto the screen once the preserve of John Wayne, Jane Mansfield and Montgomery Cliff. 'It was awesome!' On the night of the premiere, Trevor Rhone approached the cinema and assumed that there must have been some terrible accident nearby: such was the density of people on the streets leading up to the Carib Theatre that he didn't make it to within 100 yards of the cinema. Outside there was chaos: inside, revolution. The celebrity audience included the prime minister, the majority of his cabinet, Kingston's high society set and at least one lucky critic from *Rolling Stone* magazine who scrambled in with the crowds and sent back an excited dispatch:

> The rudies turned out in such jubilant force that the door gave in. They packed the Carib Theatre – till the prime minister was sitting – three to a seat. Everybody stripped down and got high and it was a hell of a hot night. *The Harder They Come* does for the rude boys what *Rebel Without a Cause* did for juvenile delinquents and *Easy Rider* did for acid-eating paranoids and *Shaft* did for Harlem.[142]

'And the music! Toots, Jimmy, mostly Jimmy,' Rhone cooed, 'the music was an instrument of repair.' My host's nostalgia for that golden era in the country's culture (*The Harder They Come* ushered in a quickening international interest in Jamaican creativity) was tempered by the prophetic power of the film. The lone rude boy; the gunman out of control, foreshadowed what has come to pass. 'Everyone's a Rhygin now,' said Rhone. 'Three M's: murder, mayhem, madness. The levers of social control are missing. Our society is out of control.'

The exuberance of his recollection of the film's premiere drained away as he escorted me to the perimeter of his gated enclave in the centre of Kingston. 'How are things now?' I asked. '*Ohhhh* not good,' he groaned like a man whose bad tooth should have been extracted long, long ago. 'No, not good. It's as if Pandora's Box has been opened.' I expected more but Rhone, pulling back from a conclusion, would go no further. As an exit line the theatricality was spoilt slightly by the fact that the gates to the gated community refused to open. While my driver fiddled with the sensor mechanism, I stood a little awkwardly with Rhone. We'd said everything we needed to say to each other but I began to sense that he was already reading my thoughts, that beyond those gates lay Pandora's opened Box. He smiled evenly and whispered: 'How seriously do you want to leave?'

Rhygin was the most visible manifestation of the violence which lies just beneath the verdant landscape of sinewy poetry that is Jamaica. Looking back, he seems to have been a rare anomaly: murders were few in 1948. Sixty years later, Jamaica has one of the highest murder rates in the world. The average of 1,500 murders per year does not appear high, but per capita of the population it is extraordinary. The percentages, if applied to Britain, would translate to fifty murders every day, or 300 per day in the U.S.A.

Some vestige of Trevor Rhone's gloom followed me to the psychiatric unit of the University of the West Indies. Professor Frederick Hickling was not as despairing: 'You have to remember, now, this country has been dealing with violence since 1494. Columbus was a very "rude boy".'

After our second meeting it was clear that my unguarded approach of faux ignorance brought out the best of him. We had settled into a pattern of tutor and pupil. He was less abrasive. His pity for me was bathed in humour – although it still barely disguised a finely developed combative streak, which surfaced when the conversation turned to neuropathology, to guns and gangs. He shrugged off my question about the extraordinarily high levels of violence on the island as alarmist. Without prompting, he suggested that we think back to the 'rude boy' era of the 1960s. 'You ready?' He waited for me to turn on my recording machine. 'We been here before, man.' A hint of patois suddenly leaked out of his voice. 'As a yout' me cyaan remember de fight at dance on a Saturday night; de scream as blood flow. Only then it was cutlass. Now is gun.'

'So, you're planning a trip to Jamaica?' Just before leaving, my sister fixed me with pity in her eyes. 'No man, don't go to Jamaica,' she warned, 'you'll return in a wooden box.'

I have made the pilgrimage to my parents' birthplace several times in the last two decades, and each time the warnings are issued. Lately though, the Cassandras have become more strident. Poring over the morning papers in the capital is an unsettling introduction to violence, Jamaican style. Today's headline in the *Star* screams: 'Cop Executed!' Gangsters have killed an off-duty policeman, ambushed in his patrol car on his way home. Two mornings later, the same headline but a different policeman, having a drink in his regular bar when gunmen burst in. They sprayed the bar with bullets, killing the officer, and then relieved him of his gun. On the fourth day yet another policeman is dead and people are beginning to ask: are the police being targeted?

The local TV crew is quickly on the scene. At the corner of the screen you can just make out the body of the dead policeman slumped over the steering wheel. The camera cuts to the disbelieving wife, trying to push her way through the police cordon. She emits a piercing scream: 'Why?' Again and again. I want to turn away from the television. What is being served up seems prurient and strangely cinematic, like some 1930s Hollywood gangster movie.

Suddenly a government minister arrives and what he says astonishes me. He advises that police officers should no longer travel alone and that they should get down to the firing ranges to sharpen up their shooting skills. There is a word to describe what is going on: hysteria. If they can kill the police at will then they can kill anyone.

There are more than 200 outlaws at large in Jamaica. Many of them are violent and nihilistic veterans of jails in the U.S.A. and Europe where they were extradited. Convicted of gun and drug trafficking, they served their sentences and have been deported subsequently to Jamaica. They, the gangsters, are well known, but many people turn a blind eye, either out of fear or because in some small way, they stand to gain, if only in the short-term, from the underground economy fuelled by these gangs. Cocaine is again flooding the capital, and with it come gangs and gunmen who have no fear of the law.

Trevor Rhone had warned of the reincarnation of Rhygin. In June 2010, Rhygin returned: he'd never really been away. The new version was a forty-one-year-old ghetto don called Christopher 'Dudus' Coke who delegated his killing to his gang, the 'shower posse' – notorious for showering their targets with bullets. The Americans requested Dudus's extradition and when, nine months later, the Jamaican authorities sent in the armed forces to arrest him mayhem ensued. Police and soldiers clashed with Dudus's supporters. More than seventy people were killed; many of them innocent victims caught in the crossfire. Dudus was eventually apprehended at a police road block disguised as a woman in a pink wig and granny glasses. But the comic dénouement was the culmination of a month-long manhunt that had taken the island to the brink of social collapse. Dudus, like Rhygin before him, has already entered Jamaican folklore.

But if the gangsters are local celebrities then so too are the policemen – with monikers such as 'Cowboy' and 'Fast Draw'. In such a climate it is unsurprising that there have been numerous accusations of unlawful killings by police officers. Kingston *is* the Wild West.

A few years ago, a strange sight greeted the traveller on the road out of town – a billboard poster repeated every few miles of an extremely handsome man. But he was neither model nor film star. He was Senior Superintendent Renato Adams, 'Policeman of the Year'. I fantasised that we were related, that he was an incarnation of old man Adams, Corporal Adams, who, family lore had it, had once faced down an angry mob in Gordon Town with his service revolver – but without firing it. This Adams, though, Renato, had a reputation for fighting fire with fire: he was the 'Papa Joe' of his day, the rudest of the latest rude boys, killing the bad guys. And in the kill-for-kill spate that gripped the country, the gangsters vowed they would take their revenge on Adams. The superintendent went on national television and announced when he would be leaving work, what time he was expected home and if they, the gunmen, cared to meet him, he would be happy to oblige. But High Noon was postponed. The gunmen didn't show.

I decide to head out of Kingston for the north coast to meet a cousin I had never met who's returned from Los Angeles to Jamaica after thirty years to run a large general store. He has sad, soft eyes that have seen most things. One eye though is permanently glued to the monitor of the surveillance camera. 'You know almost every store in Falmouth has been robbed,' he says. 'But not this one. Want to see why?' He cracks open the door, 'Spirit, come meet me cousin nah.'

Spirit is an off-duty policeman, moonlighting as a security guard, given the name 'Spirit' because of the way he manages to creep about and catch the crooks by surprise. How he does this is a mystery because Spirit is enormous, almost as wide as he is tall. And when I doubt whether he really is a policeman, he lifts his shirt and pushes back the layer of overhanging flesh to reveal the 'piece' on his trouser belt.

Just before we leave the store, my cousin reaches into the bottom drawer of his desk and pulls out his 9mm pistol. He checks it for bullets and snaps it onto his belt. 'You cool with this?' he says. I am not cool, but nod my head. I note maybe two things. One, that the bullets appear gold and two, that the gun does not have a safety catch.

At his palatial but highly secure pad just outside of the popular holiday resort of Montego Bay, it is agreed that we'll take a late siesta and hit the town towards the end of the evening. I wake up at the appointed hour. 9 o'clock, no sign of him. 10 o'clock, still no sign. And then suddenly there is a power cut. If it was dark before, it is doubly so now. I try to edge my way out of the darkness, and find myself in what appears to be a broom cupboard. And a dark thought steadily drips into my head: what if he wakes from his sleep, forgets I am here, hears me, the intruder, stumbling around downstairs and reaches for his gun. And now I can't rid myself of the enveloping thought that it is so dark in here, so very dark. Like the inside of a wooden box.

By 1965, the yards – the homes and outdoor living spaces for the impoverished in the ghettoes – were being carved up into a series of garrison communities, controlled by local dons and their henchmen – areas to which, if you were not from there, it would be unwise to venture; and areas from which the inhabitants regularly found it difficult to leave. Nonetheless, an ambitious and often brutal social experiment had begun. The bulldozers of Edward Seaga, now the minister of Culture and Development, had moved in with the explicit purpose of clearing huge swathes of slum dwellings and squatter camps in west Kingston. Seaga had steeled himself to the temporary but 'necessary inhumanity' of displacing and dislodging people who sometimes claimed they were given too little notice, and who, in any case, didn't want to move. They argued that once they left they would have nowhere to return to because the new homes were earmarked for Seaga's supporters. Just three years after Independence (though the process was already under way in the previous decade) Jamaica's political landscape had hardened into a rigid, partisan two-party system, summarised in the popular assertion: 'If your party in, you feed; if the other man party in, you starve.' This code of patronage politics extended to jobs and housing. Not only would supporters of the opposition be expelled from their homes but also squeezed out of labouring jobs, which came with the lucrative contracts to construct the new social housing developments.

But, ultimately, it was the ambition of everyone with drive and determination to move up and out of Trench Town. The immediate goal was to get out of the tenement yards (mostly rented from absentee landlords) and into the government yards. For the majority of migrants from the countryside, even that was a step beyond them, or one which might take several years to achieve. But having done so, the next stage was to try to get to Greenwich Road, the psychic border that divided north from south – downtown from uptown. 'If you reached Greenwich Road you were almost safe; beyond Greenwich Road and you'd made it.' Rousseau Road – a couple of streets north of the border – was most definitely a *residential* area (Jamaicans roll the 'r' in residential; it's a word that carries reverence). Relocating to Rousseau Road, Bunny Livingston's parents had moved in to a home of hitherto unexpected grandeur and a street which abutted a middle-class enclave. It was a stone's throw from the solid properties of civil servants and senior teachers; there was even at least one white family on Rousseau Road. The respectable homeowners there luxuriated in the one-third-acre plots of land where they could build outhouses and even plant crops for their pantries.

Bunny Livingston was welcome to stay in his father's house but he was under no illusion that he might one day become the beneficiary of 'dead lef' – no inheritance would be handed down (left by the dead). Bunny might have escaped north with his family but Trench Town was still the centre of his working and social life. When not at Studio One, Livingston, Tosh and Marley were most likely to be found hanging out at Vincent 'Tartar' Ford's yard on 1st Street, singing, playing musical instruments and dominoes. All three youths were fond of Tartar, partly because of his easy-going nature which came at the expense of his own health. He suffered from undiagnosed and, therefore, untreated diabetes – bits kept falling off him, toes especially – but Tartar gave the impression of not noticing. Perhaps marijuana numbed his concern, for the sickly, sweet-natured Rasta was a small-time dealer. Even if he hadn't had so winning a personality, Tartar would have been popular, as unsold stock was invariably smoked, and generously shared. The vibe was mellow, tranquil and very attractive to the youngsters. His home was always open to them, and Marley, in particular, had reason to be grateful. Tartar had, on many occasions, provided the roaming youth with space on his floor to roll out a bed for the night.

The record producer, Clement Dodd, certainly thought that he, too, was a candidate for Marley's affection. In his conception, he was both a father-figure and boss. Although there was no appointed leader of the band, Dodd's focus was increasingly on Marley. That attitude was not reciprocated: Marley's default position was always the unity of the band. The same was true of Tosh and Livingston. A satellite of collaborators may have orbited around the Wailers, but the core members were an exclusive band of loyal brothers whose mutually protective wall was rarely breached by outsiders. When in 1966 Marley moved out of his makeshift lodgings at the back of Studio One and began renting an apartment with his girlfriend Rita and her child on Greenwich Road, no alarm bells were sounded in the ears of Livingston and Tosh. After all, the three had made various pledges to each other, including that none of them would consider marriage until the group was on a sound financial footing. They might have sexual relations with girls, 'catch their practice' with them or, as they said in the country, 'take their rudeness to bush', but their primary focus was the band, which all three recognised as both a route to escape their destiny as 'Negro nobodies' and a potential ticket to prosperity.[143] 'We didn't have anything,' recalled Peter Tosh. 'Our aim, our ambition was to get a decent house or to move on up just as other Kingstonians did, although it was hard to get out of the ghetto.'

The Wailers had a fearsome work ethic. Marley regularly finished the day covered in perspiration, the sweat working its way down and accumulating in his shoes. They were eclectic in their lyric writing, digging into the narrative of their own lives, and borrowing from wherever seemed appropriate. Much later in their careers, Tartar would receive an important credit and the lucrative copyright ownership on at least one of the songs – 'No Woman, No Cry'. When the pathways to creativity failed to stir, Dodd would bring sample songs (demos, not-to-be-sold records) to the studio, and encourage the Wailers to listen to them for ideas. Over the next couple of years they produced a string of 'rude boy' songs, including 'Rude Boy Ska' and 'Put it On'. Each time, they might have been forgiven for thinking that their careers were about to take off, but in reality their plane was not yet on the runway; it was barely pushing off from the stand, and occasionally the controller Dodd reassigned them to a place at the back of the queue, counselled patience, and bid them wait their turn. It must have been bewildering.

They recorded dozens of tracks for Dodd but their success was no barometer of financial reward. The group was locked into a contract whose terms seemed all the more unfavourable with every hit – notwithstanding that it only took 8,000 sales for a song to be considered a bestseller.

The catalyst for change came when Rita Anderson announced to Marley that she was pregnant. And Marley, after deliberating and seeking advice from Dodd, broke the band's cardinal rule: he donned his stage suit and headed for the church. When Rita Anderson first took up with Marley, she already had a child; and she was especially impressed and relieved that Marley had welcomed mother *and* daughter into his heart. For, as Edith Clarke discovered in her survey of house-holds, Jamaica was a society where men were usually reluctant 'to father another man's bastards'.[144] Marley did not tell the other two bandsmen he was getting married, nor invite them – or his mother – to his wedding. But in a reprise of Cedella's marriage to Norval, Marley informed his new bride soon after the ceremony that he would be leaving – although unlike his father, he did have plans to return. Bob Marley had decided to join his mother in Delaware, USA to 'work some money'. Despite the local popularity of the Wailers' songs, they were still living in a way that was barely a notch above hand-to-mouth.

The idea for a concert was hurriedly put together to send off Marley to the USA. The Wailers gathered one last time. The Paragons, Alton Ellis, the Gaylads and a number of other groups agreed to perform. The police also put in an appearance. It was an evening of great intensity. The hundreds of rude boys who turned up were a testament to the impact that the young band exerted over the ghetto youth. When the Wailers broke into 'I'm Still Waiting', the police 'had to duck as pure bottles were flying towards them. It was like a storm of bottles.'

Though the police made a tactical retreat, the intensity mounted. There had been a mic problem at the stadium, so only the grandstand was used; the huge crowd was jumbled together in only a fraction of the space. Above the din of high spirits and curses, echo and feedback from the instruments bounced around the empty hall. The Wailers were bemused. The event was threatening to end in chaos. But then, instinctively, the trio pulled back from the mics, and suddenly, recalled Livingston, 'the sound became beautiful. Bob did a dramatic finale, a dying fall to the ground', and never got up: he had to be carried off stage.[145]

6

AND PRINCES SHALL COME
OUT OF AFRICA

BOB Marley's timing was poor. At the start of 1966, he was off the island; working in factories in Delaware, USA, when to be present in Jamaica in the spring of that year was to be part of one of the most momentous events in the country's history. A biblical prophecy of the coming of a black Messiah – clung to by Jamaicans and black people in the diaspora – that 'princes shall come out of Egypt and Ethiopia shall soon stretch out her hands unto God' was about to be realised with the electrifying announcement that Haile Selassie I, the Emperor of Ethiopia, would pay a State Visit to Jamaica on 21 April.

Before ascending the Ethiopian throne, Haile Selassie I had answered to the title Ras Tafari ('Ras' in Amharic denoted Lord or Prince and 'Tafari' was his family name). Selassie was venerated in Jamaica, especially by the Rastafarians who named themselves after him. In just over thirty years from the beginning of the 1930s, they had established a cult with a black Jesus (Selassie) at its centre: it was an eclectic religion, borrowed partly from the Old Testament, sprinkled with the stardust of ancient African folklore, and serving up an ideology of reclaimed black supremacy. Ridiculed for decades as the fanciful doctrine of resentful and poor black fantasists, the Rastafarian movement had taken root both in the countryside and in the wretched shanty towns of Kingston. By 1966, the Wailers had been exposed to the culture and proponents of Rastafari for more than three years, not just working alongside Joe Higgs and in the company of Tartar, but sitting in on Nyabinghi sessions, and listening to the powerful Rasta proselytisers who lived in Trench Town. In fits and starts, the Wailers had begun to shed the imagery of the 'rude boy' and to clothe themselves in the teaching of Rastafari. Not wholeheartedly, but certainly as proto-Rastafarians, they fell under its alluring spell.

The curiosity of these three young men, each in their early twenties, could have been satisfied easily in any one of dozens of Rasta yards in Kingston. But 18 5th Street exerted the biggest pull. Christened 'Open Yard' by the Rastafarian elder who lived there; it was home to Brother Mortimo Planno, a thirty-seven-year-old self-taught ghetto intellectual with abundant street-cred and smarts. When Tosh, Marley and Livingston dropped in at 5th Street, they were exposed to the rites and rituals of Rastafari, introduced to the *Philosophy & Opinions of Marcus Garvey* and to copies of the *Ethiopian World* read by young men who trembled with pride and rage, and they took part in the drumming, chanting, reasoning and praise-singing to Selassie and Marcus Garvey. The earlier black leader had played the role of 'John the Baptist' to Selassie's 'Jesus Christ'. And as far as Rastafarians, including the fledgling brothers Marley, Livingston and Tosh were concerned, in the roll call of importance, there was God and there was Garvey.

The elder statesman, Norman Manley, was undoubtedly paying him a compliment when he wrote that Garvey had shaken the country out of its denial, and 'succeeded in making people frightfully conscious of colour'.[146] The teachings of Marcus Garvey took pride of place in Mortimo Planno's Open Yard. Garvey explained the stigma of black life, and the unfathomable rage of young men such as Peter Tosh, men who knew that they were angry but didn't really understand why. In the Open Yard the Wailers gained a pass to the past. Garvey revealed what had long been whispered and suspected; that Jamaica's black population had been the victims of a crime without punishment, without reconciliation and without, therefore, the possibility of forgiveness; that the perpetrators of that crime had co-opted the compensation due to the enslaved; that the British Crown had channelled £20 million into the coffers of the plantation owners, who, after Emancipation, had been deprived of their slave workforce; and that the descendants of the enslaved, despite the broken shackles, were still in captivity. Garvey's great idea of a return to Africa where they could live under their own vine and fig tree had been embraced by the Rastas. And Mortimo Planno would have his young charges understand that Queen Victoria had actually intended that money, the £20 million, to be set aside for the repatriation of the emancipated to Africa.

Just a couple of years previously, the Wailers had been among the huge crowds who turned up early to take their places on the pavement of the streets leading from Victoria Pier in Kingston to the Roman Catholic Cathedral. They were there as part of a racial and national sacrament: the proudly black nationalist leader Marcus Mosiah Garvey was coming home, albeit in a wooden box. At about 4 p.m., clouds in the overcast sky parted and a ray of sunlight guided the double casket of oak and mahogany, encasing the embalmed remains of Marcus Garvey, as it was piped off the *Coromantee* and onto a decorated police vehicle.[147] The slow motorcade then proceeded with funereal dignity through the capital.

Great excitement and sensitivity had accompanied Garvey's poignant return on 10 November 1964, more than twenty years after he had died pathetically, alone and overlooked, in self-imposed exile in London. Garvey was now accorded the kind of respect denied him by Jamaica's ruling elite when he had departed bruised and bankrupt from the island in 1935. Back then he was a man whom, Bob Marley would later lament, Jamaicans had 'sold for rice'.[148] Now he was eulogised as 'the rugged humble son of St Ann', by the *Gleaner*, the very paper which had denounced him so shrilly and consistently in his life. 'He rose in a tempestuous lifetime to the stature of an international figure,' trumpeted the paper, 'then largely notorious, now rightly famous'.[149] In a study of splendid selective amnesia, the *Gleaner* went further to point out a truth and sentiment that it would have found unbearable to print previously, namely that 'Garvey is a symbol of the BLACK MAN, rebellious, strident, rampant.'[150]

A collective guilt, that Jamaicans had shown improper regard for the great man in allowing his ignominious funeral in London, perhaps accounted for the anxiety over the arrangements for the reburial. For twenty-four years, Garvey's duppy had been abroad in the land – a state he peculiarly seemed to have foreseen. In the darkest depths of rejection, Garvey had comforted his followers and warned his enemies with the prophecy: 'When I am dead look for me in the whirlwind or the song of the storm. Look for me all around you.'[151] Everything needed to be done properly now so that the disturbed duppy might be reunited with Garvey's corpse. Inevitably then, the alignment of the vault provoked outrage. The position was changed hurriedly after complaints that the north-to-south setting was one that was reserved for executed murderers buried in the prison cemetery. Garvey's vault was now realigned from east to west.[152]

Equally vexing was the rumour, and the ugly ensuing rancour, that the embalmed corpse had actually remained in the London vault; and that there was nothing in the stately coffin ferried through Kingston, save a few heavy rocks to give it weight. Garvey's sons resisted the gathering clamour for the coffin's lid to be raised for a public inspection: the photograph of Julius Garvey, clasping a torch and peering into the casket (along with his positive identification of his father) seemed to settle the matter, for most.

Marcus Mosiah Garvey was a determinedly black 'race' leader. In life, he had polarised Jamaican opinion; in death, he continued to do so. Then, as now, the population split into two different camps with distinct impressions of the man: wronged and sacrificial demi-god versus lowly, crooked charlatan. But twenty years on, each of the rival political parties had found a commonality of purpose (many argued it was simply naked expedience) in the return of their natural enemy to his native land. British rule had been built on a carefully cultivated suggestion of inferiority in its colonial subjects. Jamaicans were first and foremost British, and an important element of their identity was governed by feelings of proximity to the Crown. 'Tracing' of one's roots to England was a popular pastime and, during those recurrent moments of turmoil on the island, many a nerve had been steadied by the invocation of Charles II's famous proclamation of 1661: 'All children of our natural born subjects of England to be born in Jamaica shall from their respective births be reputed to be and shall be free denizens of England.'

On 10 November 1964, Jamaica's ruling elite demonstrated that they were no longer frightened of Marcus Garvey. Towards the end of his life, Garvey's political ambitions had foundered on the disenfranchisement of his obvious constituency – the Afro-Jamaican descendants of the enslaved: now they had the vote. But more than that, in the crisis of identity that followed Jamaica's formal independence from Britain in 1962, 300 years after the island's fortunes had first become yoked to the Motherland, Garvey's divisive legacy took on a unifying role.

The reconfiguration began soon after the final lowering of the Union Jack on the island. Jamaica announced its new ambitions by participating in the World's Fair of 1964. No longer would the island resign itself to being a parochial backwater of a once mighty Empire. Its flag would be unfurled alongside those of a host of nations jostling for prime pitches at the international gathering in New York. The fair, by its own estimation, was to be a 'showcase of man's creativity'; commentators enthused over the 'dizzying array of cultural come-ons', conjuring worlds of past, present and future. Shuttling through a panorama of spectacular fountains, 'time tunnels' and seven-storey-high 'space cities', passengers aboard the General Motors futurama ride glimpsed an imagined future of giant underwater hotels; the glories of the past were invoked by European countries: Italy sent Michelangelo's *Pieta*; Belgium recreated a walled medieval city.[153]

For its part, Jamaica sent a group of its most successful musicians to the Caribbean pavilion. The line-up consisted almost exclusively of the kind of performers whom the proprietors of the uptown Sombrero Club would have been happy to welcome. Millie Small, Jimmy Cliff and Byron Lee and the Dragonaires all made the grade, along with fourteen other acts. Invitations were not extended to the rude boy ragamuffin Wailin' Wailers or the ganja-smoking Skatalites. Neither did the incessant drumming of Count Ossie's dreadlocked bandsmen sound across the landscaped lawns of Flushing Meadows: Jamaica's bespoke tailored cabinet were not yet convinced that the mystical members of Rastafari, with yellowing eyes and encrusted beards, dressed in rough hemp trousers made from crocus or flour bags, possessed the modern credentials they were keen to project.

If the time was not yet ripe for those Jamaicans deemed unsavoury (and mercifully hidden away in the unsightly but unexplored shanty dwellings of Wareika Hills), then neither was it for a large section of the host nation. African-American civil rights activists gatecrashed the party at the World's Fair. In the shadow of the giant globe – the Unisphere meant as a symbol of the exposition's inclusiveness – African-Americans picketed and protested against the USA's continued segregation. They were determined to reveal the 'glaring contrast between the glittering fantasy world at the fair and the real brutality, poverty, hatred and vengeance which Negroes face'.

The fantasy world was one which the Jamaican establishment was happy to embrace. Yet many among the despised black population believed they shared a common cause with African-Americans – a fact that was further underlined the following year when Dr Martin Luther King visited the island, in a momentary escape from the constant anxiety that followed his every step in America's racial conflagration. King electrified Jamaica and, in turn, was greeted with the same extraordinary warmth shown over a decade earlier to the African-American singer and activist, Paul Robeson. Back then, according to the *Gleaner*, thousands of 'little men and women from [the ghettoes of] Denham and Jones Town' turned out for Robeson and rubbed shoulders 'with sleekly gowned women and tailored men from cool St Andrews'. [154]

Though Dr King believed Jamaica was at the dawn of the kind of new beginning that African-Americans could only dream would soon be theirs – telling packed audiences that in contrast to his own country 'in Jamaica I feel like a human being' – his visit was reported almost in biblical terms. It was as if a wise Solomon had descended from the clouds to pass a healing hand over the divisions between the classes. King ably performed the delicate task of telling Jamaicans that at this time – the passing of the old colonial order, the moment of great expectation in the nation's history – while there should be no cap on ambition, Jamaicans, like black Americans, should make the very best of their lot: 'If it falls to our luck to be street sweepers, sweep the streets like Raphael painted pictures, like Michelangelo carved marble, like Shakespeare wrote poetry and like Beethoven composed music. Sweep the streets so well that all the hosts of heaven and earth would have pause to say, "Here lived a great street sweeper."'

Parts of the speech would not have found favour with Marcus Garvey. He had argued that Jamaicans should reject the assumption that they were born to be 'hewers of wood and drawers of water'. And yet the ecstatic reception for Dr King (Jamaicans described him as 'One o' we') crested with his pilgrimage to the tomb of Garvey to lay a wreath for the great race leader, who, during his heyday in Harlem's 'Negro Metropolis', had dignified African-Americans with 'a sense of personhood, a sense of manhood, a sense of somebodiness'.[155]

The same sentiment was felt by Jamaicans and their contrite politicians who on 15 November 1964 had declared Marcus Mosiah Garvey to be the island's first national hero. Both stalwart admirer and former detractor stood to gain from this new appreciation. Ostensibly, it was allied to the commensurate objective to rid the country of the 'unsympathetic attitude of the colonial middle class to the aspirations of the barefooted man'.[156]

Students of Jamaican psychology thought they had detected a subtle shift in that barefooted man's perception of himself. After Independence, he might still be reduced to clothing his naked self in a recycled hemp flour bag, but once it was bleached and exposed to the sun (removing the logo of the flour company), and handed over to an amateur seamstress, the flour bag was transformed into a linen suit. And behold the new Jamaican! Versions of this uplifting and patriotic story were trotted out regularly in the newspapers. For others, though, with longer memories and a keen sense of history, the sighting of this new state of grace among the populace was as premature as its previous incarnation. The new Jamaican was not so new, they argued: he had revealed himself the century before. Straight after Emancipation, after the midnight hour, when the Baptist pastor, William Knibb, had counted down the hours to the end of slavery to proclaim, 'The monster is dead', the legend of the African captives' euphoria had been cemented in simple tales of transformation. A favourite was the story of the freed black woman who chastised another for 'turning back the hands of the clock' by continuing to address her formally, as had been the custom under slavery:

> 'Mornin' Missis? Why you say mornin' Missis?' said she. 'Don't we all equal now? My friend, buckra [the white man] did always say "howdye". Me will always say "howdye". If me is equal to buckra, me must equal buckra with me "howdye".'[157]

The new Jamaican was born in 1834. After that date, there was no need for the formerly enslaved to run away. But the desire to escape, to return to a nameless place called home, had not been stemmed. In 300 years of British rule, Jamaica had witnessed more revolts and rebellions than any other island colony. These violent insurrections were a manifestation of 'fits of nostalgia', says Dr Ali Mazrui, a beguiling scholar of the Atlantic slave trade 'because the memory of a life before slavery had not died out.'[158] This despite the lack of slave narratives, of glorious tales of daring escape on the underground railway. On the Caribbean islands, there had been no psychic border, no equivalent to America's metaphorical Mason-Dixon Line – dividing North from

South – to which courageous runaways might steal away and cross over to freedom. In Jamaica, the imaginative enslaved African who, emulating his African-American counterpart, sealed himself in a box and posted the man-sized package north would have been disappointed. The freedom parcel would most likely have been returned from whence it came – courtesy of the Maroons.

In 1739 and again in 1795, the British sued for peace and signed a treaty with a band of escapees named the Maroons, who for decades had waged guerrilla war and outwitted their slavemasters, as well as the 'Redcoat' troops sent to pacify them, and established a semi-autonomous region in the Cockpit country. But, after days (sometimes weeks) of hacking his way through the interior to the Maroon territory, the intrepid runaway who fled the plantation was met by a people whose fragile independence was predicated on an agreement to hand him back to his rightful owner: he was returned.

'Jamaicans damn each other and say it has no parallel in any other country.' So wrote Vere Johns in the *Gleaner* in November 1948 provoking a stew of highly seasoned responses in the country's other newspapers. In answer to the oft repeated conundrum of why Jamaicans hate each other, Professor Frederick Hickling suggests: 'Is it any wonder? Didn't the free French hate their Vichy countrymen? Is it any wonder when a system turned the driver against the cane-cutting enslaved; turned the house enslaved against their brothers and sisters in the field; turned the rebels against the informers in their midst. Didn't the resigned slaves hate the traitors in their hearts? Is it any wonder?' He trails off on a spiralling, time-travelling thought before rallying: 'But, and it's a big but,' Hickling reminds me, 'then along comes Marcus Garvey.'

Garvey acknowledged that black life had been rendered a tragic comedy in history. He likened the black man to a gambler at a poker table continually coming up with a 'poor hand', not realising that the cards were 'marked' and stacked against him. Garvey shuffled the pack, removed the joker, and dealt the black man an ace – a black ace. To those who believed themselves marked with the curse of Cain, Garvey brought a new gospel of self-worth. Blacks in the diaspora were the descendants of a once proud and ancient African civilisation, he told his followers. They should love themselves. Love would be the instrument of their repair. Too often they had been the butt of jokes – frequently at the hands of each other.

The island temperament in the Antilles is rooted in and survives through humour, believes Derek Walcott. Caribbean people walk a fine line between tragedy and comedy. In the 1960s Walcott was one of the emerging voices whose writing acknowledged the tragicomic aspect of life in the region. But tragedy was a booby trap, and comedy too. It required a fine balance to steer a path away from the denigrations and degradations of the past, but in the hands of the most venerated of his contemporaries, the Trinidadian, V. S. Naipaul, Caribbean life was freighted towards comedy. Naipaul, clinging to the islander's self-loathing, berated his Indian and Negro countrymen for striving for acceptance by the whites, 'like monkeys pleading for evolution'.[159]

From self-loathing to self-love, Garvey's message was couched in terms that needed little interpretation. Daily, the black woman was assaulted in newspapers which clearly placed a premium on light skin. 'Look how men flock around the girl with the clear, bright, incredibly light complexion,' teased an advert in the *Gleaner*. 'Don't let dull, dark skin rob you of romance [and] cheat you of charm. Try *Nauinola* Bleaching Cream.'

Even so, there had been a small but significant advance in the appreciation of blackness. In 1955, for instance, the 'Ten Types – One People' multiracial beauty contest was launched as part of the 'Jamaica 300' tercentenary celebrations. The rigid parameters – though suggesting diverse standards of beauty – were in effect reinforcing a kind of cultural apartheid. The ten separate competitions each represented a different category of skin tone, including: 'Miss Apple Blossom', 'Miss Allspice', and 'Miss Ebony'.[160] Black women like Miss Ebony may have begun to develop a new sense of being comfortable in and with their skin, yet the newspapers continued to carry sly adverts like 'For a Lighter . . . Lovelier Skin . . . choose *Lucky Heart* non-oily beauty bleaching cream'.[161]

The plethora of such adverts, which perpetuated the not so subtle Jamaican pigmentocracy, suggested that the adoption of Garvey's doctrine still had some way to go.

But then Garvey's story and message were not taught in Jamaican schools. It had been left to Rastafarians and old-time Garveyites such as Mariamne Samad to keep him alive. Even up to the generation of Tosh, Marley and Livingston, Jamaican youth were denied Garvey's insights for Africans on the continent and in the diaspora that were committed into print in his *Life and Lessons*. When they did eventually get to hear shards of his philosophy remembers their contemporary, the writer Viv Adams, they were amazed, and wondered why he had been kept a secret from them for so long. The unexplored dream of Marcus Garvey was like an unopened letter to themselves. Each of the Wailers would fashion songs from the sentiments of Marcus Garvey's speeches. In 1937, Garvey told an audience in Nova Scotia: 'We are going to emancipate ourselves from mental slavery, because whilst others might free the body, none but ourselves can free the mind.' And Bob Marley would come eventually to fold elements of that speech into 'Redemption Song' forty years later. The simple message of freeing yourself from mental slavery was one that all of the Wailers embraced, along with Garvey's advocacy that 'it was time to take the kinks, not out of your hair, but out of your mind'.

The urge to alter appearances was the most obvious manifestation of the pathology that held anything black to be retarded and stigmatised. By 1964, those ideas were starting to lose ground to a burgeoning black assertiveness and an inversion of the old colour code. 'I didn't think I would like a guy with his [fair] complexion,' Rita said of Bob Marley. Rita was dark-skinned, and, conversely, wondered whether her blackness was part of her attraction to Bob. Marley was so racially sensitised that she remembered him asking her 'to rub shoe polish in his hair to make it more black, make it more African'.[162]

'Well *helloooo*. Park your handsome self down there young man' Mariamne Samad is an immediate hit. The ninety-year-old African-American has to be the sassiest gal I've ever met. Bangles adorn each arm from wrist to elbow. The kente cloth is arranged scrupulously. A fierce and playful intelligence bursts through everything she says. Her language is rich in irony and snorts of soft sarcasm. Age has reduced her ability to move; a painful-looking oedema clogs her legs, but she has learnt to apply her stillness. She draws you in.

In the 1960s Samad left Harlem, New York, for Africa, and en route made a pitstop in Jamaica. She has been there ever since. Samad's father was a bodyguard to Marcus Garvey and a prominent figure in Garvey's African legion (a largely ceremonial military outfit whose parades through Harlem prompted J. Edgar Hoover to recruit FBI informants to infiltrate the movement). Mariamne Samad is revered as one of the last surviving Garveyites with a direct link to the Black Nationalist leader. Over the years, through a process of accretion, her home has become a shrine to Marcus Garvey. To undertake the journey to the outskirts of Kingston, as many have done, is to make a pilgrimage to an oracle. Not everyone is convinced. At least one scholar remarks, with charming condescension, that Samad is 'not a reliable witness', but I find the directness of her speech, though sometimes caustic, always sincere.

'Jamaicans despise Marcus Garvey!' She meets my sceptical eyes. 'Yes they do. Jamaicans despise the honourable Marcus Garvey!' I suggest that what she says might have been the case fifty years ago, but surely not now.

There is a pause, an intermezzo, while she weighs the level of my wilful ignorance. A firefly of recognition flickers across her face. Maybe she has met me before, or men like me, who want to confine the past to the past. Eventually, Sister Samad gestures towards a laminated poster, propped up on an easel. I am invited to read it, carefully. 'Take your time.' Printed on the poster is an extract from a handbook for the benefit of slave owners on how best to break their human property. She fixes me with hot and pained eyes, and in a sharp voice that seems to have been pushed through a grater, she growls: 'You think these people want the black man to achieve anything?'

'Yes, but that was three hundred years ago . . .'

'No. No,' says Mariamne Samad emphatically. 'That *was* yesterday. That *is* today.'

Since her teenage years, maybe even before, she has constructed a world which is completely black. 'White folk? I don't pay them no heed.' It is the white and socially white folk in Jamaica, she says, who do not revere Garvey, despite all 'the song and dance' over his elevation as a national hero. 'My dear, it is pure moonshine.'

With some effort, she rises from the chair and insists on giving me a guided tour. A back room is a cornucopia of Garvey memorabilia; yellowing editions of the *Negro World*, flags, insignia, a curious portrait of an imagined meeting between Selassie and Garvey, facsimiles of the great man's speeches. Samad is an idiosyncratic archivist, and her tale is a testimonial of enduring love. As a young idealist in 1930s Harlem, she had a schoolgirl's crush on Marcus Garvey. Even now she swoons, 'Mr Garvey? He was my *maaan*.' It may have taken twenty years but it was the devastating news of Garvey's death back in 1940 that first propelled her towards Jamaica. And like a forlorn romantic who keeps her former lover's dressing gown on the back of the bedroom door, in the expectation that one day he will return, Mariamne Samad made a promise to herself: 'I vowed that I would call his name every day, and I have.'

After several hours, with the approach of dusk, Sister Samad gets out the family album. I notice now just how far she has resisted the veneer of respectability which some embrace with old age. She is a strange mix: an unforgiving, battle-hardened race-warrior; yet one with lambent eyes and a disarming, mostly congenial manner. Except for a few portraits of her husband and her glamorous younger self, the black-and-white photos are mostly of Garvey's extended political family. She purrs over the albums. In among them is a curious little pamphlet, with photos of Garvey's two sons. 'Oh,' I exclaim involuntarily, taken aback. I feel her staring at me, intensely and defiantly, and the longer I look at the pamphlet, the more I am reluctant to raise my head from the page to meet Samad's gaze. For one of the photos of Garvey's sons is defaced, scratched out and blackened with a fountain-pen. Underneath Samad has written: 'Married white.'[163]

Ultimately, Garvey played a contradictory role in Jamaica. On the one hand, he was pressed into the service of nationalism by the home government, and by those who argued that Jamaicans ought now to stick and stay, and take possession of a land morally forfeited by the British; on the other hand, there were numerous vocal dissenters, among them Rastafarians, who, while welcoming the long overdue honour bestowed upon their man, held that his final resting ground should be elsewhere. For, had not Garvey stated unequivocally that the despised black men and women deserved to live under their own vine and fig tree? The location which Garvey had in mind though was open to interpretation. For those bent on forging a new independent nation that tree was to be planted in Jamaican soil. But for others, like the Rastas who lived outside of Jamaican society, the former colony was, just as Garvey came to believe, a 'place next to hell'; and they were adamant that, had he not been denied a passport, Marcus Garvey would surely have settled in the African homeland of his forefathers.

Rastafarian cultist groups looked to Garvey, but also drew on the Old Testament for an understanding of their life on earth. They believed themselves the chosen people, 'the seed of Israel in captivity'. The country may have adopted the motto 'Out of Many One People' to reflect its diverse population, but Jamaica was a nation of forced and voluntary migrants. There were few, if any, descendants of the indigenous peoples, the Arawak Indians who had been massacred by the Spanish 500 years previously. Enslaved Africans, indentured labourers from India and China, Lebanese and Jewish merchants and English overseers had rubbed alongside each other with varying degrees of tolerance. They were like the shipwrecked on a lost island which none felt confident to lay claim to – the descendants of Africans least of all, even though the Africans were counted among the earliest arrivals.

Equally, the privileged felt that history was not on their side. The lowering of the Union Jack signalled, if not immediately then some time in the near future, a *fin de siècle*. On 6 August 1962, the dainty Princess Margaret (representing the British government) took to the ballroom floor with the former excoriating trade unionist, Bustamante (Jamaica's new prime minister). The huge, barrel-chested, brown-skinned elderly man and the pearly white young royal danced a last waltz for Crown and colony.

Initially, the changes in island society came in small increments. Barbara Gludon, managing director of the Little Theatre, the key venue for Pantomime, the island's most popular dramatic form, first noted a shift in the world of theatre. Pantomime had been introduced by British expatriots in Jamaica in the 1940s. Boasting costumes the measure of anything found in London's West End, the Jamaican replica featured such anachronisms as 'Puss in Boots', 'Cinderella' and 'The Widow Twanky'. Few black people starred in pantomime. 'If they did appear then it was as part of a ubiquitous chorus,' recalled Gludon. But then, a local poet and dramatist, Louise Bennett, began complicating the old model by introducing African folklore, stories of 'Anancy, the spider God', and nation language (dialect), into the stockpile of pantomime narratives. This watering the wine of tradition caused a flutter in the stalls among some shocked connoisseurs. As a young reporter, Gludon remembered interviewing a board member of the theatre, a [white] lady who told her frankly that she had stopped being associated with the pantomime 'when they started giving leading roles to market women', and the lords and ladies in their frockcoats and top hats vanished from the stage.[164]

It would take many more years before Anancy's makeover of Widow Twanky was complete. Nonetheless, feeling their feathers, the ruling class trembled at the thought of 'that portion of the population [which] plainly perceived the influence it must shortly obtain in an island which in the next generation will surely be their own'.[165] The prescient observation of G. W. Bridges was penned in the nineteenth century but the sentiment could easily have applied to 1962 and thereafter. Chris Blackwell wasn't waiting for the end. Blackwell had worried about the irrevocable change that was a-coming; he boarded a flight for London before the lights of Empire went out on the island.

That sense of disquiet, of feeling a little temporary about themselves, and their surreal or unreal existence, was one which the Rastafarians also suffered from. However, they did not share the assertion of the poet Claude McKay that there was nowhere else to go. In his meditation on home, McKay had articulated an uncomplicated resignation.

> *Jamaica is de nigger's place*
> *No mind whe' some declare*
> *Although dem call we 'no-land race'*
> *I know we home is here*[166]

Rastafarians begged to differ. As Joe Ryglass of the Mystic Revelation of Rastafari was to sing:

> *Jamaica is a islan'*
> *But not I lan'*

Rastafarians did not recognise the description 'no-land race'. Rather, they were convinced of their ancestral hurt; that they had been uprooted from their African homes to which they now sought repatriation. But to where exactly? Again, Garvey proved a guide. At a time when Africa was a source of acute embarrassment – little thought about except during the pitiful Sunday sermons on its plight – Garvey instructed his followers to study the psalms and look to the east. For was it not written there that 'princes shall come out of Egypt and Ethiopia shall soon stretch out her hands unto God'?[167]

The Messiah appeared in 1930 in the noble shape of Haile Selassie, on his coronation as Emperor of Ethiopia. Selassie (Ras Tafari) traced his roots to Solomon and Sheba and was venerated and honoured with a string of impressive titles including 'King of Kings', 'Lord of Lords' and 'Conquering Lion of Judah'. As was foretold, Garvey announced that the time for the Negro 'is now come', and with measured pride he laid news of their vindication before the readers of his newspaper, *The Blackman*:

> A great ceremony took place at Addis Ababa, the capital of Abyssinia ... The scene was one of great splendour ... Several of the leading nations of Europe sent representatives to the coronation, thereby paying their respects to a rising Negro nation.

Garvey encouraged black people to see Haile Selassie as one of their own, who at long last was taking a seat at the high table of world leaders. The international coverage of the coronation *was* extraordinary, though sometimes buried not too deeply in the text were caveats which threatened to dim the romance for those who took vicarious pleasure in his elevation. *Time* magazine, for example, was not alone in focusing on the complexion and features of Ras Tafari which it maintained 'resemble those of a Spanish Jew'.[168] Garvey was scandalised by the insinuation, and fired back at plotters who would deny the race its heritage: 'Abyssinia is the land of the blacks and we are glad to learn that even though Europeans have been trying to impress the Abyssinians that they are not belonging to the Negro Race, they have learned the retort that they are, and they are proud to be so.'[169]

Ras Tafari was crowned in front of a huge crowd packed into the specially built church in the grounds of the Cathedral of St George, as Haile Selassie ('Power of the Trinity'). A batch of foreign dignitaries and correspondents descended on Addis Ababa to bear witness to the magnificent occasion. *The New York Times* drew attention to the gorgeously apparelled dancing Coptic priests and the extravagance of 5,000 cattle being slaughtered for the feast. Evelyn Waugh in *The Times* (of London), writing with restrained cynicism, reminded readers that the ceremony would take place on a site previously reserved for executions but, nonetheless, catalogued the wondrous details. The coronation coach 'formerly the property of the Emperor William, [was] drawn by six Austrian cream horses'. A gold-embroidered robe of crimson velvet swept down from the stately shoulders of His Imperial Majesty, and a 'richly jewelled' crown was placed on his head. Local chiefs 'wore lions' skins over their shoulders and rode richly harnessed mules ... Next appeared a body of servants running on foot and carrying gilt chairs.'[170]

But, at a time when black people believed themselves to be 'the footstools of other races and nations', it was the reports of European dignitaries (among them the Prince of Udine and the Duke of Gloucester) kneeling at the feet of the diminutive 'King of Kings' which caused Jamaicans to rejoice.[171] Furthermore, Garvey gladdened the hearts of his ecstatic followers with the news that 'Ras Tafari is ready and willing to extend the hand of invitation to any Negro who desires to settle in his kingdom ... Ethiopia is now really stretching forth her hands.'[172]

The cult of Selassie emerged thereafter from the dark depression of the 1930s. From the invigorating news of the coronation, Jamaicans such as Leonard Howell forged a movement. The ideology of Rastafari emerged from a cluster of ideas held by proponents of what became known as Ethiopianism. The zeitgeist was reflected in the mushrooming of black Jewish sects, calling themselves 'Israelites', which sprang up in Harlem at the beginning of the twentieth century. They were followers of Marcus Garvey and still championed his back-to-Africa ideals. In a renewed journalistic interest in Ethiopia in 1928, an entire edition of the *National Geographic* was devoted to the country and, most importantly, to the crowning of Ras Tafari himself. In Jamaica, the elevation of Selassie led some to believe that, despite all outward signs to the contrary, it was a good time to be black.

Leonard Howell certainly believed so. Armed with the certainty that is the preserve of genius or delusion, and clutching emblematic reprints of photos of Haile Selassie, the Jamaican seaman returned home from Harlem and took to his soapbox, preaching a new doctrine of Ras Tafari's divinity. The clue to Selassie's true identity, Howell claimed, lay in the gifts brought by the Duke of Gloucester to the coronation – gold, frankincense and myrrh. Leonard Howell's photographic reproductions of this living God were sold for a mere shilling. For those seduced by his vision of a new kingdom for the black man not governed by Church or State, his words and visualisation were priceless. For others, such as some of the clergymen whom he abused, he was a fraudulent conman.

On 31 October 1933, Elder W. E. Barclay wrote to the authorities, complaining, 'The Ras Tafari gang are defying British law by proclaiming their kingdom is in Africa . . . They are collecting funds from people and promising them free transportation to Africa . . . [Howell] denounces ministers, myself included, and has the audacity to call us thieves and vagabonds at his open-air meetings.'[173] Howell, in the words of the *Gleaner* 'a slight but well-knitted figure who dresses carefully, with a well-trimmed moustache,' seemed to appear from nowhere, and bemused the authorities, for 'rumour and report surround this man and his followers with an atmosphere of mysticism almost akin to awe'. [174]

The dapper orator, who spoke with a slight stutter, presided over rowdy meetings, mostly attended by a handful of curious working-class urban folk and country peasants; fairly quickly they were joined by informers and plain-clothes policemen. As their numbers swelled, the authorities became increasingly alarmed by reports that Howell's assembled masses began meetings with a rousing rendition of the British national anthem, only to be reminded by the mystical speaker that it was Ras Tafari and not George V whom they should have in mind when it came to the line 'God Save the King'. An audience with magistrates soon followed, as Howell and another 'Ras Tafarite', Robert Hinds, were put on trial for sedition. Howell was 'undefended by counsel', noted the *Gleaner*, but 'with him he brought sheaths of documents and a few books of unusual proportions. In his buttonhole, he wore a yellow, green and black rosette similar to that worn by a large number of men who accompanied him to court.'[175] The prosecution argued that while the jurors might consider Howell's utterances 'bosh and twaddle', they should consider its effect on 'the minds of those members of the community whose intelligence was not high, who were ignorant and who therefore might easily be misled.' Both Rastafarites were found guilty. Hinds was sentenced to a year and Howell to two years. The state had intended to discredit Howell, but the harsh sentence and the reported carnival of the courtroom proceedings against him provided the emerging movement with much more oxygen and credibility than Howell would have accrued if left unmolested.

Ras Tafari had its first martyr. In jail Howell wrote *The Promised Key*, with unattributed help from the Reverend Fitz Balintine Pettersburgh's *Royal Parchment Scroll of Black Supremacy*. Both tracts were to become key texts for a group of like-minded sufferers who began to call themselves Rastafarites or Rastafarians. *The Promised Key* and *Royal Parchment* and a third text, *The Holy Piby*, were coded handbooks for the government of the self, with an inversion of the old order in which the black man was ranked first. The nuggets of truths hidden in the texts would serve as balm for the black soul. 'Alpha & Omega, the Black man & his wife, was here on Earth before Adam and Eve.' 'The Ethiopian Dynasty [will] triumph.' Readers should hold fast to the warning: 'Before I trust a white person, I trust a snake,' and finally take note that 'Black Supremacy starts 23 December 1925', at about 7 p.m.

The new order was ten years overdue when Howell emerged from jail. The emblems, such as a crowned lion with a spear in its mouth and inscribed beneath in bold 'King of Kings and Lion of Judah', were embraced and the doctrine expanded. The movement received an unexpected boost at the hands of an Italian propagandist called Federico Philos.

'Up from the depths of the jungle,' Philos had discovered, 'blacks are flocking to a new organization . . . Its name Nyabinghi means "Death to Whites" or "Death to the Europeans".' The secret society, he claimed, had been formed in the Belgian Congo in 1923 to drive out the Europeans, but since then had expanded to the whole continent. Philos went on to warn that Haile Selassie had become its supreme head and that 'whenever one mentions the word "Negus", the eyes of blacks gleam with mad fanaticism'.[176] Designed to lend justification to Italy's invasion of Ethiopia, Philos's propaganda had a profound and unexpected consequence: it fired the imagination of black people, including Rastas, who would have flocked to the organisation if they'd been able find it. The suggestion of some historians that overnight the Rastafarians formed themselves into groups who swore allegiance to Nyabinghi and took the oath of 'death to the white man and his black allies' seems a little fanciful. Nyabinghi as a name and idea may have crossed into Jamaica; the seed may have been planted but it took much longer to germinate. Nyabinghi would not register as part of the Rasta lexicon until at least two decades later.

There was no unity among the early Rastas, and no clear division between militants and moderates. Though the accent was on the individual and an absence of any hierarchical structure, their customs were invariably designed by those who proposed themselves as leaders.

Despite his rhetoric of fire and brimstone, Howell's code was built not on battle but on withdrawal and retreat.

The colonial administration didn't quite know what to make of the mystic and his followers. Eventually, when fear of imprisonment seemed not to have curbed his seditious tendencies, they fell back on the old familiar way for treating 'dangerous leaders of millenarian cults': Howell, like Bedward the decade before, was incarcerated in Bellevue mental asylum. Unlike Bedward, he was eventually discharged, surfacing a couple of years later with the news that he and 700 loyal Rastafarian supporters had purchased land to live in a commune at Pinnacle. The retreat was an attempt to find a haven away from the harassment of law-enforcers and their abusive and 'grudgeful' countrymen, who were prone to stoning meetings and breaking down the zinc-fence boundaries of their compounds. But in just over a decade that Eden, at Pinnacle, in a dry and mountainous region on the outskirts of the capital (a caravan of buckets of water needed to be dispatched every day) was broken up by club-wielding policemen. Many of its inhabitants fled to the squatter camps and shanty towns of west Kingston where small bands of Rastas had established themselves among the 'sufferers'.

Some found work on plantations like that of the former politician and acerbic journalist Morris Cargill. Cargill fulminated in the pages of the *Gleaner*, venting prejudices leavened with wit. At home he was far more liberal and humane. Cargill drew a distinction between genuine and counterfeit Rastas. He employed a Rasta who was known by the generic 'Brother Man', 'for he would give us no other name. The workers on my farm at first took the view that he should only be allowed to work if he cut his hair. But I managed to persuade them out of this unreasonable attitude.' Cargill grew fond of 'Brother Man' and saw first-hand how prejudice against the Rasta could be translated into violence when one day 'Brother Man' ventured to the capital and returned in bad shape, 'limping painfully. He has a large bruise under his left eye, and the eye is nearly closed. He takes off his shirt and shows me that there are bruises all over his back and one on the right side of his ribs.'

'"What on earth has happened to you?" I ask him.

'"De police boss. De police do it."'[177]

Brother Man's experiences would not have been atypical: Rastas were harried constantly by the authorities. Cargill developed a sympathetic understanding of the growing band of Brother Men on the island: 'Behind all the Ras Tafarian fundamentalist gobbledegook is, nevertheless, a sound psychological truth.' Assailed by daily humiliations which robbed the black man of respect it was perfectly logical that he would 'drop out of the society which insulted him, developing a religion, a culture and a way of life which totally excluded the white man and all his works'. At a certain level Cargill believed they were better off than their brown compatriots who strived to be socially white. 'The Rastas preached love, peace and reconciliation between people and races. Freed from the daily impact of white-supremacy doctrines, they gained self-confidence and shed the chips-on-the-shoulder with which more "respectable" Blacks were constantly burdened.'[178]

But to Cargill's middle-class readers *why* and *how* anyone would become a Rasta remained a mystery yet to be solved. One day you realise you haven't seen your houseboy, Peter, for quite some time. Perhaps he's returned to his village in the bush without informing you. It has happened in the past. Then weeks later, wandering round the untended rough patch at the bottom of the garden, you poke your head through the door of a broken-down hut, and there's Peter. But, whereas he was once neat and trim, now he is unkempt and unwashed. His hair is long and knotted. The khaki uniform you bought for him has been replaced with 'bag-o-wire' (trousers of crocus bags held up by a wire belt). He is crouched in a circle of fellows with a similar dress code and attention to hygiene, running their mouths over some vexing subject, muttering dark oaths and chanting down Babylon. You have no choice but to let Peter go. He is already lost to you and the civilised world.

But whereas middle-class parents could keep their children away from Rastas, in the ghettoes, the Lord-loving and aspiring lower classes, including Revivalist captains like Toddy Livingston, lived cheek by jowl with the brethren, and in fear of their moral contamination, as if Rastafarians were carriers of some deadly virus. In a sense they were: a ghetto youth's chances of making his way in Jamaican society was already slim; once he graduated or converted to the Rasta movement he had no chance at all. Conversely, Rastas would argue that poor folk had bought a lie; that they were deluded in holding out for the possibility of change, and that the reality of the Jamaican masses would always be grim. Rastafarians acknowledged that to survive, temporarily, they needed to seek a reality that resided in the Immanent and Transcendent.

Only through repatriation to Africa (Zion) could they find a permanent 'solution to the hopeless hell of Jamaica.'[179]

Reverend Hugh Sherlock, the saviour of Boy's Town, agonised over the growth of Rastafari, especially in ghettoes like Trench Town, a development which in his view was born largely of despair. In 1950, he prophesied gloomily that trouble lay ahead. 'Some of these people are so frustrated that we have lost their allegiance. They have a new cult instead of our religion, and talk in symbolic terms instead of using our language.' Jamaican society, he observed, had chosen to look away from the 'human degradation and misery which many are now experiencing. It may yet be the spread of epidemic disease and bloodshed.'

More often the blood shed was Rasta blood, though the urban myth was that the inverse was true; that they were wild men, guilty of wielding knives and machetes against innocent victims. The perception of Rastafarians as outlaws and criminals was popularised by a few widely reported acts of violence perpetrated by men who shared the ideals of the back-to-Africa movement. The most notorious was the strange case of Reverend Claudius Henry, the leader of the African Reform Church in Kingston who styled himself the 'Repairer of the Breach'. Henry was first brought to island-wide attention in 1959 when thousands of blue cards were distributed (in exchange for 1/- each) with a simple and unequivocal message:

> Pioneering Israel's scattered Children of African Origin back home to Africa, this year 1959, deadline date Oct. 5th . . . Holders of this certificate is requested to visit the Headquarter at 78 Rosalie Ave . . . No passport will be necessary for those returning home to Africa. Bring this certificate with you . . . for 'Identification'.
>
> Prophet Rev. C.V. Henry, RB[180]

Henry also wrote to the British administration demanding aid with the repatriation scheme. The 'Repairer of the Breach' continued his message of redemption from the pulpit of his church on Wednesday and Saturday nights where, on at least one occasion, according to undercover police reports, Henry warned his audience that unless the British provided ships, 'they should prepare for bloodshed' and in the violence that would ensue, 'Jamaica will be left desolate as a graveyard.'[181]

As 5 October approached, hundreds of Rastafarians, having sold all of their possessions, arrived in trucks, taxis and on foot at the grounds of Henry's church in time for the deadline for repatriation. The ship did not materialise.

In February the following year, Henry was brought before magistrates after a visit from immigration officers to the church ended in acrimony. The immigration officers were looking for Henry's son Ronald, who'd returned recently to the island with some African-Americans, and complained of being 'terrorised' by the threatening language of Henry and his followers. Allegedly, Henry had shouted that 'they were going to free Africa and that any white man or black man who stood in their way would be killed'. The 'Repairer of the Breach' was fined £50 and sentenced to keep the peace for a year.

Two months later Henry's church was raided by police who found an arms cache that included 2,000 detonators, a shotgun, a .32 calibre pistol, eighteen sticks of dynamite, a large quantity of machetes, sharpened on both sides, conch shells filled with cement, clubs and a spear. Despite this arsenal, it was a letter, signed by Henry and more than a dozen of his followers, which the authorities considered most sinister. Though unposted, the letter was addressed to Fidel Castro, whose revolutionary victory barely a year before had electrified supporters and terrified detractors the world over.

> We are getting ready for an invasion on the Jamaican Government and therefore we need your help and personal advice. We have the necessary men for the job ... The Cuban prime minister will be leader of Jamaica in the near future, as we do not want Jamaica but to go home [to Africa].

On the night of the raid, Ronald Henry and his African-American 'fighters' slipped out of Kingston and made their way to Red Hills, where they set up camp. They had already gathered a small stash of weapons and had been busy attempting to recruit Rastafarians to their cause. Once the plot had been detected the Rastafarians were no longer enthused about the prospects for a positive outcome. A dispute arose and the 'disloyal' Rastas were executed. A week later the Rasta camp was raided by police and soldiers. Ronald Henry and a handful of his men shot their way out of the ambush, killing two soldiers from the Royal Hampshire Regiment. After a month-long manhunt, with several hundred troops and police, Ronald

Henry was eventually apprehended and put on trial at the Supreme Court for murder and treason. Down the road at the Half-Way Tree Court, his father and inner circle was put on trial for treason. Reverend Claudius Henry was sentenced to ten years. His son was sentenced to death. At 8.30 a.m. on Tuesday 28 March 1961, he went to the gallows but on the short walk across the prison yard, before the hangman pulled the lever, he uttered a final defiant cry: 'I die for Marcus Garvey!'

More than 500 people – some sombre, a few openly weeping and others fizzing with excitement – had gathered outside the St Catherine District Prison in Spanish Town to witness the hanging. A hush rippled through the crowd as the warden pinned the death-notice to the concrete prison wall. But, in the days that followed, Jamaicans were not reassured by the execution of Ronald Henry and the imprisonment of his father. Having woken from a bad dream they could not turn over and go back to sleep. What if there were more Claudius Henrys out there? It was entirely possible.

If Jamaicans were petrified by the idea of bearded enemies embedded in their midst, then Rastafarian elders also realised that they had a huge public relations problem that needed to be addressed. Although there were numerous groupings of Rastafarians in the capital, increasingly, in west Kingston, they deferred to an intellectual cluster that 'moved' with Mortimo St George Planno.

Planno was only thirty-one at the time, but, in Trench Town, he had a reputation for being both shrewd and fearless. After a succession of clashes with the police his face was already beginning to settle into the battered shape and bruised dimensions more associated with a seasoned pugilist. The tales of his defiance were legion. Planno was known to lead bands of Rastafarians on pilgrimages to the major hotels (like the Myrtle Bank hotel) for the benefit of camera-snapping tourists, who'd be charmed into paying ('for a small money') for their unusual holiday shots. Stopped by the police with a crowd of brethren and questioned about what they were doing and where they were heading, Planno was said to have bellowed: 'Why you don't ask us if we belly see food since morning?'[182] Mortimo Planno could gorgonise foes with a stony stare, but his deep baritone voice was seductive and unexpectedly disarming. In west Kingston especially, Planno was a heroic figure. He was famed for having established the Ethiopian World Federation Local Charter 37 on Salt Lane in Kingston, and had been instrumental, a couple of years earlier, in helping a Rasta elder called Prince Emmanuel to convene the first 'Universal Grounation of the Rastafari' – a three-week-long drumming and chanting convention, attended by 3,000 locksmen, held in the slum of Back-o-Wall. The Grounation sought to establish some unity and shared tenets among the disparate groups of Rastas.

The Wailers were just one of the groups of young men lured by the drumming, and by the spirited and spiritual talk at Mortimo Planno's yard on 5th Street. The grounded reasoning and rhetoric complicated their thinking, sometimes with dizzying results. Bunny Livingston admitted that though the intellectual rigour was impressive, it was not always rewarding for the three youths: 'Vibes at Planno was never good for rehearsing – too much philosophers and learned guys, too many distractions, too many people a-come want weed.'[183]

The Wailers, in the early 1960s, flirted with Rastafarian ideology but their commitment was more to the lifestyle, the rhythm and pace of life, and the easy access to ganja. They were drawn into the orbit of Planno's world – indeed, Livingston felt Planno was also courting them – even if his intentions and motives weren't always clear.

Mortimo Planno *was* something of a strategic thinker. He was also much given to letter-writing. Even before the fallout from the Henry rebellion, he and his associates had devised a plan to rescue the reputation of Rasta. Early in 1960 Professor Arthur Lewis, the first black principal of the University College of the West Indies, opened his mail and found a letter from the Trench Town Rastas. Planno suggested that the professor send colleagues to conduct a survey of Rastafarian life as a corrective to the rumours, myths and propaganda that had become attached to the movement. Coming just weeks after the hysteria surrounding the manhunt and capture of Ronald Henry, the proposed survey had added urgency – though some professed to be scandalised by the legitimacy such research might confer on the cult.

Even more remarkable was the subsequent news that the government proposed to include representative Rasta brethren on a mission to five African states (including Ethiopia) to investigate the feasibility of Rastafarian repatriation to the continent. Middle-class outrage reached previously unsurpassed heights of hypocrisy. It was a tale of two hands. One prominently made into a fist raised in anger at the expense of it all; and the other, hidden behind the back with fingers crossed for its speedy success.

Writing in his monthly journal in November 1960, the lawyer and amateur historian Ansell Hart summarised the prevailing sentiment: 'the biblical exegesis affecting a hardcore of some 15,000 Rastafarian cult-ists,' unless fulfilled, would continue to be 'a festering sore in Jamaica; and that it would be worth Jamaica's while to spend £5 million to remove the feeling of spiritual frustration from [them]'.[184] Stripped of its lawyerly language, Hart's argument was that the Rastafarians be given every encouragement to leave.

A dispute arose between the Rasta representatives (including Planno) and the government task force to Africa about the terms and pres-entation of their objectives to the Ethiopians. Mortimo Planno was convinced that the government delegates were trying to sabotage the mission with 'the Edinburgh type approach to schedule time', so that few substantive points could be made. Watching how the untutored Rastafarians were outmanoeuvred, Planno wrote that 'the British deserve a marks here . . . [they] was not interested in giving the true feeling of the Rastafari Movement.' Planno, whose 'emotions was often time above my conscientiousness', was clearly vexed. But what troubled him most was a feeling of lost opportunity through the disunity of the delegates, which he likened to 'a cow giving her milk and kicking it over'.[185] Nonetheless, the mission returned bearing encouraging messages from the King of Kings. The Emperor confirmed that he had 'set aside 500 acres of very fertile and rich land [to be] given through the Ethiopian World Federation, Inc., to Black people of the West, who had aided Ethiopia during her period of distress.' During the Italian invasion of Abyssinia, Jamaicans had been among those who volunteered to fight with the Ethiopian army and this had not been forgotten. There were few caveats to Selassie's offer but it was stressed that potential migrants 'must be of the pioneer calibre . . . and be prepared to forgo many of the things to which they are now accustomed.'[186] As it was a common view among Rastafarians that Jamaica was 'an open prison surrounded by water,' the sacrifice would not be so great.

The highlight of the trip was undisputedly the Rastafarians' private audience with the Emperor. Three brethren presented the Emperor with gifts. They included a map of Africa carved in wood, photographs of the Jamaican locksmen, a painting of Errol Flynn's Navy Island off the coast of Jamaica, and a woven scarf in red, green and black.

Planno and his compadres returned to a hero's welcome. A tide of euphoria swept through Rastafarian communities, and Planno's stock, already high, rose even further.

Mortimo Planno watched with great satisfaction the flowering of his teaching in the fertile minds of musicians like the Wailers who hung around his yard. He'd shown a special interest in them, more so because they were curious but cautious. Marley had proven the most reticent of the three young men but even he now was not so guarded in the company of the scholarly Rastafarian. As Planno remarked, everyone, including Marley, sought him out. He had talked to Haile Selassie and therefore, to Bob Marley, conversing and parleying with Mortimo Planno was like talking to God by proxy.

So many musicians turned up at 18 5th Street that at one stage, someone christened them the '5th Street All-Stars'. Those who had enrolled at Mortimo Planno's unofficial 'university' included Alton Ellis, Bob Marley, Peter Tosh, Bunny Livingston and Jimmy Cliff. The latter's song 'King of Kings', with lyrics that put the giraffe and elephant in their place as also-rans, establishing the primacy of the lion, may, on the surface, have sounded like a simple children's parable; but it didn't take too much decoding to unearth the truth: the lion was the Conquering Lion of Judah. The King of Kings, who reigned in the jungle, was the Lord of Lords, Emperor Haile Selassie I of Ethiopia. The genius of Cliff's pop song was that the subliminal message could, if one chose, simply be ignored; it need not tax the middle-class mind or interfere with the uncomplicated danceability of the beat.

All of the musicians were inspired by their time at Planno's Open Yard to be more overt in reflecting the beliefs of Rastafari in their songs. In any event, by 1965 popular music in Jamaica had taken yet another turn in its evolution: it had slowed down with the emergence of what became known as rock steady. The slower beat was better able to carry the message, to give space to the lyrics of musicians who had become more conscious of their history and identity. Men like Planno could rightly claim to have planted the seed of Rastafari in the souls of these young men and women. And now, almost overnight, the saplings sprang up throughout Trench Town and west Kingston. The sly 'King of Kings' would soon make way for more explicit songs like Alton Ellis's 'Back to Africa', imbued with lyrics expounding the tenets of the Rastafarian faith.

Ideas were exchanged and songlines suggested in endless, cyclical rounds of discussion and music-making. The vibe at Open Yard, not readily replicated elsewhere, always felt creative, even if it didn't yield tangible results. And as far as Bunny Livingston was concerned, there were also unwelcome distractions, and not just ganja. Planno seemed consistently to have a stream of young women at his elbow who peeled away and attached themselves to the Wailers every time they walked through the door. Livingston came to suspect that Planno was procuring girls for the band, as part of a larger scheme to lure them away from Clement Dodd. Although Dodd had hinted (or the Wailers convinced themselves that he'd hinted) that he considered them almost as junior partners in Studio One, Livingston recalled, 'Coxsone was actually building an empire for himself.' The Wailers had become so disaffected and disenchanted that, ordinarily, it would not have been difficult to prise them from Coxsone, but there was the small detail of the five-year contract to see out: it would take another two years for it to run its course.

'Knickerbacker' was the word Bunny Livingston most often used to describe Clement Dodd. It was a term of reproach. In Jamaican parlance a 'knickerbacker' was someone who hopped onto the back of the bus or tram for a free ride, without the conductor realising. It was a feature of Bunny Livingston's character that his ears were cocked permanently for the sound of people hurrying behind to leap onto his back. That which was Bunny's was Bunny's. Even as a young man, it was said of him: 'You can't take him make jackass,' meaning you couldn't take him for a ride, and you tried to exploit him at your peril. 'Bunny is a different kind of man,' said W. J., one of his old friends. 'Bunny is a man who have him little pipe, somewhere down in the back, and him no want nobody smoke from him pipe.'[187] His pipe was an exclusive medium of communication with Jah (God).

Bunny Livingston wasn't yet entirely sure whether Mortimo Planno could be counted among the knickerbackers. But certainly his doubts about Planno would have been put to one side, at least temporarily, on 21 April 1966 – one of the most memorable dates in Jamaican history.

Ethiopia's imperial aircraft, emblazoned with the insignia of a roaring lion and stripes of red, green and gold, dipped beneath the clouds on its journey towards Jamaica's Palisadoes airport. This was no ordinary scheduled flight. On board was a diminutive man whose angular features were softened by a neat moustache and beard and shrouded by a larger than necessary military cap, His Majesty Haile Selassie I. And down below, tens of thousands of Rastafarian necks craned towards the sky, waiting for their 'God' who was now descending from the heavens. The heavy rains suddenly stopped, remembered Donald Manning (a future member of the group the Abyssinians), when the imperial plane touched down. All weather and meteorological reports from the time confirm this strange coincidence but there is no agreement on the singer's account of an accompanying 'flock of white bird coming from the East'.

Manning had pedalled as fast as his racing heart would take him to the airport and arrived to witness 'the most people I ever see from I born'.[188] They'd trekked down from Wareika Hills, from Accompang, from the Dry Harbour Mountains, from Sligoville, from across town and from every squatter settlement and ghetto on the island. Some were dressed from head to toe in white, others were barechested and in rags. They carried banners, Rasta and Ethiopian flags, flaming torches, palm branches and cow-horned chillum pipes packed with ceremonial weed. The air was thick with the cloying smell of burning ganja and a droning cacophony of conches and drumming. People had gathered in such great numbers at the airport that not an inch of tarmac could be seen.

When the King of Kings looked out of the aeroplane's window he saw that every building was decorated with Rastafarians, perching on balconies, and sprawled out over the rooftops. On the runway, the guard of honour lining the red carpet had been overwhelmed by the crush of people who broke ranks and pressed towards the plane; they reached up to touch the undercarriage. In what John Hearne, the resident humourist at the *Gleaner*, dubbed 'the Battle of Palisadoes', regimental swords were lowered, held in the kissing position or returned to scabbards in a scandalous 'defeat of ceremony and protocol'.

For almost an hour the plane stood silent on the tarmac. There was no movement from within the cabin, and no one emerged. The official welcoming party, including Selassie's Jamaican equerry and the Governor-General pushed their way to the top of the stairs. When the doors opened and Haile Selassie I stepped out, he was confronted by an extraordinary spectacle – a sea of unbridled near-hysterical adoration. 'It was louder than the sound of thunder rolling,' recalled Mitsy

Seaga, 'louder even than an explosion.' People swarmed all around the base of the steps. Selassie retreated towards the door.

Mortimo Planno had not been invited to be part of the official delegation. He was hemmed in with the crowd on the tarmac. But now he heard his name being called through a loudspeaker. Jamaican officials had become so anxious about the mayhem that was unfolding that they summoned Planno to calm the crowds.

Mortimo St George Planno climbed the steps and, in his account, addressed the multitudes with a psalm:

> Why do the heathen rage, and the people imagine
>   a vain thing?
> The kings of the earth set themselves and the rulers
>   take counsel
> Together against the Lord and against his anointed,
>   saying
> Let us break their bands asunder, and cast away
>   their chords from us
> He that sitteth in the heavens shall laugh.[189]

The effect was immediate and magical, recalled Donald Manning. 'Did you see the film *Ten Commandments*? When Moses stretch forth his hands towards the sea and the sea part in two? And Mortimo just put his arms out and say "His Majesty want to come off the plane now."' The country's newspapers were to capture this extraordinary moment. Planno was pictured on the steps (with locks and camera) in front of Emperor Selassie I, appealing to the masses to make room for H. I. M. to pass. The crowd parted and the Emperor, tears streaming down his cheeks (whether from 'sorrow at the uncontrollableness of the vast throng . . . or out of joy', the *Gleaner* couldn't tell), climbed down and into the open-topped royal car. The Rastafarian scholar had spared official blushes: the local papers were to crown him 'Prime Minister for the Day'.[190]

Bunny Livingston and Peter Tosh were not at the airport. They were broke, and had gone to Clement Dodd's for the ritual humili-ation of waiting for some money. Dodd passed them many times in the courtyard that morning, rushing back and forth on some imagined hugely important business matter. Eventually, he handed over the 'little money (£3)' that they were owed. They rushed to Spanish Town Road before the Emperor's motorcade was due to pass. 'Nothing had ever happened like it,' recalled Livingston, 'nothing had come close since Christ Hosanna, Christ passed through Palestine and people waved palm leaves at him.'

None of the Wailers were, as yet, full converts to Rastafari, but if Bob Marley's new wife Rita's account of catching a glimpse of the diminutive but mesmerising Haile Selassie, waving at the crowds as his car sped through Kingston, was indicative of their intent, then the group were not far off from full immersion. 'There was something about the middle of his palm that struck me – I saw a small black print,' claimed Rita Marley, 'and I said, oh my God, the Bible says that when you see him, you will know him by the nail prints in his hand.' Thereafter both Rita Marley and Bunny Livingston became besotted with the idea that they had seen the resurrected Christ. 'One look at his [Selassie's] face and I was changed for he was the Almighty,' said Livingston. 'You look at the creator of all things and everything inside you changes, everything changes, it was like a current passed through you.'

7

ON BECOMING RASTA

'WHEN Selassie came, we stopped the kind of dancehall, whorehouse life,' recalled Bunny Livingston. 'No more drinking beer, no more nightclub vibe.' The Wailers made 'a Nazarite vow neither to drink nor cut our hair'.[191]

The state visit of Haile Selassie I gave a huge boost to the Rastafarians. As John Hearne put it succinctly in the *Gleaner*, it was a case of 'Rasta Day Come'.[192] At last they had some kind of validation and, if not something to crow about, then at least to chant about. Musically, Peter Tosh was first out of the blocks. He composed a tribute to the Lion of Judah and his explosive three days in Jamaica that was a simple statement of fact: 'Rasta Shook Them Up'. Tosh, though, was not so forthright in his burgeoning beliefs on those rare occasions when he returned to Westmoreland and came under the scrutiny of his mother. Alvera Coke was curious about the unusual hat that her son had pulled down scrupulously over his ears. She considered it a lame attempt to disguise his lengthening locks: 'I asked him why he did not cut it. He said, "Mama when I cut my hair it expose my mould and cause me to catch cold." He did not tell me about the Rasta business.'[193] The shake-up, evidently, did not extend to Lord-loving Jamaicans such as Alvera Coke, who continued to disdain the group even after the Emperor's visit.

For its part, the Jamaican government, while extremely respectful, even reverential, towards Selassie, calculated on the Emperor of Ethiopia introducing a note of sobriety among Rastafarians by puncturing notions of his divinity. Principally this would have been achieved through owning up to the fact that he was merely mortal. Selassie hadn't quite performed in the way they had hoped. Mirroring the enigma of the Rasta elders who asked for some signifying statement that he was 'the one', the 'messiah' whom they'd longed for, Selassie is alleged to have answered: 'I am who you think I am.' This was close enough to the biblical 'I am that I am', for them to interpret it as his majestic modesty.

Rastafarians did not ordinarily find themselves on the guest list for receptions at King's House, the official residence of the Governor-General. But on 21 April 1966, an elder called Ras Amos ranked among Jamaica's high society – a position he attributed with gratitude to the munificence of Selassie: 'He lifted us from the dust of the earth and let us sit between princes and kings.'[194] Amos was also able to scotch the rumours circulating among some brethren that the diminutive man feted by the authorities was not the *real* Selassie, but an impostor foisted on the Jamaican people to placate them. Ras Amos's testimony would eventually be supported by Brother Mortimo Planno. Though *his* earlier invitation and new-found status was spoilt somewhat when he was escorted away from the red-carpeted honour guard, through which he had attempted to make his entrance to Gordon House where Selassie was to address the island's politicians. The 'Prime Minister for the Day' could perhaps be forgiven for not appreciating that his term of office had already expired.[195]

Throughout his brief stay, Selassie was both overwhelmed and bemused by the tumultuous Rastafarian welcome in Jamaica. Protocol perhaps prevented him from enquiring too closely into their appearance but then, at yet another of the gala events, his curiosity got the better of him. Selassie sent one of his ministers to ask the Rastafarians present at the reception why they grew their hair long. Back came the response that 'the answer to the question would be found in the Bible: Numbers 6 and Leviticus: 21. The Emperor smiled and nodded.'[196]

The Wailers signed up to the Nazarite law that 'All the days of his separation there shall be no razor come upon his head . . . he shall be holy, and shall let the locks of the hair on his head grow.' Long matted hair – dreadlocks – were to become emblematic of Rastafari. As yet, the Wailers had some way to go, none possessed hair that fell below their ears, never mind their shoulders. Without 'locks' they could still pass as regular Jamaicans; with locks they would be identified forever with Rastafari. To display your locks, then, was to 'come out'.

To grow your hair was not simply to adhere to an obscure passage from scripture. Rasta was an attitude to life expressed perfectly through hair which appeared to have been left to run riot. In a society bound by an unspoken convention which placed a premium on 'good' hair (soft and manageable) over 'bad' hair (dry and wiry), the locksmen provoked disgust and dismay. Not all Rastas conformed to this image. In the 1940s, Leonard Howell, who considered himself 'damn good looking' sported a pencil-thin Hollywood matinee-idol moustache. The only bearded brethren among his flock were the guards, fierce-looking mountain men whose appearance was designed to inspire fear. Other Jamaicans believed the adoption of locks owed more to the Mau Mau rebellion against the British in Kenya in the 1950s. Rastafarians venerated the Mau Mau; they were pin-up revolutionaries made glamorous in photographs printed in the *Gleaner*. And, finally, by the time Livingston, Tosh and Marley turned more fully towards Rastafari, a younger generation of Rastas had emerged, calling themselves 'Dreadlocks' who, as well as declining the razor blade, also spurned the comb.

To the young Peter Tosh the unkempt Rasta who abandoned not just the comb but all materialism and worldly possessions was a romantic and heroic figure, like India's Sadhu holy men whose abstemiousness and integrity he could not help but admire. 'When you see how some isolate himself, live upon a bush, and start walk without a home, canvas all upon top of him and old clad make himself look a way that you don't think of walking near him. That man is a scientist ... him just dealing with the Creator.'[197]

One of the appeals of Rastafari, at the point of the Wailers' entry into the religion, was its lack of prescription. A loose set of ideals wedded members together. But there was no governing doctrine or unifying set of rules. So that, as well as Dreadlocks, there were Rastas known as 'turban-men' who wrapped their hair at the backs of their heads, and also 'comb-cuts' who kept their hair short. None of the Wailers was especially hirsute. Tosh, in particular, possessed hair that refused to sprout into anything but mini-locks. But even if their hair had been willing, the Wailers' transformation into Rastafarians was never going to happen overnight; there would be no blinding

Damascene conversion from rude boy to Rasta. Years would elapse before the gap between vow and practice was closed. Becoming a Rasta was a work-in-progress.

Perhaps it was too soon to say just how Selassie's visit had shaken up Jamaican society but, undeniably, it had. After all, Rastas had stood in line with the evening-suit and ball-gown brigade on the Governor-General's lawn waiting to be presented to His Imperial Majesty. Yes, it was an aberration, but emboldened by the knowledge that this strange departure from the norm couldn't possibly last, some in the upper-crust, Myrtle Bank crowd had confessed to a frisson of radical chic in being in such close proximity to the bearded men. Even in the shanty towns, the scales had tipped favourably, if temporarily, in the brethren's direction. Rasta was now kind of cool. Maureen Rowe, a member of the faith, recalled the shift in attitude. The same neighbourhood rude boys, whom she trembled at the sight of and crossed the road to avoid, suddenly began to address her respectfully as 'daughter', albeit 'in the very same macho ways; the term "daughter" had been substituted for "ting" or "beef."'[198]

Rastas also made up ground on the Revivalists who had held sway in the ghettoes for decades. George Eaton Simpson who conducted anthropological field work in the 1950s noted that there was great rivalry and antagonism between the two groups. Even though they shared a love for Ira D. Sankey's Christian hymn book, *Sacred Songs and Solos*, they parted company on features of Revivalism – 'rejoicing', 'spiritual' dancing and "procession trance', which Rastas regarded as backward. Sometimes a Rasta and Revivalist camp would face each other but the two groups did not 'take tea'. They also differed in their organisation. While the 'shepherds' or 'captains' (such as Toddy Livingston) presided over devoted Revivalist congregations, Rastafari was a 'flat religion'; there was little or no hierarchy, although there were rotating 'chairmen' or 'table-men' and, increasingly, elders such as Mortimo Planno, whom the youths looked to for spiritual guidance; and in the case of Planno, material guidance, too.

Rasta camps were refuges of reasoning, drumming and ganja-smoking long into the night. Tosh, Livingston and Marley were to find in these camps a respite from the shifting, airless oppression of ghetto life. The musicologist Verena Reckford conducted fieldwork in these impoverished settlements where music was the obvious balm. 'One man said,

"Suppose, for argument sake, I come home one evening and I really feel downpressed – like I don't make no scufflings [money] all day – instead of beating I wife or roughing up I children, I tek out I drum and start a little ridim, you know? Before yuh know what happen, the whole yard is wid I. Yuh no see it? Next thing you know I man come off the worries so much so, sometimes I get a little insight into how fi tackle me problems."'[199]

The researcher did not record if the brethren had gained insight into the age-old question for Jamaican men of whether it was a good idea to beat women in the first place. Even so, the drumming and vibe was demonstrably powerful and transformative. The previous governor of Jamaica, Sir Hugh Foot, had pointed out as much when he conceded generously that it 'would be a mistake to assume that all Rastafaris are criminals'. Foot offered the assessment that 'certainly the Rastafaris provide an interesting example of reaction against the normal conventions and they also illustrate a commendable desire to escape from squalor and poverty by evolving some new pattern of communal life.'[200]

Three months after Selassie's visit the honeymoon with the authorities was over. Bulldozers moved in as part of Seaga's social experiment to clear the Back-o-Wall Rastafarian squatter camps in west Kingston.

Five years on from Independence, there seemed to be even fewer employment opportunities for the sufferers of Trench Town. However, recalled Bunny Livingston, there was always something that the enterprising might do. Even on a trawl through Trench Town, 'you could pick up scrap iron and sell it, or go to a dairy farm and pick up all the lead from milk tins, and the lead could be sold.'[201] But when there were no empty bottles to be found, copper-wire to be gathered, mangoes, ackee and gulnip to be picked up, when you had exhausted your credit line with the Chinese-Jamaican shopkeeper, then, especially if you were a Rasta in west Kingston, you might turn to men like Brother Watto and Mortimo Planno. Several Rasta camps were dotted around Trench Town from 3rd Street and beyond. With the passage of time they'd acquired colourful biblical names like 'Bethelehem' and 'Calvary' on 13th Street and Lindus Lane.

But when it came to Trench Town, Planno represented its royalty. He was the ghetto's philosopher king who held court on 5th Street and whose address book included professors at the University of the West Indies, nightclub owners and police administrators. When the head of the Ethiopian Orthodox Church in Jamaica visited Kingston, Morty Planno was one of the first men he'd call on; he also established channels via intermediaries both to the government and to the opposition. Known affectionately as 'Brother Kumi', Mortimo St George Planno was connected; Bunny Livingston described him as a kind of Rasta Don who could get things done. At a time when the children of Rastafarians were routinely turned away from Christian schools, Planno as being invited to hold impromptu seminars at the university. He was a man whom the authorities, when they weren't singling him out to be put 'under heavy manners' and roughed up, accepted grudgingly was worthy of attention. On occasion, outside promoters and producers sought the services of Brother Planno in gaining entry to the west Kingston music village and some of its Rasta-oriented recording artists. Planno was always keen to enlarge his sphere of influence and for much of 1967 that included keeping the Wailers, and especially Bob Marley, in his orbit.

By then, the Wailers had recorded over one hundred songs for Clement Dodd but, frustratingly, they had little to show for their years of labour. While Marley was in America, Tosh and Livingston had clashed repeatedly with Dodd, mostly over money. 'Coxsone treat me like a commoner,' remembered Livingston, 'but I put up with it for the love of music.' But, on at least one occasion, Tosh and Livingston had become embroiled in such a heated argument with Dodd that the police had to be called. Their working relationship deteriorated: by the time Marley returned from the USA neither were on speaking terms with the record producer. Marley went to meet Dodd without them because they were 'at war with Coxsone'. The meeting did not go well. 'Coxsone was trying to use his brains 'pon Bob,' suggested Livingston. He concluded that Dodd had tried to sow a seed of discord between the Wailers by asking Marley: 'Are you still going to use them? In those two years, you were in charge, and I want to know if you still are.' When Marley relayed the news of the meeting to the other two, they were enraged; the end was inevitable.

The Rasta elder, Planno, offered an alternative to toiling for the man. Never mind that, in this instance, *the man* (Clement Dodd) was also black. Bob Marley had returned from the USA with money in his pocket and a plan. The foundations for the plan were to be found in his luggage. Marley had been busy working on his compositions in

America. The trunk was crammed with notepads and with lyrics scrib-
bled on scraps of paper. Danny Sims, an American producer who was
to be significant in Marley's future, reckoned that Marley had already
composed 500 songs by the time they met in January 1967. Even after
adjusting for Sims's master-showman's hyperbole, Marley's creative
output had been prodigious. Though there was at least another year
of the contract to see out with 'Mr Downbeat' himself, the plan did
not involve Clement Dodd. Bob Marley was determined to cut out the
middleman; the Wailers would record their songs themselves. Mortimo
Planno declared himself ready to help. In the first instance, he offered
himself up as a mentor and educator, but Planno also had musical
ambitions, which would surface later.

Marley was just twenty-one, but though he seems to have had
some kind of epiphany in Delaware, of ensuring a future musical life
independent of any knickerback producers, he was grounded enough
to take cognisance of practical considerations. At their new headquarters, a shack which Bob Marley purchased on Greenwich Park Road,
the Wailers would form their own record label, 'Wail N Soul M' (an
amalgamation of the Wailers and Rita Marley's group, the Soulettes)
but, in the first instance, they would continue to record songs at Studio
One, and Dodd would be given the licence to distribute them. The
arrangement would have worked perfectly had the records been a flop;
both parties would have had a share in nothing. Unfortunately the first
song, 'Bend Down Low' was a major hit in the Jamaican charts and
Dodd's superior earnings, courtesy of the lucrative distribution deal,
were hugely contentious. Marley had wagered on the successful outcome
of the arrangement redeeming Dodd in the eyes of his compadres, but
the financial disparity between their reward and Dodd's served only to
damn him further. After November 1966, the Wailers would have no
further dealings with Studio One.

Money was tight as Wail N Soul M Records was financed solely
through Marley's measly American savings. Rita Marley was cast as the
group's unofficial banker. Resources were pooled – only nickels were
to be withdrawn for food and the rest put aside for recording.

Typically, the Wailers would hire a studio, quickly lay down as many
tracks in the few expensive hours allocated to them, and leave with the
master tapes. They'd hire a stamper and press as many copies as they
could afford, attaching blank white labels to the 7-inch singles. The

song's title would later be handwritten on the label. Initially, blanks were sold for 21 shillings, then dropped to 12/6, and eventually to 7/6.

The Wail N Soul M business model – not that it ever involved a bank manager – was to deal directly with the record stores and other outlets. They packed up records in boxes, divided them into three equal stacks – one for each Wailer – and, balancing them on the handlebars of their bicycles, set off around the capital. Livingston reminisced fondly how they targeted potential clients: 'One of us to the jukebox men, one to the sound-system guys, one to the record shops like GGs, Clancy Eccles and Matador.' The Wailin' couriers ventured as far as Doncaster and Franklin Town, careful to avoid certain lanes lest they were ambushed by known 'bad men'.

In the course of the day, Tosh, Marley and Livingston passed each other several times, heading off in different directions, though they couldn't always be sure. Often, the records were piled so high they could hardly see over the tops. Distribution by bicycle came with the inevitable, occasional slapstick scene straight out of a Laurel and Hardy or Jaques Tati film, recalled Livingston. 'Bob had too many records balanced on the handlebars once. The bike got out of control on the corner of Brentford Road and Bob ran straight into a bus. Pow! Records all over the place!'

On rare occasions, they might attempt to sell straight to the public outside of a cinema or theatre, or after one of the sessions at the myriad clubs, where they continued to perform. Roadside competition, though, was always fierce. As well as cold-supper vendors, there was a host of buskers and other street performers. Arguably, the 'legs man', Maurice 'Persian the Cat' Samuels, was the most entertaining. Since the disbandment of the Skatalites whom he'd accompanied, the Cat hadn't 'dropped legs' (danced) so regularly or appeared formally on an evening's billing. But no matter who was playing inside the Success Club, or Garvey's Liberty Hall, outside, 'Persian the Cat' would often prove a bigger draw. Minutes after he'd begun to dance in the street, people would be lured outside to watch him 'flick 'n' fly'.

'Persian the Cat' was an unusual Rastafarian whose dress sense owed more to Fred Astaire than to an idealised Africanness. He never went anywhere without his handcarved walking stick with its silver-tipped end. And for his shows he would don a top hat and a scissor's tail jacket. Not for him the footlights and raised stage: 'Persian didn't step inside the dancehall. He just rode his bike to the events, jumped down and started dancing.' Apart from a handkerchief, no other prop was required for his performances.[202]

The show-stopping act would culminate in Persian the Cat flicking the handkerchief above his head and letting it fly before launching himself after it, pirouetting in the air, flipping round and catching it before it hit the ground. His approach to the inevitable necessity of occasionally earning money – manifest in his casual and spontaneous performances – chimed with the pattern of life in Trench Town. Alert to opportunities but mostly operating on need, like many Jamaicans he lived a life of 'occupational multiplicity.' In Trench Town, there were many, including the Wailers, who'd mastered this particular skill; Mortimo Planno ranked first among them.

If a Venn diagram was drawn of the networks that made up ghetto life in late 1960s Trench Town, then one name would fall at the intersection of those concentric circles – Mortimo Planno. The Rastafarian elder exuded power. He was, wrote the Canadian anthropologist, Carole Yawney, 'solidly muscled, rangy, over 6 feet tall, with an extraordinarily broad forehead, luminous smile and mane of locks'. At a time of intense, anti-white feeling, Yawney took the unusual decision, at the start of the next decade, to live among the Rastafarians in Trench Town – one street up from Planno on 6th Street. Although clear-eyed in her judgement, she was enthralled by the man she described as a great communicator, capable of both 'intimate dialogue and flamboyant oratory'. And as well as recording a diary and notes of her fieldwork, Yawney acted as Planno's unofficial amanuensis. He would command her to run and fetch her typewriter whenever he sensed the imminent arrival of inspiration.

Invariably, ganja was the medium which fuelled Planno's reasoning, as it did for most of the brethren, as well as the regulars and stragglers who patronised his yard. Though it was known locally as the 'Open Yard', it was not conspicuously so. Like many dwelling spaces in the ghetto, it was difficult to locate, as it was near impossible for all but the cognoscenti to discern the boundaries between one yard and the next in the ghetto. Neatly trimmed gardens, which would suggest the tidy minds of their owners, had only ever existed in the imagination of the Trench Town planners. But the corrugated iron and cardboard fencing of the shanty town, a tangle of overgrown bush and profusion of fierce-looking cacti that gave 'the Rock' – as it was known by locals – its idiosyncratic topography were no reflection on the inhabitants' self-regard; more often these borders had emerged by design, to obscure the growth of 'herb yards' (plots of cannabis). Planno's high profile required greater discretion on his part. Though Bunny Livingston was irritated by the constant traffic of souls in search of a draw of herb or a 'bleaching' of the chillum pipe, life at 18 5th Street pulsed to a low, but detectable, level of fear from the threat of raids. Notwithstanding his caution, or maybe because of it, Mortimo Planno also posted lookouts, solicited tip-offs from local businessmen and other informants on the fringes of the authorities, who were close enough to glean the whispering of police intent. Most importantly, Planno retained the services of a prominent Kingston lawyer.

The tenancy of Open Yard was shared with four other independent families, only half of whom were Rastas, and none of whom, except for Planno, wore dreadlocks. But at times the 5th Street residence more resembled a Rasta camp than tenants' communal dwellings. This was especially so on those occasions when circumstances called for a 'reasoning'; when, for instance, the country seemed to lurch from one near cataclysm to the next, when colour drained from life to a monotonous monochrome, heralding a darkening of the mood in the country, and a descent into a stultifying collective anxiety. Then the drumming and chanting would begin, the chillum pipe would be packed and lit. On one such occasion, Yawney recalled Planno warning those assembled in his yard of future hardship and the need for sacrifice. '"These were turbulent times which they were passing through," he said. "Everyone wanted to go to Heaven, but no one wanted to die."'[203] Yawney did not record the presence of Peter Tosh that night, but the truth of that line would resonate in a Tosh song called 'Equal Rights' a few years later. Bunny Livingston tended to play down the influence of Planno on their lives, but Donald Manning recalled that the Wailers were so often to be found at Open Yard that he suspected that they actually lived there. 'The Wailers used to sing a lot of song that Morty Planno write . . . Johnny Nash would come down there and all kind of man from foreign country . . . The whole of us was around there in the night, play bongo drums, smoke a lot of herb, and we sing praise to God.' In fact, so much ganja was consumed, noted Yawney, that often 'by the time the [chillum] pipe was burned no one was able to move off the porch'.[204]

Rasta sessions were not governed by time. The brethren might start arriving after work, stopping off to smoke at 6 o'clock in the evening, noted the elder, Pa Ashanti. The gathering would continue uninterrupted from dusk till dawn, so that a man might only realise when 'daylight catch him' that the temporary pitstop had turned into a major detour. Reasoning and recitation went 'from psalm to psalm, chant to chant, right around the clock. Is Nyabinghi right through. Sometimes a man don' reach him gates [his home] for the whole week.'[205]

Rastas, such as Ashanti, drew a distinction between the secular entertainment of drumming ('jollification' was the word he used) and its amplification of sacred Rasta rituals; between those drawn spiritually to the movement by a sense of vocation and others merely attracted by the lifestyle. Planno, by contrast, was a curious mix of fundamentalist and pragmatist: *all* were welcome at Open Yard.

The Rastafarian Movement grew slowly in its first twenty years. A Special Branch report of the Jamaica Constabulary on the 'Rastafarite Cult' in 1957 estimated that there were fewer than 2,000 members throughout the island. The report (which struggled to disguise the mirth of its authors) drew attention to the lack of cohesion among the Rasta-farites. Most regarded 'Haile Selassie as their spiritual leader', but at least one group 'declared their allegiance to King Saud of Saudi Arabia'. Rasta groups were observed to hold Sunday-night services and, occasionally, 'processions where mystic and religious utterances may be heard.' The authors of the report concluded reassuringly that the cult was 'not likely to attract intellectuals . . . the majority are of low mentality . . . and apart from encouraging wayward youths to smoke ganja and creating minor disturbances, the Rastafarites have no real influence on the communities in which they live.'[206] However, the much-publicised survey conducted by the University of the West Indies researchers (with a great sense of urgency) a few years later, which put the Rasta population at 30,000, suggested either an extraordinary fecundity on the part of the Rastas, or an equally extraordinary myopia on the part of the police.[207]

In the thirty years since its inception, followers had established them-selves in rural enclaves and urban camps, presided over by charismatic elders with an emerging set of rites and rituals and self-defining language. The violent rhetoric and the use of words like blood, thunder, lightning and fire were designed to inspire fear. But in other regards, the reliance on puns, metaphors, rhyming and double entendre was simply another example of Jamaicans' playfulness with language, sometimes designed to obscure meaning (from others) rather than clarify. Elements of this obfuscation were a hangover from the days of slavery, when linguistic gymnastics had evolved to wrongfoot the overseer, or to avert punish-ment through too transparent or direct a response to a question. Such subtleties were lost on the planters, though, even liberally minded ones such as Monk Lewis, who pronounced himself bedevilled by the evasive-ness of his slaves. 'Unless a Negro has an interest in telling the truth,' Lewis confided to his journal, 'he always lies – in order to "keep his tongue in practice"'.[208] The eighteenth-century habit of self-preservation (mistaken as mere evasion) was transplanted to modern life. Whether Rastafarians or not, Jamaicans readily recognised the verbal conceits of individuals who 'play fool to catch wise'.

Jamaican English continued to evolve alongside its Rastafarian cousin. The verbally witty Peter Tosh was especially adept at riffing on Rasta-speak; he dipped in and out of it, like a bilingual speaker, depending on the setting or audience. Almost daily, Tosh coined phrases which became part of the lexicon – 'shitstem' for system; 'polytricks' for politics, 'head-decay-shun' for education, the list was endless. But as Tosh matured so too did stories multiply of flummoxed journalists who turned up at the stage door and left, after a fleeting audience with the singer, with a vague feeling of having been mocked or insulted by him in some way, just like the exasperated eighteenth-century planter. Bunny Livingston was also capable of Rasta parley, but mostly he seems to have made it a point of honour almost to speak as near to the Queen's English as was likely to be heard on the island; his 'speaky-spokiness' became even more pronounced when angered.

Of the three Wailers, Marley most often sought refuge behind language; at times, the completeness of his jargon rendered him almost incomprehensible – when it suited him. Such a state of being, though, was still largely a decade away. To some extent then, all three Wailers adopted the language of Rasta. Benjamin Foot, who'd later work as a tour manager for the group, confessed that he often found it impossible to decipher what was being said.

On a practical level, exclusive use of jargon, familiar only to the initiated, was an inevitable product of being crammed into overcrowded shanty towns where there was little privacy. Perhaps also the rigorous

adherence to a code (or in this case a coded language) is a mark of
the new converts' commitment to a group. But Rastafarian veterans
such as Mortimo Planno felt under no such obligation. Indeed Planno
abstained. Constant use of Rasta-speak could serve 'to get the brethren
"off track" by focusing on the vehicle rather than its contents.'[209] And
further, he tended to view too conspicuous a reliance on Rasta-speak
as an impediment to reaching out to potential members. And as the
Wailers, especially Bob Marley, were to find, Planno took his pros-
elytising of Rastafari very seriously. Mortimo St George Planno even
wended his way to the racetrack to commune with future converts.
In the stables at Knutsford Park he found jockeys and stableboys
like Donald Manning who thirsted for what he had to say. Planno's
weekly trips to the track might, of course, have had more to do with
his predilection for gambling. A stableboy's tip was likely to be more
robust than a ganja-induced vision of a winning horse, and perhaps
a fair exchange for the wisdom he imparted. Rastafarians might have
forsworn materialism but for Planno that rejection did not extend to
the racetrack. One day in the future, the spiritual investment in a return
to Africa would be made manifest in a ship docking at Victoria Pier or
a plane landing at Palisadoes airport, but in the meantime, life might
be made temporarily more bearable by a return on a 2-shilling wager
on the 3.30 at Knutsford Park.

Planno's willingness to engage in both the spiritual and material
worlds might have marked him out from other Rasta elders, but in his
love of gambling he was one with the many residents of Trench Town
who daily slapped dominoes on tables and flipped cards. This passion
for gambling continued unabated despite the unlikelihood of a favourable outcome, made worse by the intervention of predatory gunmen
who had perfected techniques for beating the odds. The notorious local
thug known as 'Batman' was the worst.

Batman was a superbad bad guy who could not pass a poker or
dominoes table without trying his luck. But for an inveterate gambler
Batman had one peculiar feature: he was not entirely at ease with a
concept which at least allowed for the possibility of losing.

Batman's long shadow would precede him as he carried out his
rounds through the narrow alleys of Trench Town. He would happen
across a card game and before the terrified players could scamper
away, Batman would pull up a chair and lower himself into the game.

Politely, he would ask whether they minded him playing. 'Of course not,' came back the reply. Always there was the small matter of his lack of money but Batman offered his gun as surety. The pistol was placed on the table. The game was on and, despite the efforts all the other players, Batman never succeeded in winning a hand. At the end of the evening, Batman would be in debt to one of the gamblers. 'OK, tek the gun.' The trembling gambler would demur. 'No, no,' Batman would insist, 'you win, tek the gun. Is yours.' Eventually the man would draw the gun towards him. Whereupon Batman would kick over the table, reach behind his back, pull out another gun nestled in his waistband and berate the winner for trying to t'ief what didn't belong to him. For good measure Batman would relieve the other gamblers of their winnings, then let off one or two shots in the air – which was the cue for everyone to vacate the scene.

Barely a week passed without news of some daring theft or shocking violence which, though the culprit had escaped undetected, bore the imprint of Batman. But Batman craved recognition. At some point in his career he had decided to nominate Bob Marley as his confessor. He would wait for the first editions of the tabloids and scour the pages until his eyes alighted on the report of some nefarious act. Delighted, with his finger poised over the copy, Batman would rush around Trench Town in search of Marley, and on finding him would proclaim loudly: 'Is me do that!'

If Marley had no fear of molestation from tough guys such as Batman, then, overnight, his alliance with Rastafari freed him from the prurience and malice of black folk who had questioned his identity. Becoming a Rasta put the issue beyond doubt. Later on, when journalists prodded him about his complexion, about the difficulties of his mixed-race heritage and where his true allegiance lay, Marley would bat away the questions, saying that because he was a product of both black and white, he 'dipped on neither side'. The truth was he didn't just dip on the black side: he was totally immersed in it. The proof was his embrace of Rasta. Becoming a Rasta signalled a seismic shift in the convert's identity. To become a Rasta was not to whisper, but to shout out your identity: you were black *and* African.

*

The alignment with Africa and the nostalgia for that continent as the root of one's being was graphically expressed in the work of the artist who simply went by the name 'African'. But on the floor of the Jamaican National Gallery where African's art was exhibited, I fought hard to resist the thought that both his name and the fetishist switch that he clung to were props, that his Africanness was a received emotion. That same sentiment articulated in the sculptures of Woody Joseph appeared more heartfelt, all the more so because he failed to comprehend it himself.

'It can't mek dog, so you have to mek a fish out of it.' Woody Joseph picked up a rough piece of wood from the stream to demonstrate the secret of his art. 'This is a fish.' He smiled sweetly, baring seventy-year-old teeth that had lost their battle with sugar cane. Too much saliva and too little dentition rendered his speech almost inaudible, but the admirers at his bush retreat (I include myself) hung on his every word.

The day before, when I had suggested to my guide that I wanted to meet this famed mystical and intuitive artist, she had looked doubtful. Woody Joseph lived deep in the interior, without benefit of electricity or telephone. We would have to send word to him, she said mysteriously. It might take a week before an answer came back. In the event, we travelled the next day and when we pushed on through the bush to the clearing at Woody's compound, I struggled to contain my disappointment. Given the guide's account of the extraordinary difficulty that a visit would entail, I was bemused to find several pilgrims had simply stepped off a tour bus to arrive before me.

The intuitive artist was giving a demonstration, working on his next creation. The reflected light, when the sun caught the shine of his machete, flickered across our faces. Joseph worked with impressive speed, slicing through the wood, chipping away at an eye, carving, almost caressing the tail into a curve. Had Joseph heard of Michelangelo, one of the tourists wanted to know. He hadn't. Yet, like the Old Master, he too believed the sculpture was trapped inside the wood and that he was merely freeing it. As he carved, the ground thickened into a carpet of wood chippings.

Woody Joseph began humming an old mento work song. A few years back it would have eased the toil of digging a ditch or cutting sugar cane. Yellowing cataracts clouded his eyes. He rocked back and forth, working the song into a kind of mantra, and one by one each of us yielded to its beauty.

'How much for that?'

One of the pilgrims wanted to know the price of the sculpture he was working on. Woody Joseph pretended not to hear. The pilgrim repeated the question.

'It not finish!' answered Joseph.

There was a sting in his response. The old man was clearly upset by the impertinence of the question. Almost imperceptibly he turned his back on the small crowd. The pilgrims seemed perplexed, and when it was clear that Woody Joseph would not be drawn on any more enquiries, they slowly started to drift back down the hill towards the waiting bus, until only the guide and I remained.

He beckoned us to follow him into his hut. We passed a pile of rough-looking and red-stained wooden heads neatly stacked in a corner, each wearing an expression of being trapped in varying stages of agony. A curtain made from old crocus bags divided his studio from the living quarters. Inside, his wife was gutting a freshly killed chicken. The room was warm with the smell of blood. She tore angrily at the carcass; the dog started to sniff near the entrails slopped into a bucket before she kicked it away.

'Wha'appen?' asked the guide.

'You tell me,' she replied.

Her husband cut in: 'You nah have any sour-sop or coconut water give them?'

She threw down the knife and wiped her palms on the apron. I was not looking forward to the drink.

Without prompting, Woody Joseph began to explain his unusual journey from tenant farmer to international artist. 'My work? No one learn me.' He studied his wife as she, with much deliberation, handed us cups of warm coconut water, flavoured, it seemed, with chicken offal.

'I was sick and I go to a river to heal my foot,' Joseph continued, 'and I saw a piece of wood was swimming down in the water. I take my cutlass and draw it in. That cause me to be an artist. I was working for eight years. I never sell piece. My plan was very obstruct by my wife.'

He must have told the tale countless times before but Woody Joseph still seemed to marvel at the turn his life had taken. Eight years on, he was at the head of a small band of intuitive artists whose work, retaining vestiges of an African idiom, was highly regarded and sought after. Yet he had had no training.

'It just come out. Just coming out of all my traditions in Zambia. Well, Zambia is red. Nothing beat Zambia is the red – the sun of God, the gold of the earth.'

Joseph paused. The thought needed to be rounded off but it had obviously been considered many times before and was impossible to complete. Woody Joseph didn't know the answer. The work he produced remained an enigma to him.

'When I dream, I fly over Africa, Zambia and all those places, and I didn't know them before.'

Pilgrims in search of the mystical in Jamaica stretch in an unbroken line, beginning, in the 1930s, with the Harlem Renaissance writer and some-time anthropologist Zora Neale Hurston. Occasionally, the pilgrimage was purposeful. In Hurston's case it culminated in the publication of *Tell My Horse: Voodoo and Life in Haiti and Jamaica*, more often it was the result of an accident.

Thirty years after Hurston, in the winter of 1966, an African-American record producer arrived in Kingston, Jamaica, a man who in his own estimation was considered by the US authorities (namely the FBI) as dangerous as the leaders of the Black Panther Party for Self-Defense. But unlike Huey Newton and Bobby Seale, who terri-fied officialdom when they organised legally-armed Black Panther members to assemble and police the police, first in a protest at the California state capitol in Sacramento, and then later on the streets in cities around the country, Danny Sims was guilty of nothing more than producing a commercial which included the provocative track 'Burn Baby Burn'. America's cities had gone up in flames in riots in Los Angeles, Detroit, Chicago and elsewhere – ipso facto – Danny Sims was thought to have provoked, and to have been a key architect of, the racial conflagration that had engulfed America. That, at least, was Danny Sims's explanation of why he had fled in self-imposed exile from his own country. 'We were going to be killed by the CIA and

FBI,' Sims recalled of his flight with his business partner, the singer Johnny Nash. 'The police were killing black people. I was at the top of the list.'[210] Shrewdly, the pair sought safety in the peaceful back-water of the Jamaican capital. A rather less colourful explanation owed more to the cheaper record production costs in the Caribbean. Whichever version was more likely, what was beyond dispute was the fugitive record producer wound up renting an upmarket house in Russell Heights, the Beverly Hills of Jamaica.

Just a few weeks after their arrival, on 7 January 1967, the Ethio-pian Christmas, Johnny Nash embarked on an unusual adventure. He attended a Nyabinghi session chaired by Mortimo Planno in west Kingston. The uninitiated were often overwhelmed by the spectacle of such ceremonies but, according to Danny Sims, the focus of his partner that night was not on the drumming, chanting or chalice smoking, but on a single voice: 'That night, Johnny came home raving about this guy he had met named Bob Marley. He said every song he heard him sing was an absolute smash and that we should sign him immediately to our label' (JAD Records). The next day the Wailers, accompanied by Planno and Rita Marley, made the trek uptown from Trench Town to the exclusive Russell Heights for an impromptu audition, during which they played about thirty songs for Sims. The American producer was especially struck by Marley and invited him back for breakfast the next day. Marley was giddy with the prospect of what the meeting might lead to, but there was no danger of him immediately losing all sensation of the ground beneath his feet. His compatriots had a way of restoring gravity. En route to Russell Heights on his bicycle, Marley was stopped by a police patrol. The guffawing officers impressed upon him a fact with which he was surely familiar: a dutty (dirty) ghetto youth had no business breathing in the rarefied air in this residential middle-class suburb. Marley, as previously noted, was ordered to turn around his bicycle and head back to where he belonged. It took a further hour before he was able to find another way and safely circumvent the police cordon. But his ordeal was not over. When he did arrive at Russell Heights, the black American host later reported the perplexing spectacle of his servants refusing to serve Marley. They were adamant, recalled Sims, 'and walked out: they would not serve a Rastafarian'.[211]

In any event, a record contract, despite Johnny Nash's effusions, was not immediately forthcoming. There would be a period of reflection on both sides. The Wailers' association with Mortimo Planno was still informal but increasingly he was beginning to advance himself as their manager – one who could broker the beguiling prospects of a big deal with an American record label. But not everyone in the group, least of all Bunny Livingston, was reconciled to the arrangement. Friction greeted him at every corner. Planno possessed such an overbearing personality that anyone who came into contact with him was in danger of being bamboozled. There was an expectation in Rasta circles that initiates would surrender to the teaching and wisdom of the elders, and this further complicated their relationship.

The anthropologist Jake Homiak witnessed the enormous influence wielded by Planno when he ventured to a Nyabinghi gathering at Bull Bay. Halfway through the proceedings, as the sparks from the huge campfire criss-crossed the air and the drumming began to mesmerise, Homiak gradually felt more and more discomfited. The hundreds of Rastas were transfixed by the ceremony but the anthropologist sensed that for at least one of the brethren *he*, this lone white man, was the focus of attention. Homiak felt a pair of eyes boring into the back of his brain, and he knew that when he turned around he would immediately lock onto that person in the midst of the huge congregation. He turned slowly. Standing on a rise, barechested, his arms crossed, was Mortimo Planno. 'It was intimidating as hell. Clearly from his expression, I was just a dutty white boy,' remembered Homiak, 'a white piece of scum, invading his sacred space. I could hardly get a word out. He dusted me off, and then proceeded to move to a lignum vitae tree, followed like the Pied Piper by all the young males. They sat around him and Planno held court for several hours.'[212]

Livingston felt that 'Brother Kumi' was planning to 'take over' the young Wailers. There were numerous examples of this. One of the more disturbing was the occasion, Livingston recalled, when Planno contracted them to give a concert without first securing their agreement.

The arrangement at the Wail N Soul M label added to the tensions. Notwithstanding the early chart success of its first releases, their fledgling independent label did not thrive. 'We had no real money,' said Livingston, 'the records were selling but the money was being diverted.' Livingston suspected that Marley had been coerced into 'giving it to Planno to do his business'. But then Livingston was beginning to divine plots in every action undertaken by their self-appointed manager.

There were no reserve funds to draw on in these straitened times. In the spring of 1967, the Wailers decided to beat a retreat to the countryside. At least in the country, if you had no money, you could plant some crops and live off the land. All three went on the trip, as well as Rita Marley, Livingston's girlfriend Jean Watt, and a singer called Vision. It was a return to Nine Miles and their childhoods, a return to a romanticised Eden and a respite from the oppression of Trench Town and the tentacles of Planno.

Everywhere they went people implored them to come and stay. Livingston and Jean Watt took a room in the house of a woman called 'Miss D' who had had two children with Toddy Livingston. Marley moved nearby into his grandfather's old house which was attached to a small piece of land – Smit's farm – between two mountains where they were able to plant yams, cocoa, corn and cabbage; they also cared for Marley's childhood donkey, Nimble, who'd grown feeble from neglect. Dragon stout, the strong Jamaican brew, seemed to revive him. And each morning, in the early hours, they trekked three miles into the hinterland to bathe at a place called 'Spring'. They brought coconut oil tins with them to ferry water back to the village. And they made traps for birds, or killed them with home-made slingshots, then cooked them or made soups. 'Food was entertainment,' recalled Livingston.

Nine Miles lacked electricity. Candlelight and kerosene lamps illuminated the domino and card games. They sat outside in the evenings, smoking the Tampi herb that grew freely in the region, and reasoned until the cold penetrated their bones.

Marley's first home, at the top of the hill, where a big pimento tree had fallen, was used for rehearsals, and the rudiments of the harmonies for songs later to be known as 'Burial', 'Wisdom' and 'Comma, Comma' were composed there. The songs would though need to be completed in a studio.[213]

But their return to Kingston was delayed when Marley, working on the farm, injured himself on an upturned hoe. He was stoical, and merely cleaned the wound and kept off the damaged foot as much as possible. But the unspoken truth was that none of the Wailers were in any hurry for the injury to heal. Each stage of improvement edged them closer to the date when they could no longer defer their re-entry into the cauldron of Trench Town.

8

BATTERING DOWN SENTENCE

THERE was no police station in Trench Town. But then it wasn't necessary. It was difficult to hide – all of life was exposed – in the arid and over-crowded shanty town called the Rock. There were few solid walls between the various yards, mostly they were divided by wire fences. Coming up the west road, the patrolling policemen needed only to stand up in their jeeps and they could see virtually the length of the ghetto. Any kind of suspicious activity would be spotted immediately.

The residents of Trench Town needed to be particularly vigilant and discreet since the draconian reformulation of Jamaica's drug laws, which had made possession of marijuana a criminal offence, and those prosecuted liable to a mandatory custodial sentence. There was a sliding scale of offence, remembered Bunny Livingston: 'If you were found with a single [unlit] spliff on you, you went straight to prison, charged with possession. If caught with seed you went in for cultivation. If held with some rounds of ganja for sale, you'd go in for trafficking. And if arrested for planting a ganja field you would get three to five years.' All came with custodial sentences. The only exemption was being charged simply with 'smoking', then the culprit was given a choice: pay a fine or face imprisonment. But under no other circumstances were those convicted of convening the Dangerous Drugs Law allowed to pay a fine – it was not an option.

When Bunny Livingston felt in need of a draw of herb, he would take himself off to Vincent 'Tartar' Ford's yard in Trench Town. The vibe was particularly mellow at Tartar's. He had cultivated a herb camp, so that there was never a shortage of ganja. But the yard's popularity derived mostly from the makeshift shop and soup kitchen

Tartar ran for the locals. It never brought in much money. But in those days, Livingston recalled, 'a few pence could take you far'. With nine pence in his pocket, a man could afford 'a dozen crackers, maybe an ounce of butter, a pound sugar, a little piece of ice and one or two limes,'[214] and still come away with change. Tartar could just about get by on his food sales and promissory notes. Occasionally, if he had money, Livingston would throw in his lot with him to help replenish his stock. And when times got really rough, Tartar could always count on supplementing his income by selling weed.

Tartar was 'safe': he could be relied upon. Four years on from their formation as a band, the life of the Wailers was still little more than hand to mouth. Any anxiety over loss or theft of materials, though, was tempered by the fact that their possessions were few. The one consistent worry was to keep their musical instruments in good working order and, more importantly, to keep hold of them: they would be expensive to replace. The Wailers had two guitars. The bigger one, christened 'Betsy', they would take on the road with them; the smaller one would be stored away. And it was a mark of Tartar's trustworthiness that there was never any doubt about where the spare guitar would be left for safekeeping.

One afternoon in the spring of 1967, on a particularly slow day, Bunny Livingston found himself lounging at Tartar's. People were constantly dropping by, taking in the vibe. Nothing much was happening. A local guy called Tom was strumming on a guitar, and one of the yardboys, Pucu, was preparing a 'takeaway' – a 2-shilling draw of ganja to go and sell to a neighbour, the caretaker of the local park. Pucu was always a cause of a minor irritation for Livingston: 'Pucu was a little youth trying to help when we were short-handed, but he didn't want to do things the right way. He just take a short cut all the time.' The received wisdom was that Pucu was one of those youths who shouldn't use ganja because 'his brains are too light'. Livingston cast a drowsy eye in Pucu's direction and noticed that, peculiarly, Pucu was taking the whole bag of weed with him. It would have made more sense to just take the one ganja stick that the caretaker wanted and to return the rest to its hiding place.

Bunny Livingston didn't have time to berate the youth for his foolish behaviour because just then, out of the corner of his eye, he thought he saw a patrol jeep passing along Collie Smith Drive, a policeman

standing up and peering over as it made the slow trawl along the
perimeter of the ghetto. Researchers have made clear that 'hallucina-
tions are not an invariable consequence of marijuana use' in Jamaica.[215]
Bunny Livingston was under no illusions but he had to adjust his eyes.
The police seemed to zoom into view from background to foreground
in no time at all. 'The cops looked over the wall and saw Pucu doing
his stuff.' Livingston was no longer smoking. He was just listening to
Tom playing and singing but his reactions had slowed as a previous
joint had worked its magic. 'Suddenly I saw plain-clothes policemen
come through the gate and a next one jump over the wall ... I said
to Tom, "You have anything on you?" Tom said, "No!" So I said,
"Well, here come the cops."'

Pucu was not so sanguine. He panicked and, dodging and weaving
through the yard, he ran straight into the arms of the law. The police
charged all three of them with possession, even though the guitarist
and Livingston were only 'in the vicinity'.

By the time the case came to court, Pucu had been transferred to
a juvenile centre, and the charge against Tom had been mysteriously
withdrawn. Livingston was left alone, charged with sole possession of
the bag of ganja.

Bunny Livingston was determined to give as good an impression as
possible. He borrowed a suit jacket which he wore to the trial. When
the judge looked up he simply saw a force-ripe youth, not yet sporting
locks, but undoubtedly a fledgling Rasta. There was no jury. The judge
found him guilty, and when it was pointed out that Bunny Livingston
was just twenty, 'the judge just leant back in his chair and said: "That's
old enough to go to prison."' He sentenced Livingston to eighteen
months' hard labour. Livingston was 'taken away and stripped and
thrown into General Penitentiary, together with some rude boys'.

Bunny Livingston later complained that his own lawyer hadn't put
up much of a fight, because he secretly sympathised with the prosecution; ganja was frowned upon, and the harsh sentence reflected the
paranoia about the imagined threat to the status quo and civil society
posed by groups like the Wailers, Rastas, rude boys and other miscreants. Livingston, understandably, took the sentence personally, but the
judiciary had been guided by the government in its promotion of zero
tolerance towards marijuana.

Jamaicans had been drawing an equation that put Rastafarians and ganja on one side and the breakdown of law and order on the other, for the past two decades. As far back as 1951, the *Gleaner* had editorialised about the 'ganja gangs' that they believed were proving a growing menace to society. Evidence to that end had been provided by a chilling incident on 11 June that year. Jamaicans had woken to horrific newspaper headlines of the murder of a young man, and the ravishing and wounding of his virtuous girlfriend, by a suspected bearded man. The couple had gone for a swim in Palisadoes. They were sitting on the banks, singing the popular, new Roman Catholic hymn 'Our Lady of Fatima' when the 'bearded man' leapt out of the water with a knife and a club. He bludgeoned and stabbed the young man to death, then raped and stabbed the girl, throwing her body into the water with the words 'You dead there too.' Remarkably she survived and identified her bearded assailant as the known Rastafarian Alton 'Whoppy King' Jolly. Newspapers and other media outlets stoked the flames of outrage over the heinous act. Jolly had carried out the robbery to feed his drug habit. 'Deprive these wretches of their ganja,' thundered the *Gleaner*, 'and they are exposed at once for the craven idlers that they are.'[216] It was a measure of the shock and alarm felt by Jamaicans that the Rastafarian's crimes elicited a dyspeptic outburst from the otherwise genial host of *Opportunity Hour*, Vere Johns. In the first instance, Johns suggested, 'They should be deloused and made to take a bath, then treated to a haircut and have their abominable beards shaved off.' He also advocated that some Crown Lands be set aside to establish new prison farms for the Rastas, 'not on the mild Richmond Farm plan'. And Johns closed his sermon, bringing down a gavel on his pulpit: 'Let the bearded brethren be rounded up and placed where they can do no harm.'[217]

'Whoppy King' had been caught and executed, but since then, in the perception of large parts of the population, there had been an incremental growth in the outrages perpetrated by the Rastafarians each year. The terror sparked by the botched rebellion of Claudius and Ronald Henry had been reprised just two years later at Coral Gardens near Montego Bay. On 11 April 1963 a gang of six Rastafarians 'launched a Holy Thursday rampage' at a Shell petrol station with spears and machetes. A posse of civilians and police then pursued them. On hearing the news the Prime Minister and heads of the Defence Force had flown to Montego Bay, and troops and armoured cars were sent to the area

– actions which fuelled the media's mistaken stories of a 'Rastafarian uprising' (which was actually the settling of a local vendetta between local Rastas and a farmer). By the end of the conflict eight people were dead including two policemen and three Rastafarians. The surviving 'bearded men' were subsequently hanged, and scores of Rastafarians (more than 150) were rounded up under the dangerous drugs, unlawful possession of property and vagrancy laws.[218]

In the hysteria and soul-searching that followed Coral Gardens – as with the 'Whoppy King' affair, the Coronation Market riots, and the Henry Rebellion – reactionary measures, like stiffening the penalties for ganja possession, had been widely applauded.

The government was not going to lose any friends by howling that it would no longer tolerate the noxious trade in dangerous drugs. In the dragnet thrown over the island, Rastas were always more likely to be snared than any other group. And after a number of 'bearded' men were arrested and charged both with possession of ganja and with chillum pipes, some speculated sarcastically that the offence should be amended to 'suspicion of being Rastafarians'.

The draconian measures appealed to the more conservative elements in Jamaican society (regardless of class) but even they drew a distinction between the abstract mass of Rastas and the individuals with whom they had good personal relations. When the patrician *Gleaner* journalist Morris Cargill heard that one of his workers, Brother Man, was intent on visiting Kingston, the right-wing columnist and landowner grew anxious and apprehensive. He confided to his diary: 'I begged him to be careful, and not to carry any ganja with him in public places.'[219]

The police went about their business with unbridled enthusiasm. The jails began to fill. Livingston's arrest and imprisonment would coincide with the sentencing of other well-known singers for ganja offences. In 1967, Kenrick 'Lord Creator' Patrick received a similar sentence when he was stopped on a motorcycle and an ounce of ganja was found on him; and most notably, the prominent singer Freddie 'Toots' Hibbert of Toots and the Maytals also landed a term in jail – a miserable and shameful time that was offset perhaps by its inspiration for his hugely popular song '54-46'. Weekly, the papers ran stories of police raids which destroyed huge ganja fields, of ganja found in suitcases and crocus bags, and of youths arrested when sticks of ganja fell out of their pockets. Only occasionally would a story be published questioning whether ganja was any more harmful than Scotch whisky, or pointing out the hypocrisy and 'pompous moral attitudes about ganja . . . preached and promulgated in an alcoholic haze'. Bunny Livingston drew little comfort from such arguments or by the larger suspicion anonymously aired in the *Gleaner* that the legislation against ganja had done 'more than anything else since emancipation to convince people that the law has been designed to oppress the poor'.[220] At first, he was more concerned about the shame and ignominy of his criminal conviction than the hardships that lay ahead.

General Penitentiary, a decrepit maximum security institution, built in the 1840s over 11 acres of sloping land in east Kingston close to the harbour, was not a sight to gladden the heart. The 20-foot exterior wall was rimmed by barbed wire; an armed officer was stationed at each octagonal guard tower with his rifle cocked. Inside, the two-tiered cell blocks faced onto courtyards. More than 1,000 men were crammed into them, even though the prison had been built to accommodate 850. The floor space of the average cell measured 5 feet by 8, and was just big enough for a mattress. Prisoners lived in fear of kicking over the bucket jammed in the corner in to which they had to urinate and defecate. A narrow window – close to the ceiling in the 9 ft high cell wall – that let in little light, was fit only for the purpose of much-needed ventilation. Every aspect of prison life seemed formulated to feed the notion of punishment.

Yet the architects of the General Penitentiary (GP) congratulated themselves that they had embraced the same Enlightenment ideals that had led to penal reform in England, namely that a custodial sentence was not just punitive but should prepare prisoners for their eventual rehabilitation into society – notwithstanding that constant surveillance and a discouragement of communication were still central to the ethos of Jamaica's main prison.

The very idea of imprisonment was especially shameful and repugnant to the island's black population. Work had begun on GP's construction less than a decade after the full emancipation of the enslaved, and the prison and the system it enshrined, were seen by many as a continuation of slavery by other means. Backbreaking employment on public works programmes, though not quite on the scale of the convict lease system imposed in the American South after the Civil War, was the lot of the island's prisoners. Inmates at GP could expect long hours of limestone-cutting and brick-making; worse still, their fellow convicts on the prison farms were forced to re-enact the humiliations of their ancestors wielding machetes in the sugar-cane fields.

But sympathy was more likely to come from the Devil than any other section of society. Cynical Jamaicans believed that the convicted had brought their plight on themselves, and endorsed the maxim of the first governor of GP that prison was 'a state of self-inflicted slavery, without its alleviations'.[221]

That cynicism was further expressed in an ironic song about the General Penitentiary composed during the Second World War:

> *Dear GP that's the place for me*
> *You get a haircut and trim for nothing*
> *And three tidy meals every day . . .*
> *When Germans drop shells*
> *I'll be safe in my cell*
> *Back in dear GP*

Nineteenth-century Enlightenment, never particularly bright, had dimmed to a point of near-invisibility by the time Bunny Livingston was bundled through the iron gates of GP in 1967. His first impression was one of bewilderment; the penitentiary was 'a hell world' patrolled by 'ugly guys with long sticks and cuffs' – an animated Hieronymus Bosch canvas of sadistic half-naked creatures fornicating, vomiting, pissing and shitting over each other while they picked at the chigger eggs embedded in their bare feet.

You had to be wily to make your way through life in Trench Town but Livingston found that nothing had prepared him for the dangers of General Penitentiary. The brutality was staggering. 'Some men when they get crazy, sharpen long pieces of steel, and you see two guys just punching each other's flesh with them. Nobody's running. Nobody's dodging. Just give and take until somebody drops. It's ugly-looking shit.'

In quiet moments, before the break of dawn, Livingston reflected on what he had done, on how *he*, a promising musician, wound up in jail with the detritus of Jamaican society. While he clung to the burning belief of his innocence, that he was not guilty as charged, he accepted the greater truth that he *was* guilty (defiantly so) of association with Rasta, and of surrendering to the reasoning and ritual of smoking ganja.

He'd heard a small voice in his head whispering such thoughts, and the point was further reinforced by unwelcome taunts from his father. After much prevarication, Toddy Livingston had dragged himself reluctantly along to the jail with one consoling thought in mind; he would remind his son that it wasn't 'just him one', that he had brought disgrace 'pon the whole family'. 'My father did come and say: "Rasta business done now? You supposed to wise up to that.' Whereupon, Bunny rolled up his shirt to reveal 'the button of King Selassie I that I wore inside of it.' Toddy leapt immediately at his son, throwing a punch at him, 'not an angry box', more out of frustration and disappointment. His ire subsided almost as quickly as it had arisen, and he dropped his fists. Only then did Bunny Livingston turn to his father and speak candidly about his belief that the Ethiopian Emperor was his protector. 'I told him, "All who praise Jesus freak batty inside here" – namely the Lord-lovers had been weak and had been raped in the jail. "Only those who praise Selassie I live."'

From its inception, General Penitentiary had acquired a reputation for acquiescing to the practice of 'the beastly act of sodomy' among its inmates.[222] Bunny Livingston believed that he possessed a fine nose for detecting the 'batty men' who perpetrated such antics. Early on in his term of imprisonment, the dread of 'nocturnal communications' and the real risk of getting caught up in the lottery of violence – to be subject to random acts of physical abuse – pushed him towards a strategy of isolation. He trusted no man in prison, and turned himself into 'a lone lion, observing what is going on'. What was happening was that with irregular regularity a fight would break out, with the certainty that someone's 'belly is going to be cut out . . . to be gutted'. Prison brought out Livingston's tendency towards withdrawal, but also a determination to be strong and in control of himself, for he was among wolves. 'You have to learn the art of winning without fighting, that is the greatest martial art ever . . . You have to think like a lion and these wolves pick up on that vibe and they don't fuck around because they know you are going to fuck up some of them.' For eighteen months he would embark on an internal migration. He would not hold conversations, and would perfect the mantra that only 'a damn coward' needs company. The one flaw in Bunny Livingston's strategy was other people; unsolicited visitors turned up at the penitentiary, until he made plain his displeasure. A visit from a close friend of the family convinced him that he was right to spurn outside contact when he detected pity in her eyes. Bob Marley turned up only once but his visit heralded another from the man he least wanted to see – Mortimo Planno.

Livingston had no idea that he was coming. 'They bring me to a room and he walks in and say: "You can still sing?" Yes, Planno walks in his big old dutty nasty self and goes on like he's God! "Still sing?" "More than ever,"' answered Livingston drily. Bunny Livingston held the unshakeable opinion that Mortimo Planno was 'using his brains', trying to undermine and sideline him. In Livingston's conception, Planno was all too cognisant, and jealous, of his intimacy with Marley. He, Bunny Livingston, was an impediment to the grand design that Planno was working towards. Conveniently he'd be incarcerated for over a year but once Livingston had served his sentence, he was sure Planno didn't relish his returning to the fold; he wanted him out of the way. Out of earshot of the other visitors, Planno whispered to him: 'You know it was your father who set you up and sent you to prison?'

Bunny Livingston was enraged. But after a while he reflected that it was 'a psychological move' to try to 'make me give up . . . If my father did that to me what reason did I have to go on living?'

Livingston consoled himself with a biblical analogy. He cast himself as Joseph in the dungeon, or Daniel in the lion's den; and he held firm to the belief that there was a divine reason for his incarceration: Jah (Jehovah) was testing his faith and endurance. 'Jah wanted me to know . . . when your brother, sister, mother, father, everybody forsake you, HE will take you up.'

In prison Livingston learnt to exert greater control over his emotions, to curb his frustration. He told himself the punishment should not be taken personally because in the penitentiary 'you are received as a body, not as a person'. Boredom and tedium remained formidable opponents but even they could be marshalled. 'You just let time be your friend . . . just say, "OK, Brother Time, I'm yours."'

But Livingston didn't just lose his liberty in July 1967. In a development that couldn't have been better designed to torment him, he missed out on the group's most lucrative contract to date. For Bunny Livingston's incarceration did not diminish the enthusiasm of Johnny Nash and Danny Sims to work with the Wailers. The deal with JAD Records eventually brokered by Mortimo Planno secured a weekly retainer (Sims claimed it was $100 per week) for Tosh, Marley and for Rita Marley whom it was agreed would stand in for Bunny Livingston for the duration of his imprisonment. Their brief (which would mostly fall to Marley) was primarily to write songs for Johnny Nash.

For much of 1967, Bob Marley's dedication to lyric composition was matched by a deepening immersion in the Rasta faith. Increasingly, he surrendered to the tutelage of Planno. As well as bleaching the chillum pipe and reasoning at Open Yard, Planno also encouraged him to attend ceremonies at the makeshift temple which he and his immediate circle had fashioned in the shadow of the municipal garbage dump, smouldering away all day at the Dungle. The Rastafarian tabernacle, rimmed by dozens of flagpoles, had been spared the bulldozing visited on the nearby shanty town dwellings on the Foreshore Road, three months after Selassie's visit. It served a multiplicity of functions – primarily as a place of worship but also as a social club and centre of learning for Amharic lessons. The temple, stretching 60 feet, was made mostly from corrugated zinc and scraps of wood, decorated with photographs of Haile Selassie and Marcus Garvey. Divided into three sections, a semi-subterranean chamber, with a dirt floor, served as the main site of worship and other sacred functions. Much of its interior – the beams and even the metal chairs – were painted sea-blue; and on feast days and other anniversaries, red, gold and green bunting stretched across the ceiling. At the height of religious intensity, as the drama of the occasion crested, the fervour and fire of the incantations became intoxicating and irresistible; the weary hymns melted the heart; and Marley, along with most of the crowd, was mesmerised by Planno's commanding voice as he led the prayers and chanting from a platform mounted on oil drums.

It was during this time that Bob Marley seemed to slip into a self-imposed internal exile. For a period he stopped talking to anyone except his wife and his Rastafarian tutor. If a third party posed a question to Marley, he would not answer directly but rather mutter a response to Rita or Planno which would then be passed on to the enquirer. Marley's bizarre behaviour was reminiscent of the remedial actions taken by Jamaicans who believed themselves the target of an Obeah curse. Typically such a victim would be advised to dress fully in white and forgo all physical and social contact, until such a time as the curse expired and the danger had passed. Psychiatric textbooks might, of course, have offered another explanation: the anxiety over his future; the fitful starts and stops of his dealings in the record business; the unwelcome attention of envious neighbours and sniping over the Babylonian success afforded by the association with Nash and Sims in the midst of grinding squalor of the west Kingston slum; all these stresses and frictions had converged, had taken root in his delicate mind and had triggered the 'screw-faced depression' which the otherwise joyful musician occasionally suffered from throughout early adulthood.

To many, Babylon represents an ancient Persian civilisation, but to Jamaicans in general, and Rastafarians in particular, it conjured passages from the Bible on the plight of the Israelites in Exodus, wandering in the wilderness for forty years, resting their weary bodies by the rivers of evil Babylon, and dreamily remembering that they were heading for Mount Zion. Rastafarians transposed that story so that *they* now represented the true Israelites held in captivity for centuries, and were comforted by the revelations in the Bible that one day, on Judgement Day, the great city of Babylon, the mother of harlots and the abomination of the earth, would fall. Modern-day Babylon in Jamaica was represented by all the decadent and oppressive forces arrayed against the 'sufferers'.

Shrewd analysis or righteous posturing? Either way the semi-detached Rasta approach to life on the island often proved vexing even to sympathisers. Norman Manley (the founding father of Jamaican Independence) had shown much more interest in Rasta thinking than most of his political class. He even had a former Rasta on his payroll as a bodyguard. But finally, while acknowledging that in its short thirty-year history the movement had disclosed 'an alienation from society',[223] Manley counselled Rastafarians to throw in their lot with their fellow Jamaicans, for 'there are no Moses for modern man, and the Promised Land will be won under the curse of Eden'.[224]

Dealing with Babylon (an inventory of Babylon's trappings ranged from small items of materialism to naked corporate capitalism – from wallets and car keys to big recording studios) was always problematic for Rastafarians. Rastas themselves tried to make some sense of the varying degrees of engagement; they drew a distinction between practical 'statical' or 'secular' Rastas and the 'churchical' Rastas who were more explicitly religious. To some extent, of course, all Rastas had to deal with Babylon – it was a necessary evil – but the underlying Rasta ethos held that too close an association was corrosive and corrupting.

Danny Sims described how this conflict was played out in the febrile mind of Bob Marley when it came to the choice of recording studios in Kingston. 'Marley refused to record in what he called "the Babylon studio" so we recorded at Randy's. He wouldn't go into Federal Records or Byron Lee's studio. He just didn't want to do anything with those kind of people.' Though Randy's was run by a Chinese-Jamaican family, as was Byron Lee's, the subtext was that there were levels of association with 'those kind of people', degrees of selling out to Babylon. Randy Chin was not as 'socially white' as Byron Lee, and could therefore be patronised. 'In those days,' recalled Sims, 'being around a Rasta was like being around a Black Panther'.[225]

The authorities looked on anxiously at the rise of racial feeling in Jamaica, and the ill winds which they detected were blowing in from the USA, manifest in the seething hatred between black and white displayed not just on the freedom marches at Selma, Alabama, but more worryingly in the gun battles between Black Power militants and America's police forces and National Guard.

Two foreign lecturers arrived in Jamaica in 1968 whose reception displayed the full range of Jamaican sensitivity to race. One was the Guyanese scholar Walter Rodney who, according to his security file, was 'a convinced Communist with pro-Castro ideals, [thought] latterly to have taken an interest in Black Power'. The other was a Canadian, Theodore MacDonald, who garnered just as much suspicion and unwelcome attention from his students. MacDonald charted an ascent in a radicalism that was somewhat less than chic. Towards the end of the decade, he noted that violent slogans such as 'It's time to put down pen and take up the bomb' had begun to make their way to the campus at the University of the West Indies on protest placards. One day, the professor found himself at the wrong end of a student sit-in which he was invited to attend. Held prisoner in the basement of the student common room, MacDonald managed to escape after three days, once the overheated tempers had cooled and the excitement abated. No matter the philanthropic attitude that had propelled him towards Jamaica; caught in the heat of the times, the gentle Canadian academic was recast as a virulent agent of Babylon.

The black temper did not improve as one moved out to the countryside. After a fashion, MacDonald found that when driving through the rural parishes, even though his car lacked air-conditioning, it might be prudent to keep the windows rolled up. The lesson was harshly learnt. On several occasions, indolent youths had been roused by the sound of an approaching car whose occupant, it was speedily broadcast, was determinedly white. 'They'd run alongside, maybe yards from the road, and when parallel take aim with a handful of goat or cow shit, and, with alarming frequency, found the gap exposed by the car's opened window.'[226]

Such antipathy was always likely to be expressed in more sinister forms in the ghettoes. By the time MacDonald's fellow Canadian, Carole Yawney, arrived in Trench Town, she was already aware that Mortimo Planno 'had acquired a reputation for being highly suspicious of white people'. The description was an even closer fit for his Rasta associates, some of whom were sufficiently outraged to free themselves of any restraint in their violent criticisms of the man who'd brought the enemy into their midst. Yawney recalled the roiling and rancorous discussions of the Rastas who, like Hobsbawn's Andalusian anarchists, 'lived in argument'.[227] Her sponsor had suffered the ignominy of challenges to his authority and occasional death threats. However, after much delicate reasoning among the brethren, Brother Planno had established an 'escape clause' which allowed for the movement 'to work with non-Blacks [such as Yawney] under special circumstances.'

Mortimo Planno was the ultimate yard politician but even he could not legislate for the actions of other visitors to his yard. Highly charged currents of discontent continued to course through Open Yard. None more so, wrote Yawney, than in the shape of 'a certain local psychopath, a "sober mad" in their terms, as opposed to a "mad mad", [who] set upon me'. On that day the 'sober mad' man drew a knife and putting its tip to Yawney's neck backed her out of Planno's yard. He slashed the knife at anyone who tried to interfere. A large crowd gathered to witness the commotion, and hours passed while the anthropologist calmed him down by 'entering into his fantasy with him'. Yawney also noticed sanguinely that the hostage-taking occasioned yet another reasoning session among the brethren 'about whether a Black man should injure a Black brother to protect a white woman'. They mostly found in her favour but, in the event the conclusion of their reasoning was not put to the test. Suddenly, 'three tough-looking youths on motorbikes arrived, pistols drawn, whips bristling'. They were undercover cops, Papa Williams among them, whose strange visage disoriented the sober madman even further. Yawney was rescued and her kidnapper invited to accompany Papa Williams to police headquarters, and thereafter to the psychiatric hospital.

When the madman escaped a few days later and turned up outside her house, even the courageous Yawney was sufficiently unnerved to take temporary leave of the island.[228]

From the 1960s onwards, bitterness towards white people swept in and out of Jamaica like so much foul-smelling flotsam and jetsam. But it did not herald any final settling of the score for the wrongs of the slave past or the continued 'downpression' of Babylon. The Nyabinghi curse of 'death to the white oppressor and his black ally' was marked more by rhetoric than any real call to arms. Most Rastas who moved to the beat of 'one love' would have been shocked had anyone been so foolish as to take them literally. When conducting fieldwork, another contemporary researcher, Sheila Kitzinger, observed that although the Rastas bore a frightening countenance and spoke in 'a formal and ritualised verbal aggression', they were courteous and dignified. Kitzinger wrote that she was careful never to touch them lest 'I should contaminate them unwittingly with my own unholiness and sin,' but she also readily confessed: 'No thoughts of harm entered my head when I introduced my two-year-old daughter to them. Nor was I the least bit alarmed by them, although our Jamaican maid fled.'[229]

It was always Planno's preference to express what Rastafarians were in favour of, rather than what they were against. To that end, music was a powerful vehicle. The songs he wrote and recorded with the Wailers in 1968, tracks such as 'Selassie is the Chapel', were much more Rasta chants than ska or early reggae tunes. That particular song was a confirmation of Rastafarian faith and a warning of imminent 'dread judgement' for the infidels, for those who clung misguidedly to the belief that salvation might be found elsewhere, outside of the chapel of Selassie. But if this was music intended as a tool for spreading the faith, then the handful of records pressed did not express an overarching confidence. Twenty-six copies fell somewhat short of the mass production requisite for scaling the pop charts. Perhaps Planno envisaged 'Selassie is the Chapel' becoming the collector's item it has proved to be. But at the time, apart from on the gramophone of a rented house in Russell Heights, it would never have played in the living rooms of middle-class households. Rather, these initial collaborations with the Wailers were confined to a few Rasta camps, and the jukebox of the local tearoom that Planno frequented, and whose owner was happy for him (after hours) to play his songs again and again. Although the record label for 'Rastafarian Prayer' and 'Selassie is the Chapel' credited the Wailers (Bob and Rita Marley, and Peter Tosh featured), the songs really belonged to the Rasta elder.

Nonetheless, the tracks reflected a spiritual awakening, while the secular 'Bust Dem Shut' (Burst Their Shirts) and 'Pound Get a Blow' were compositions which showed that the Wailers were still very much working in the trenches, producing powerful narrative songs about the unremittingly harsh economic climate under which the majority of Jamaicans struggled to eke out a living.

Bunny Livingston might even have argued that life was somewhat easier in jail, especially at the prison farm in Richmond where he was transferred after a few months at the General Penitentiary. The dorms were larger in Richmond with rows of double-decker cots. Each of the two dorms accommodated about 100 men. The provisions were plentiful – coffee, cocoa tea, buttered bread, rice'n'peas and chicken. 'Guys got fat and round and thick, big and shine and muscular,' recalled Livingston. In those days when an inmate was discharged, 'a man could look at you and say enviously: "Where you coming from, a foreign land?"'

There was the inevitable price to be paid for such comforts. Guards armed with rifles watched over the prisoners as they went to work cutting cane in the despised sugar plantations. But Livingston found that prison existence might be leavened through the exegesis of a hitherto unhidden talent. As soon as he picked up a bat and ball it was apparent that he was a better than average cricketer. Relative to his fellow inmates, Livingston's cricketing prowess was test-match standard and put him, in their minds, on a par with the celebrated West Indian batsman and bowler Garfield Sobers. Prison staff placed a premium on cricket. Cricket matches were played across the street from the Richmond Farm establishment. Prison rules allowed for up to three inmates to play in the warden's team, and they were especially eager to see Bunny Livingston pad up.

Going out to bat for the Richmond Farm Eleven granted prisoner Livingston certain privileges. He did not take up the offer of near-unlimited visiting rights for friends. But Bunny Livingston more than availed himself of the privilege to 'burn a little spliff' as often as possible. 'I smoked herb every single day I was in prison from GP onwards. The wardens bring it, sell ganja.'

'Crackie', one of the biggest ganja kings in Jamaica, supplemented his illegal income with full-time employment as a prison officer. His competition came largely from 'Coolie Boy', another warden/ganja merchant whose notoriety was forever captured when the ska trombonist Don Drummond titled an instrumental after him. Both men bore out a truth which many in Jamaica testified to, namely that the hypocritical guardians of social order were some of the biggest traders and contraveners of the Dangerous Drugs Law. When researchers into cannabis consumption on the island asked a local man why he didn't purchase his ganja from local farmers like everyone else in the village, he answered that there was no need to because his generous policeman son-in-law often returned from his shifts laden with a bag of marijuana, and always kept him in plentiful supply.[230]

Reflecting on that time, Livingston admitted that smoking was more recreational than a medium for communing with Jah. 'You might as well smoke herb and meditate . . . you can channel herb high.' Smoking also dulled the frustration over the lack of an outlet for his musical creativity, made all the more poignant when he caught snatches of music unexpectedly. There'd been little music during his months in GP save for occasional reverberations from the many sound systems punching out their music in the south of the city. On the radio, Livingston listened with some trepidation when the DJ announced tracks that the Wailers had composed without him. And it was with a sense of gratitude and pride (untainted by schadenfraude) that he later drew to the attention of anyone who'd care to listen that none of those tracks on which his voice was missing – 'Pound Get a Blow', 'Hurting Inside' and 'Don't Rock My Boat' – ever became hits.

By contrast, it was during his imprisonment that Livingston began to compose a song which would later be recognised as one of his greatest achievements: 'Battering Down Sentence'. Even in its rudimentary form, the power of the song was immediate. 'Whenever I'd sing it one of the senior warden always begged me not to . . . He'd say, "Please nah sing that one. That will make a prisoner get a spirit that encourage man to run away."' The song reminded inmates of thoughts they'd pushed to the back of their minds during their incarceration. Everyone knew prison life was a sham, was a warped and phoney existence – reality lay just beyond the prison gates. No one really spoke about it. 'Battering Down Sentence' was a pitiful and mournful reminder. It introduced a profound note of sobriety to the Richmond Farm Prison. The guards bowed and trembled when he sang. 'The warden became extremely nervous,' remembered Livingston. 'He thought the song would incite a riot.'

Riots, though, rarely occurred. Richmond Farm inmates knew that any transgression might not simply lead to a withdrawal of privileges, but a return to General Penitentiary. And if you misbehaved in GP you were sent to the dumb cell where it was impossible to stand; you had to sit and crawl. Prisoners who tried to escape, when caught, were locked up in a section of the jail called 'Escapee'. And if you tried to escape from 'Escapee' your final destination was a place given the name 'Belgium', where they housed the most notorious criminals. Rhygin had famously broken out from there in 1948, but it was rumoured that no one since then had ever escaped.

After eighteen months, Bunny Livingston walked away from prison, still smarting from the injustice of his sentence, and reflecting on the trauma of the experience. 'You have to go to hell to know what the Devil's about,' he said. 'I have been to hell!'

LET IT BURN

WHEN the gunshots were fired at the vehicle carrying Norman Manley, the leader of the opposition party, he ducked instinctively. For several hours on Sunday 12 February 1967, Manley had toured the west Kingston area, standing in the back of a pickup truck, accompanied by supporters on bicycles who cheered him along the way. At key moments, when the truck rolled through the neighbouring shanty towns, Manley placed the loudspeaker to his lips and exhorted residents with a simple message: to turn away from the gunmen and refrain from violence in the forthcoming elections. As the pickup turned at the intersection just beyond Majestic Pen, Manley had his answer: a crack of gunfire sounded and half a dozen bullets whizzed past his head.[231]

The seventy-five-year-old elder statesman escaped without injury, but in the following days he lashed out in unstatesmanlike fashion at the gunmen and the real culprits who had hired them – the governing party. Except Norman Manley did not refer to the Jamaican Labour Party as the government. The name this most genial and assiduous former barrister reserved for them was the 'enemy'. Manley's son, Michael (who would inherit the mantle of leader of the People's National Party), backed his father's assessment, pointing out that, at the height of what was then called 'the West Kingston War',[232] they had buried several of their supporters each week in the months before the attempted assassination. But the truth was that there had been casualties on both sides, and when detectives from the Flying Squad swept down on west Kingston on the following weekend, they raided the hideouts of suspected gunmen from both the JLP *and* PNP.

Non-alignment was one of the central tenets of Rastafarian ideology. Rastas paid no allegiance to the state, only to Haile Selassie. When they were 'seated' and inhaling on the chillum pipe they were aligned solely with Jah. But Edward Seaga's social experiment, sending in the bulldozers to level the slums of Back-o-Wall and erect the government housing project of Tivoli Gardens, exposed the extent to which the ghettoes had become politicised. When Rastas and other tenants and squatters moved out, they did not return. If they had wanted to go back they were unlikely to be offered the keys of the new houses. Critics argued that Seaga was guilty of cementing Jamaica's patronage politics in only housing people in Tivoli Gardens who were known supporters of his JLP party or who'd pledged future allegiance. The seeds of division which Kingston still experiences in what has become known as its 'Garrison Constituencies' were sown back then, says Reverend Webster Edwards. 'When people are living together, co-mingling, you do not have a problem. When you create an homogenous group of people who feel that they are one, "us against them", then you set the stage for the sort of problem we are experiencing at this time.'[233] That categorisation of friend or foe, ally or enemy, would evolve, so that rather than being challenged about which race he belonged to, Bob Marley was more likely to have to answer insistent questioning about which side of the political spectrum he leant towards. The time was coming, whether Rasta or not, when you would have to declare for one party or the other. Further down the line the question of allegiance would not need to be asked. Who you voted for was defined just by dint of where you lived, and straying into an enemy neighbourhood carried with it the real possibility of violence.

The political activist Neville Graham was just a schoolboy when he first caught sight of the 'stickmen', the local political enforcers who imposed their will largely through the use of pickaxe handles. In those days, recalled Graham, your political allegiance was also tempered by practical considerations: there were two grocers' shops in an area of JLP activity. Mr Eddie was JLP and Miss Reenie was PNP. But everyone flocked to Miss Reenie, and spurned Mr Eddie. Even though his shop was cleaner, 'it was emptier; [Mr Eddie] did not give credit.'[234]

Trench Town ranked among the most targeted and contested strongholds. 'We were a bit scared to go out,' recalled Anthony Doyley, 'because when you leave out of Trench Town you'd be putting yourself to jeopardy.'[235]

The incremental growth in political violence came to be accepted with a certain degree of cynicism. It was inevitable: a version of Professor Hickling's 'then was knives; now is gun.' 'Bragga', a local amateur historian of Trench Town, charted the rise of the hard-men, the enforcers who graduated from sticks to guns: 'Some of the men never had the heart to kill people and all that. But they did have ways to monopolise the vote.' There was no big political machinery. Parties depended on the hard-men 'to intimidate the electorate to vote' in the approved manner.[236] The political violence in 1967 and beyond was marked by an escalation of abductions, woundings and murder in the West Kingston War, but the ongoing intimidation could be traced back to the 1940s.

It started with rhetoric; in the bar-room or rum-shop philosophy of colourful figures like Wills Isaacs who even scandalised his own party with the frank assessment that it might be necessary for a new nation to crack a few heads on the road to realising democracy, because 'a broken skull or two did not matter much in the growth of a nation.'[237] By 1968, Sir Alexander Bustamante, the first Prime Minister of an independent Jamaica, was settling into retirement and an impregnable veneer of respectability, but just over a decade before, in an earlier incarnation, he'd been among the first to rush to the scene of political disturbances at Gordon Town, in a car laden with pipes and rocks, as if it was some kind of gangland rumble. More recently, the political landscape had been shaped by the bad-man style of politicians who'd notoriously brandished guns on the stump at election rallies. All had played a part in a coarsening of the culture. Even Bishop Blair buckled up and attended to parishioners with a .45 gun on his hip.

Just as the mood darkened in the country, so too did the music take a turn. The reverberations from the devaluation of the pound, articulated in the Wailers' 'Pound Get a Blow', were felt strongly in former colonies like Jamaica. And as Niney the Observer was to sing, it was not a time for weak hearts: it was an occasion for 'Blood and Fire'.

Bunny Livingston emerged from prison to an uncertain future and no immediate source of income. He was not party to the $100 a week contract with JAD Records, and was reliant initially on his compadres for a helping hand. 'Bob and Peter would give me a little pinch every time they get stuff.'

The group's contract with JAD was welcome but creatively the association was proving something of a cul-de-sac. Danny Sims would argue that the fault did not lie with him. He had attempted to help them fashion music that was exportable but the American DJs had not taken the bait. Frank Crocker's response was typical, remembered Sims. 'He said, "Danny, you bring your gun, your dope, your money but this material here, you gotta bring a translator. It'll never be played on the R&B stations."'[238] The association with JAD exposed certain tensions between the three young men. Livingston was sensitive to the charge (largely imagined and authored by himself) that he was 'excess baggage' and was being carried by the group. Others, on the fringes of the Wailers, noticed an unexpected consequence of even a little improvement in their finances – the greater ease of procuring ganja. And although ganja might free up thoughts, and perhaps also suggest lyrics, it could also act as an impediment to creativity.

'Peter Tosh was equally as talented as Bob,' recalled the DJ Wayne Jobson, 'but he was not as disciplined. If Peter was in Kingston and he heard there was a particularly good draw of herb half an hour from Negril, he'd immediately hit the road.'[239] Perhaps the musical impairment had not so much to do with consumption; after all each of the Wailers became heavy smokers. More important was the use of time each made *between* smoking. There are scores of witnesses of the dedication Marley showed towards songwriting – among them Anthony Doyley, a young Trench Town admirer and future reggae star (as the lead singer of Knowledge): 'Each morning he would come and go into park . . . and I would be standing there listening to him make these sounds until one day he put it on record . . . I think that just came naturally because Bob sings like eighteen hours a day. When Peter and Bunny would be gone to their respective homes Bob would be sitting there until four o'clock in the morning playing his guitar, and tuning the voice.'[240]

Rita Marley maintains that it was her husband's sense of frustration about the limits of their music at this period that led to the Wailers' next move, linking up with eccentric producer Lee 'Scratch' Perry.

You gather after only a few minutes in his company that Lee 'Scratch' Perry has spent decades refining the art of sowing confusion. I track him down at Hellshire Beach on the outskirts of Kingston. Behind the idiosyncratic style there is method. A baseball cap is studded with jewels to resemble a crown. Chunky rings adorn each finger. Half a dozen gold chains loop from his neck to navel. Tasselled Aladdin's slippers round off an effect which is less carnival and more cockney pearly king (an earlier version of ghetto-fabulous bling). His eyes travel: they cannot be caught because they will not rest. Almost immediately the clowning begins. He doesn't even remember his whereabouts from this morning, let alone the day he struck a deal with the Wailers. I finally settle on a strategy that is akin to taking a run-up to the jump. Let's travel back to arrive at that moment of launch.

'Where were you on Independence day?' I ask.

He has a smile as slow and even as a lift rising: 'I don't rightly know, you know, sah.'

A day that *every* Jamaican alive at that time can instantly recall is 6 August 1962. It's like asking Americans where they were when the news came through that President Kennedy had been shot.

'C'mon,' I plead, 'you *well* know where you were. Where were you?'

Perry's eyes lock onto the Aladdin's shoes. A joker's cackle is just about stifled.

'So, where were you?' I ask again.

He shuffles about like a school child who's just been caught playing truant.

'Whereabouts? One of those parts, sah. Who can say?' Perry's slippery, studied linguistic (and very Jamaican) obfuscation is best practised on non-Jamaicans. It was a manner that was already fine-tuned by the time he met the Wailers, but they recognised it for what it was, and were generally not amused. Tosh and Livingston least of all.

Lee Perry, who styled himself 'the Upsetter' had emerged from the ranks of Studio One where his first task had been to make himself familiar with brush and broom. By the time he left Clement Dodd's care he'd transformed himself into an indispensable producer. Perry was not shy of pointing out his attractions: 'When people hear what I-man do them hear a different beat, a slower beat, a waxy beat – like you stepping in glue. Them hear a different bass, a rebel bass, coming at you like a sticking gun.'[241] Ultimately, the mixing-desk wizard parted company with Dodd in a fit of pique over the studio boss's differing assessment of his worth. Notwithstanding his irritation over the irreverence shown to

him, Perry did not much care for propriety – a characteristic which was
evidenced by his immediate disregard for the dynamics of the trio, and
his transparent favouritism towards Bob Marley. He seemed unperturbed
by Peter Tosh's resentment about being marginalised from the creative
heart of the Wailers. In a group of three vocalists, only one could lead,
and though Perry conceded that 'Peter Tosh was an artist by himself,'
he preferred to concentrate on Marley, believing his musical intelligence
matched his own. Perhaps Perry sensed that Marley was by temperament
far more given to experimentation and accommodation. Bob Marley was
more likely to be intrigued than alarmed by Perry's eccentricity (bordering
on psychopathology) which saw him, for instance, 'planting' an LP in
his yard each time a record album was produced. If Tosh's displeasure
centred on the business of production, then Livingston's jealousy was
personal. He had always felt closer to Marley than anybody else, and
believed now that Perry was trying to 'take over' his soulmate, his 'inch
man'. His suspicions seemed to be born out when the producer invited
Marley to move into his yard, all the better to hone some of the creative
ideas forged in the intense heat of their musical collaboration.

Something of Perry's impish and mischievous nature crept into the
records he produced for the Wailers. The tracks were by turns innova-
tive, experimental and exuberant. 'Duppy Conqueror' was a prime
example – a playful and satirical exposé of the superstition about Obeah
and duppies that was still abroad in the land. Perry's account of the
origins of that song revealed the sympathetic mutual understanding that
he and Marley were developing. 'I said, "Well look here, Bob, I want
you to write a tune with 'yes me friend, we on the street again' in it."
He gave me the third line, I gave him the fourth line and so on. We
started to work together and the ideas started to flow till finally we
made the tune 'Duppy Conqueror'.[242]

In part, Perry's genius was to team up the three Wailer vocalists
with the extraordinary rhythm section of the Upsetters – the Barrett
brothers, Carlton on drums and Aston on bass. Both were graduates
of the Trench Town School of music: make your own instruments
and teach yourself to play. Starting off on tin pans and a one-string
banjo, they'd become consummate musicians whose skills were in such
demand that they appeared on numerous line-ups, including not only
the Upsetters, but also the Hippy Boys, and now the Wailers. Their
own prodigious output was born out of a financial necessity to service

various commitments, Aston's more obviously than his brother's. Aston was commonly known as 'Family Man' – a reference to his latitude towards family planning that had rewarded him with a tribe of children by the time he was out of his twenties.

Though a year older than Bunny Livingston, it was a mark of his reverence towards the Wailers that Aston Barrett referred to Livingston as "Sir". Of the three vocalists Barrett found him the least approachable, 'not too chatty, chatty'. Nonetheless, Barrett was privileged to be associated with the Wailers. He was not alone. Even rival groups such as the Paragons expressed that veneration of being 'let into a secret' when watching the Wailers rehearse. 'It was like being on a spaceship, listening to the music of the spheres.' A sensation, no doubt, enhanced by 'licking the chalice' or drawing on a spliff.[243]

But Family Man's deference towards the trio was in sharp contrast to the attitude of their new producer, Lee Perry.

In reinventing the Wailers' sound, Perry too often gave the impression of erasing all that had gone before. His critique of the Wailers' earlier proven successes irked. Strangely, for a man who considered himself something of an amateur psychologist, his distinct lack of deference appeared either clumsy or wilful, or both. Lee Perry's armchair psychology had been learnt at the dominoes table. He claimed that, 'Through dominoes I practised my mind, and learnt to read the mind of others.' Though Perry was astute enough to realise that Livingston was 'a guy that don't like you to rough him', there was a gulf between observation and practice. He ought to have been capable of greater empathy, having been on the receiving end of Dodd's disfavour. 'Coxsone never wanted to give a countryboy a chance,' Perry later reflected. 'No way. He took my songs and gave them to people like Delroy Wilson. I got no credit. Certainly no money. I was being screwed.'[244] But Perry seems to have been of the school of thought which said: 'Do unto others what you have had done to yourself.'

Perry had a reputation for being reluctant to part with cash. Yet he cast himself as a generous patron who once provided Aston Barrett with a car, a Ford Anglia, in lieu of wages or royalties. With his lion's share of subsequent sales, such apparent generosity came to be seen in the same light as the Conquistadors' trinkets exchanged with the natives for gold. Musicians' wariness towards him was not uncommon.[245]

Initially, the Wailers were prepared to put their misgivings to one side. While they were in the trenches, still struggling to find their way – despite some success – working with Perry, and the musicians associated with him, was undoubtedly leading to a maturation of their music. Money was still tight though, and the Wailers were forced, once the songs were ready, to search for record studios who might offer their services on 'trust' (credit). Musical equivalents to Miss Reenie were increasingly hard to find.

Livingston described a further breakdown in trust when they took their business to the usual recording studio outlet at Randy's. The Wailers had gone there to record the track 'Duppy Conqueror', but they hadn't paid up front. Unbeknown to them, Randy Chin's confidence and largesse had diminished somewhat during the economic downturn. From now on, he'd advised his assistants, they might put their faith in God, but everyone else would be obliged to part with cash. The Wailers wrapped up a final take of the recording but they had no money to pay for the session. Of course when the record was released they'd settle up – maybe even with a little interest – but, in the meantime, the recording would have to be on 'trust'. Randy Chin wasn't at the studio that day, and his assistant, Errol Thompson, mindful of his boss's edict, wouldn't release the master tape. In the ensuing fracas, Bunny Livingston, by his own admission, 'had to resort to violence'. He swung a piece of timber at Thompson. At first, the assistant managed to avoid it but then Livingston swung again into his ribs. The timber broke in two, leaving a jagged edge which Livingston pushed under Thompson's throat. It was enough of an inducement. Thompson 'trembled as he went for the tape'.

If Bunny Livingston was not being too liberal with the truth, then the Rastafarian approach to settling a dispute through reasoning (even if at times a frank and heated 'nose-to-nose' variety) had deserted him that day, and would do so in the future. He increasingly displayed a preparedness to threaten violence as a means of conflict resolution. And in the coming months, the mercurial Perry would find himself on the wrong end of Livingston's ire.

The first inkling that something was fundamentally amiss in the Wailers' relationship with the producer came with the artwork on the sleeve of the album *Soul Rebels*. Judging from the cover, the group's Rasta sensibility was not shared by Lee Perry. Instead of a demure and conservatively clothed Rasta woman, the album *Soul Rebels* was emblazoned with a female guerrilla fighter brandishing a machine gun and sporting a khaki shirt, tantalisingly parted to the tips of her nipples.

The soft porn look of the album's cover did not gel with the righteous image the Wailers had started to forge for themselves. But it wasn't just 'the photo of the titty business that upset we', remembered Tosh. More problematic and disturbing was the fact that the group had been kept in the dark. No one had bothered to canvass their opinion.

The dispute over the cover was a mere dress rehearsal for what lay ahead. The tipping point came at the bar of the Sombrero Club when the excited band members met the producer to discuss the chart success of 'Duppy Conqueror', and the album *Soul Rebels*. Despite their oral contract, when the record started to sell, Perry informed them that contrary to expectations 'it wasn't a 50–50 situation' any more. He could only afford to pay 10 cents per record sold. While Marley argued ineffectually with the producer, Livingston stood to one side, listening and growing more and more impatient. He imagined having to explain the position that the Wailers now found themselves in to disbelieving friends. He could already hear the mockery: 'But oonoo idiot. After all you go through with Coxsone. After all you go through with all them people, you come back again and go deal with Scratch, and you have no agreement!' All the while he was listening to Perry's justifications Livingston's hands clenched the back of a chair. He kicked it over now, and began turning over tables at the bar. He picked up a chair to break over Perry's head and had to be restrained by Marley and Tosh.

Furniture was righted. In the lull that followed, there might still have been a possibility of reaching some accommodation, but the Wailers insisted on returning to the subject of their royalties and to the level of record sales. Suddenly Perry sent one of his retinue to fetch a bottle from the car, and when she returned, he directed her to put it on the table. A conciliatory gesture perhaps to change the mood over a drink? But when Tosh asked Perry what was in the bottle, at first he wouldn't say. Eventually, he answered calmly that it was acid. Peter Tosh was livid. He demanded to know who it was intended for. Perry refused to speak further. Tosh opened the bottle and threatened to pour it over him. Perry didn't blink. Perhaps it was just some strange hoax? Peter

Tosh was incredulous but, according to Livingston, when he eventually smashed the bottle, a strange vapour issued from it. 'It smoke, it smoke.'[246] The meeting broke up without Perry explaining his bizarre behaviour.

Perry remembered the encounter differently. The veiled threat was all in the mind: 'That was [Peter's] suspicion; there was no acid there. That came out of his thoughts. They always think me have something to do them something, but it was only in their thoughts because they know I wasn't chicken.'[247] Whichever version is correct, one thing is sure: all three Wailers turned against the producer. Their dispute did not rest solely on the belief that Perry had short-changed them on royalties, but also on the revelation that Perry had credited himself as the author of a number of their songs. The Wailers (as a group) would never work with Perry again.

They had hoped for better from Perry. The Afro-Jamaican expected to be cheated by the Chinese-Jamaican, the Lebanese-Jamaican or the Anglo-Jamaican, but on some primitive level, black men and women carried in their collective DNA a memory of both the desirability and possibility of cleaving together, 'colour for colour' and 'blood for blood'. Time and again, in the face of a welter of contradictory evidence, black Jamaicans (the Wailers were no exception) continued to champion the dream of black unity. If Tosh, Livingston and Marley still doubted its unlikelihood, then their dealings with Perry confirmed that black people were just as capable of donning the uniform and practices of Babylon to exploit each other. Consistently, throughout their careers, hoping that the longed-for ideal of unity might be realised, they would find disappointment. In this, they were like the gambler addicted to losing, and disoriented by success.

Even so, the Utopian New Jerusalem – a society where the black population was no longer exploited – seemed a little closer in the late 1960s with the rise of a radical new movement, Black Power, which had emerged from the civil rights campaigns in the USA. To be a black man walking the streets was to be in a permanent state of rage. The meaning of Black Power was apparent in America. It had a certain cachet. You could imagine it referring to the aspirations of a minority group who were still disempowered but sensed change. But what did it mean in countries like Jamaica? Transplanted to the Caribbean, Black Power created confusion. When the Trinidadian writer, V. S. Naipaul, wrote about it, he attached an ironic question mark to the phrase. Black Power? Blacks were already in charge, weren't they? Didn't they already have power? What exactly was it then? Well, in the first instance, it had to be acknowledged.

Even the former prime minister, Norman Manley, who had stressed that the harmony of Jamaica was best expressed in the nation's motto: 'Out of Many, One People', was alert to the everlasting appeal of Black Power. 'We have to understand ourselves and dare not ignore Black Power,' Manley told PNP delegates in 1968. 'I salute Black Power.' In his final speech as leader of the party, Manley acknowledged that talk of 'Black Power' had reignited the fears that some of the more privileged sections of society had articulated when adult suffrage was granted to a country with an overwhelmingly black population. But to the fair-skinned elder statesman, Black Power meant 'the acceptance with joy and pride of the fact of blackness, of black dignity and black beauty'.[248]

Manley wrote his treatise in the autumn of his career and in the fallout from the strange affair of Walter Rodney, whose allegedly dangerous extracurricular activities had led to a political farce that had engulfed the country.

Walter Rodney's brief eight-month stint in Jamaica coincided with a growing disquiet in the government about the importation of a black American model of racialised politics which falsely described the problems which beset the island. The 'hundreds of black men in the US [who] were working towards an Armageddon in which Whitey is to be either destroyed or forced to his knees',[249] would find their equivalent in Kingston's ghettoes if the black American propaganda took root. Jamaica's paranoid elite believed themselves to be the substitute for 'Whitey'.

Almost inevitably, this prompted a number of reactionary measures to contain the virus of the Black Power movement. In July 1968 for instance, the Ministry of Home Affairs banned any publication authored by Stokely Carmichael, Malcolm X or Elijah Muhammad.

Rodney entered the stage as the drama was unfolding. An exceedingly bright twenty-six-year-old, the peripatetic Guyanese scholar arrived in Jamaica with his wife and child in January 1968, to take up a post at the University of the West Indies as a lecturer in African History. He found an eager audience for a novel discipline which was treated almost as a vocation, and he would find that Jamaicans outside the university were equally enthralled.

Had Peter Tosh the funds and the qualifications, undoubtedly he would have enrolled on the course. Tosh consumed all of the African literature – especially African history – that he could get his hands on. When Bunny Livingston compiled an inventory of their reading during their time together, he recalled that he was a 'top literature man, reading Shakespeare especially. Bob read a lot to get his lyrics, and for direction. He read books on music technique and others which dealt with rhymes. Peter read about martial arts and African history.' The idea of Africa loomed large in Tosh's imagination and through his songwriting he would arrive at the stark and simple conception that 'As long as you're a black man, you're an African.'[250]

Tosh translated his words into action when he demonstrated on behalf of his black brothers in Africa. Earlier in the year black Jamaicans were outraged by the Smith regime in what was then Rhodesia, when it hanged a number of its black citizens in an act which many equated with judicial murder. Tosh, alongside the producer Prince Buster, took his protest to the streets. Demonstrators from Trench Town and beyond converged on the British High Commission. On 12 March 1968, the *Gleaner*'s front page was dominated by news of the demonstrations. Inconspicuously, towards the bottom of the page, the paper reported that Winston McIntosh of 19 West Road, Kingston, was among protestors who refused to be dispersed by the police, and was arrested and charged with obstructing the traffic. Tosh was not identified as a member of the Wailers, perhaps the editors were not familiar with him or the group but as far as Trench Town was concerned he was a local hero and champion of Africa.

The idea of Africa had undergone a transformation in the popular imagination in recent decades. No longer did it elicit pity and embarrassment; rather it conjured ancient glory and pride. In those days, remembered Viv Adams, the very name 'Africa' contained a certain magic. And sections of the population's news-gatherers (guilty of the Jamaican reliance on approximation in lieu of absolute truth, namely: 'If it nah go so, it nearly go so') had impressed their neighbours with the *fact* that Walter Rodney, the visiting Guyanese lecturer, was actually an African. To the authorities, he more resembled an agitator. He wore dashikis and an Afro, possessed a beard, and professed an admiration for Che Guevara and the Black Power and Black Consciousness movements in the USA. Central casting could not have provided a more worthy candidate for a security file. Jamaican intelligence services duly obliged. Students were electrified by his lectures, but out of hours he made a point of limiting his time on 'the most bourgeois of campuses' among the 'rum-sipping, soul-selling intellectuals' who were classed as his colleagues. Rodney wrote to a friend back home:

> I try to find some meaning among the mass of the population who are daily performing a miracle, they continue to survive! Kingston is meaner than when you left it . . . Today, all that matters is the question of action . . . against imperialism and its cohorts . . . Che Guevara is the ideal Revolutionary man. All that is required is that one should extract the essence of his life's experiences, rather than attempt to embrace his numerous suggestions concerning guerrilla warfare . . . I doubt whether the situation is explosive, and I doubt whether I will be here long enough to witness the explosion.[251]

Briefings from the security forces suggested otherwise. Undercover policemen, dressed as Nyabinghi dreads, followed Rodney to Rasta yards where he reasoned with the brethren and tapped into their 'cosmic powers'. Rodney was later to reflect in his *Groundings with My Brothers* that he was humbled in their company and that the pampered, educated fools at the university should sit at the feet of the Rastaman and 'hear him tell you about the Word . . . You have to listen to their drums to get the message of the cosmic power. And when you get that, you get humility, because look who you are learning from. The System says they have nothing, they are the illiterates, they are the dark people of Jamaica [but] I got knowledge from them, real knowledge.'[252]

Rodney may have sounded like a starry-eyed convert, but the Special Branch operatives were more concerned about what the Rastas might be learning from *him*, and about the effect on them of his powerfully seductive message. They shadowed Rodney wherever he went. Robin 'Bongo Jerry' Small, who'd dropped out from the middle class and a privileged education at Jamaica College to live among the poor, often acted as a guide for Rodney. Small noted that the ghetto people didn't really know anything about Rodney but that 'the news spread about this African doctor, everybody describing him as an African doctor who come to get involved in the black struggle. Him was just a doctor of philosophy, but people refer to him as an African doctor, and you know how powerful a title that is.' Small arranged an itinerary which included stops at Local 37, a chapter of the Ethiopia World Federation, which had been set up by Mortimo Planno, and also a session at Planno's 5th Street yard. In particular, a visit to the Clarendon stronghold of Reverend Claudius Henry, recently released from jail, was viewed suspiciously. And even more potentially incriminating were the gatherings Rodney convened at the university, sometimes attended by irreverent Rastas. On one occasion, Small recalled a flurry of note-taking by police informants when a 'Rastaman got up and say in reference to the academics led by Walter, "You have the brains, we have the brawn, just give us the guns and we will do the rest."'

In general, the report cards of the Special Branch officers scored low on precision but high on drama. Ultimately, they struggled to build an indictable case against the lecturer, and even conceded that despite the personal appeal of the man who could talk the talk, occasionally addressing himself as 'I man Irie, I man dread', and an intellectual whom Rastas respectfully referred to as 'Brother Wally', he was a man they were 'unwilling to accept as a leader'. Nonetheless, the agents concluded that Rodney was just about to set light to a blue touchpaper under Jamaican society. In particular they claimed to have received intelligence that at the height of the tourist season (more than 70,000 cruise-ship visitors arrived in the first nine months of that year), instead of posing for snapshots, he was 'trying to incite [Rastas] to attack tourists'.

The security file was bulging by October 1968, when Walter Rodney was invited to attend a black writers conference in Montreal. No sooner was he off the island than the prime minister summoned the vice-chancellor of the University of the West Indies, Sir Phillip Sherlock, for urgent talks. Sherlock tried to disabuse the PM of some of the queer notions that he held about Rodney: for example, that the Guyanese lecturer had shaken students out of their usual concerns about the canteen food and was shaping them into mini-revolutionaries. Though sceptical, the vice-chancellor left promising to conduct his own investigation, though he had in mind a more considered longitudinal study than a snap survey. The next day Sherlock was bemused to hear, along with the whole nation, an emergency government broadcast on the radio that

The Wailers in relaxed mode

Colin Grant with the local herbalist, Brother D, at his church in St Thomas, an area renowned for its Obeah-men

Grant with Sister Mariamne Samad, who turned her home into a shrine to Marcus Garvey

The Wailers pass the 'Old Grey Whistle Test' in BBC television studios in 1973

The Wailers pose for a publicity shot for the album
Catch a Fire – their first for Island Records

Peter Tosh goes solo with *Equal Rights*.
He would sacrifice 'peace' for 'justice'

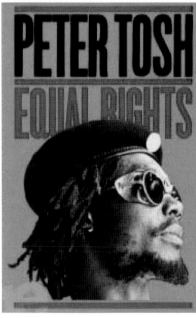

Peter Tosh in harmony with Mick Jagger –
on tour with the Rolling Stones in 1978

Bunny Wailer, once more in his element on stage, in communion with Jah

The gates of Bunny Wailer's property

Bob Marley and band members are joined on stage at the One Love Peace Concert in 1978 by the prime minister, Michael Manley and the leader of the opposition, Edward Seaga

The Natural Mystics
away from the crowds
in splendid isolation

Rodney had been refused permission to re-enter Jamaica as an undesirable person – a move underscored by the subsequent newspaper headline
blazed across the front page which read:

GOVT. ACTED TO SAVE THE NATION

In breathy, fulminating prose, the *Gleaner* revealed the discovery that Dr
Rodney had been at the centre of a plot to stage a 'Castro-type revolution on the island', and that the lecturer had turned the 'Mona campus
into a hotbed of anti-Jamaican organisation'. A pamphlet, 'prepared on
the university', was uncovered which allegedly gave 'instructions for an
insurrection and for maximum violence and destruction including the
burning down of the university'. Outlining the scale of the conspiracy,
the prime minister had ominously informed the house that 'the animosity
and talk of rebellion', under the guise of Black Power, was not just
to be directed at 'whites alone but against mulattoes and all brown-
skinned persons as well'.[253] Presumably, the brown-skinned students
were to be exempted.

The barring of Rodney unexpectedly induced the very act it was
designed to forestall, as student protests quickly escalated into violence
and destruction. Detecting the shoots of dangerous radicalism among
the left-leaning 1968 student population had become a favourite pastime
for acerbic newspaper columnists and middle-class households. Caroline
Cooper, a contemporary student, recalled that at the time of her enrol-
ment, her parents were so anxious that they solicited the prayerful services
of their pastor to accompany her – in much the same way, suggested
Cooper, 'that other believers would have taken their child to an Obeah
man for protection from bad-minded and grudgeful people'. Nonetheless,
Cooper joined the marchers.[254]

In the days that followed, the *Gleaner* was pained to report a
strange and disturbing sight, one never before witnessed in Jamaica:
brown-skinned middle-class students clad in their red, blue and purple
academic robes protesting alongside scruffy and hardened agitators,
'some identifying themselves as Rastafarians', and bizarrely shouting
slogans of 'Black Power'. Cars were overturned and buildings set alight.
The police and army were called out and curfews were imposed. They
fired teargas and clashed with the demonstrators. Fires raged. Cowed
and besieged officers of the fire brigade refused to man units. There

was no more water, as Niney would later sing, 'to put out the fire. Let it burn. Let it burn!' Buses of the Jamaican Omnibus Service were set ablaze or hijacked. Inevitably, people from Trench Town and the other ghettoes were drawn to the flames. Ranked among the protestors and gangs of young men roaming the downtown area was Peter Tosh.

Tosh was a man given to larks and high jinks. He had an enormous capacity for fun, recalled Wayne Jobson. 'Peter was running jokes the whole time.' As well as humour, he possessed a store of courage and daring that sometimes tipped into recklessness. 'He was a man,' concluded Jobson, 'who liked to take chances.'

Tosh arrived in the midst of the uproar and demonstrations, and towards the end of the evening, buoyed by the heightened mood and extraordinary events, he took it upon himself to commandeer a hastily abandoned coach. Sat behind the steering wheel of the forty-seater 'weedy' bus, he headed for a shopping precinct. Tosh rammed the bus through the glass front of a store, and Kingston's finest went in and helped themselves to the loot. The happy shoppers climbed into the bus and Tosh reversed out and sped away to Trench Town. Everyone considered it to be 'well cool', remembered Livingston, 'but Papa Joe Williams was vex!'[255]

At Palisadoes airport Walter Rodney had not been allowed to disembark from the plane bringing him from Montreal. He was never re-instated, and, after a few days in which scores of the street protestors had been injured and several killed, the demonstrations petered out. Armed soldiers had encircled the university and prevented students from leaving. In any event the students' enthusiasm for protest had dimmed significantly after the police made plain their intentions to no longer discriminate between the street people and the students, and to dispense with teargas and use live ammunition should they not desist.

Few doubted that Jamaica had been through a seminal moment in its history. After the smoke had cleared, Mortimo Planno even commemorated the Walter Rodney riots in a poem. Rastafarians identified with Brother Wally and found common purpose with the man whom the state had declared *persona non grata*. The Rodney affair gave a fillip to the Rasta movement. The orbit and reach of Rasta crept insidiously beyond Trench Town and the other settlements. Not only had Rodney invited Count Ossie and his drummers to the senior common room at the Mona campus, but the traffic also began to go the other way; Rasta centres like 'Open Yard' increasingly became the preferred destination for disaffected left-wing intellectuals and students who began to place a greater emphasis on the unexplored position of Africa in Jamaican history. Their plans for re-ordering society along more equitable lines might be given a sympathetic hearing among the Dreads, but not unreservedly so. Rasta parted company with the university-educated brethren on ideology. There was no place, for instance, for Marx in the Rastafarian make-up, and nor for faux revolutionary rhetoric.

Down in the hole of Trench Town, Mortimo Planno was occasionally lured to the uptown homes of Rasta sympathisers. Carole Yawney recounted an episode on one such evening when Planno, invited to a poetry reading, challenged a rum-soaked student who had been full of fiery talk. Did the student know how to make a gun? Did he even know how to procure one? After the fire and explosions, what then? Chances were the dashiki revolutionary would slip back into the comforts of his middle-class existence.

Mortimo Planno passed 'dread judgement' upon those for whom revolution amounted to little more than an intellectual exercise; Rasta was *living* a revolution. For all the talk of solidarity that night, it was apparent that ganja-smoking would not be welcome at the poetry reading. As Yawney explained, that attitude illuminated the gulf that for all the righteousness and good intentions had not yet been crossed by the start of the 1970s. Locksmen, she wrote, possessed a keen eye for weeding out the dilettantes who professed 'to love Rasta but not his herbs'.[256]

While clergymen worried that 'the growth of the Rastafarian Movement, even among the middle class, threatens to outpace the birth rate', other anecdotal evidence suggested the uptake was far more modest; the uptown embrace of Rasta was limited to one or two students who started sporting locks, buying Rasta art, playing reggae records and even 'licking' the chillum pipe.[257] But middle-class seekers of Rasta enlightenment (or even those who just wanted to hang out) could find moving around the shanty towns intimidating, if not menacing. Not all Rasta yards were equally welcoming or willing to authenticate their passports to righteousness. Bongo Joseph's yard in Trench Town, for instance was definitely off limits. Not even combsome brethren (who combed their hair) could venture there. 'A lot of the elder Rastaman was very touchy and very funny [suspicious] when it come to educated youths,' remembered Small.

Even if a university graduate gained entry to a Rasta yard, the cultural mores could be difficult to negotiate. Yawney found in her research that wherever she went she was expected to be 'seated' and have a draw of herb. Yawney ended up smoking more than her hosts, with an inevitable adjustment of her faculties. The lifestyle did not lend itself to the kind of excuse that might be offered for turning up late to your 9-to-5 job or university class.

A gradual 'middle-class-friendly' change would come with the formation of a new branch of Rastafari, the Twelve Tribes of Israel. The organisation which emerged on the streets of west Kingston in mid- 1968 was the brainchild of Vernon Carrington, a former sky-juice vendor. Carrington brought a salesman's simplicity to what he believed to be the problem with the Rastafarian movement – a lack of structure. The template for his sect was taken from the Bible. Carrington and his followers considered themselves the true descendants of the Old Testament patriarch Jacob whose sons – Reuben, Simeon, Levi, Judah, Dan, Naphtali, Gad, Asher, Issachar, Zebulun, Joseph and Benjamin – had founded the twelve tribes of Israel, later scattered to the four corners of the earth. Under Carrington's scheme, each new member of the sect would be assigned to one of the twelve tribes. And further, building on the idea that contemporary equivalents might be found in ancient fables, the Twelve Tribes Rastas placed special emphasis on the Holy Book as a repository of historical and prophetic truths.

Such a conception was perhaps not so remarkable in a society whose population turned to passages of Scripture almost as a tradesman might refer to his manual. Tosh, Livingston and Marley did not differ markedly from their compatriots or even other Rastas in their curiosity over the Bible. For Marley especially, it was almost an appendage: he was forever to be found with a Bible in his hands. 'At one time,' said Esther Anderson (who'd form a lengthy attachment with Marley), 'I told him, "Why not get it over with and sing the Bible?"' But Bob Marley kept a Bible nearby not just because it proved a limitless source of inspiration for lyric writing but also because one of the central tenets of the Twelve Tribes of Israel was that members should read a chapter of the Bible *every* day. Adherents could expect to complete the task in three and a half years. Never mind that as your eyes stretched from Genesis 1 and neared Revelation 22, like the painters of very long bridges who readied themselves to embark on another coat just as they reached the end, the Rastafarian bible-student might need to be re-familiarise himself with what had gone before. Something of that duty and dedication resided in Marley's requiem-like 'Redemption Song' and the mournful plea, 'We've got to fulfil the book.' The secrets of the Scriptures, hinted at in that phrase from 'Redemption Song', would reveal themselves through microscopic analysis. That principle, established by Vernon Carrington in 1968, formed a bedrock of the faith – along with the primacy of obedience to the constituted authority of the sect, headed by Carrington, who was soon to answer to a name more suited to his standing as a visionary: 'Prophet Gad'.

As Bob Marley's commitment to his chosen faith broadened, he began to display an independence of thought beyond the reach of his early mentor, Mortimo Planno. Tosh had never been as taken by Planno's magnetism: his cynicism would not allow it. On his part, Livingston viewed the elder's sincerity as merely an affectation, a veil for command and control; he'd moved swiftly from resistance to Planno to outright rejection. In any event, given his temperament, Livingston's spiritual quest was always likely to be more private. In the Rasta conception, God resided in the individual; there was only 'man and God' or 'I and I'; there was no need for Livingston to worship at any temple other than his own.

But neither Livingston nor Tosh had been subject to the full range of Planno's charm. From the outset, he had locked onto Marley, and, as with others so honoured, the young Rasta had found that the terms of their courtship demanded total submission. His association with Planno was always intense and often suffocating Even so, the inquisitiveness that had first steered Marley towards Planno also made him a prime candidate for the seductive proselytsing of Prophet Gad. And notwithstanding Planno's aggression and determination to maintain pole position in the recognition of Rastafari throughout the island, he would be forced reluctantly to loosen his grip on Brother Bob – but not entirely.

The uptake of The Twelve Tribes of Israel among the middle class, exaggerated by those who saw it as a preface of doom (more than a decade later the scholar Frank Jan Van Djik estimated their membership to be less than 1,000), was, nonetheless, just another manifestation of the escalating interest in Rastafari on the island. The yearning for an identity not governed by a moribund association with Britain, now that the Union Jack had been lowered permanently, was one felt not only by the 'sufferers' in the shanty towns but also by the sons and daughters of the ruling elite. Into that void would step visual artists such as Robert Cookhorne (African), Woody Joseph and Ras Daniel Hartman (a.k.a. Lloyd George Roberts) whose works were snapped up by collectors. But more accessible than the intuitive artists – much more so – were the reggae singers whose lyrics, spoken with heartfelt surety in an uncertain age, were both alluring and irresistible. It was a testament of youth and a nod to an unassailable truth that the black man's time had come.

Leslie Kong sought to capitalise on reggae's rising popularity. He owned the rights to a back catalogue of Wailers' tunes, and he now set in motion a plan to release the best of them. For years, it seemed that the Wailers had been like an anchorless boat, rolling and yawing in a boiling sea. Despite their street smarts, the end result of their endeavours appeared on paper as if they had been no better than gullible novices. It was galling enough then, especially for Marley, for the group to find no better a deal than signing on with Leslie Kong, the man who'd produced his first song for an imagined handsome fee which was in reality small change. Against their better judgement (and, more fundamentally, contrary to their wishes) Kong proposed to release a *Best of the Wailers* album, but as Bunny Livingston pithily observed, the Wailers hadn't yet done their best work so how could there be a 'best of'? Kong would not back down.

Bunny Livingston was presented with yet another challenge to his idea of anger management. The singer is alleged to have tracked down Leslie Kong to his ice-cream parlour/restaurant (on the ground floor, beneath the studio) which also doubled as a record shop, and immediately reverted to type, at least as it was most recently known. The nose-end reasoning did not elicit the positive outcome that Livingston hoped for from his 'lady-like' adversary. Although no blows were exchanged, it has often been alleged that Livingston left the record shop calling down a murderous 'dread judgement' on Kong, vowing that he would not live to see the profits of his treachery. Livingston was rumoured to have then sought out an Obeah-man to put a curse on Kong, much to the amusement of the Chinese-Jamaican producer.

Bunny Livingston's version of the events is, inconveniently, not as dramatic. He does not dispute that all of the Wailers were vexed over the forthcoming issue of the album and mightily annoyed with Kong. But realising that there was little they could do to influence him, they were adamant that at the very least they'd extract some kind of financial compensation. They chased Kong around the island and eventually received a satisfactory amount.

A few weeks after sales of the *Best of the Wailers* had started to rocket, the thirty-five-year-old Kong suffered an unexpected heart attack and obligingly died, fulfilling Livingston's alleged prophecy.

Actually, when it came to the cause of the music producer's demise, Livingston could only speculate, along with everyone else: 'He could have been one of those illnesses that kill someone fast ... some kind of baby germ ... He died fucked up in any event. He just came to the studios to work on some records, felt bad, sick, went home and died.'

Leslie Kong had been the first producer to spot the talent of not just the teenage Bob Marley but also the equally youthful Jimmy Cliff. But if Marley and his group were floundering at the start of the 1970s, then Jimmy Cliff's career was just about to shoot off into the stratosphere. As previously mentioned, Cliff had been lined up to star in a small locally made music and gangster film, *The Harder They Come*.

The film, which substituted the original 1940s rude boy, Ivanhoe 'Rhygin' Martin, for a 1970s wannabe reggae star up from country, who turns bad, as 'bad as sore' as Jamaicans say, broadcast a raft of songs which would become the soundtrack to the 1970s, not just in Jamaica but in many countries around the globe. At its centre was a portrayal of the extraordinary vibrant world of reggae with scenes and attitudes which perfectly mirrored the reality. It offered up fantastic opportunities for Cliff and a scattering of other singers. None of the Wailers, however, made it into the film. Later the director, Perry Henzell, would explain that he'd never considered Marley for the lead role because 'Bob Marley had not really surfaced at that point ... not for me anyway. Jimmy [Cliff] was much bigger ... at this time in terms of selling records and all of that.'[258] However, Rasta artists such as Ras Daniel Hartman and the elder Mortimo Planno were among those offered parts. But Planno was sufficiently concerned about the film's sub-plot, which put aspects of Rasta life on screen, that he spurned the overtures from the film's producers for him to take a starring role.

Planno worried about the negative association that the film seemed to posit, namely a link between Rasta and the criminal underworld controlling the cultivation and distribution of marijuana. When the credits rolled, filmgoers would leave *The Harder They Come* associating Rasta with criminality, that the two were fused together like 'batty and chamber' in Jamaican parlance. That was the fear, but Planno need not have trembled. Almost single-handedly that film raised the profile of reggae in ways that individual artists had struggled to achieve in the previous decade. *The Harder They Come* played everywhere, and even ran non-stop for eighteen months, three times a day, 500 viewers per show, at an independent cinema in Boston.[259] It was the epitome of cool. It was 'well cool'.

And a more compelling lesson for Marley, Tosh and Livingston was the defiant stance of the protagonist Rhygin on the folly of paying attention to the prophets of the hereafter. *The Harder They Come* was a wake-up call to all reggae artists, including the Wailers, that they should seize their share 'here and now'.

EAT THE FISH BUT SPIT OUT
THE BONES

'ME always live in the ghetto. Me don't feel like the ghetto should be my future, like we should always love live inna shit.'[260] Bob Marley yearned for a life beyond the confines of the shanty towns that seemed to be his destiny. His daily 'screw-face' countenance was a visual record of the gulf between the present and the hoped-for future. The frowning features of this youthful family-man registered that this was not the way things were supposed to be. The Marley household was little better off than those of thousands of other west Kingston residents, observed Michael Thomas, with 'nothing except a formica dinette, a glass cabinet for the family china and a radio blasting'.[261] No one deserved to be in the ghetto, Marley would contend. On a good day, he might surrender to the peculiar glamour of Trench Town, which Bunny Livingston alluded to when he described it as a 'magical town like Hollywood, full of stars.'[262] But Marley was a 'big man' now, and when his mood was less sunny, Trench Town became an airless empire of dust, overridden with smells you did not want to give a name to. Then the Rock's famed social cohesion barely disguised an attitude of 'misery likes company', and a desire to see your neighbour remain just like you, a hopeless 'crab in a barrel'.

Marley shared the anxiety of his compadres about where their career was going. After some local success, the Wailers seemed in danger of stalling. All now had children, and were further 'tied up' with each other as a result of these unions. Namely, Tosh had fathered a son with Shirley Livingston (Bunny's sister). As noted earlier, Bob Marley and Bunny Livingston shared a sister, Pearl, from the liaison between Livingston's father and Marley's mother. The Wailers, already a band of brothers, were now knit closer by the ties of blood. Though many Jamaicans laboured under the myth that children didn't cost anything, Marley, in particular, felt stretched by his own family commitments; the twenty-six-year-old musician now had four children.

The record label, Tuff Gong, was supposed to have relieved some of the stress. During the Perry period, JAD Records had given the Wailers the latitude to develop their own projects. Tuff Gong was the first venture. Myriad explanations later surfaced as to the origins of the title. Most common was that it denoted Marley's street name. The early Rasta elder Leonard Howell was also known to his followers as Gong; and Marley is said to have proclaimed that he was 'tougher than Gong'; he was Tuff Gong. Livingston was adamant that the explanation was much simpler. The Wailers had first proposed the title Tuff Gang, but then worried that it might 'send the wrong message'; so Gang slid to Gong. More likely the clue to the name's secret was to be found in the films of J. Arthur Rank. Tuff Gong referred to the semi-naked strongman sporting a loincloth who beat the giant gong with a huge hammer, announcing the start of each film. The various versions highlighted the extent to which as early as 1971 the Wailers' biography was already subject to the old Jamaican adage: 'There is no such thing as facts, only versions.'

As well as this group label, Tosh and Livingston also formed individual labels. Tosh started Intel-Diplo, an abbreviation of Intelligent Diplomat; Livingston weighed in with Solomonic, in deference to the Old Testament's King Solomon. These labels were no exercise in vanity, but rather recognition both of the aspirations of maturing men, and the escalating competition between the scores of talented musicians on the island. Jamaican society was closer to a tradition where you made up your own music; the stories are legion of people discovering their impromptu ditties preserved on another man's record. Batman, for instance, took issue with the Slickers over ownership of the song 'Johnny Too Bad'. He claimed the lyrics, *walking down the road with a pistol in your waist*, were words sung about himself, as he roamed the mean streets of Trench Town.

Each week more and more records were produced for an industry which, given the modest size of the record-buying public, could not possibly accommodate them all. The concept of 'less is more' was anathema in such a scenario: Tosh and Livingston believed that they had to multiply in order to maximise.

By 1971, despite the range and competence of their music, the Wailers had little to show by way of pecuniary reward for their eight years of labour. Indeed, they were even forced to 'diversify their portfolio', and move into other commercial enterprises. When times were tough the group defaulted to the Soul Shack – a record shop/café which they opened in Kingston, and from which they sold cooked food and home-made products like Tosh's hand-carved combs.

In the summer of 1971, a few months before the group severed ties with Lee Perry, Marley's proven skills as a songwriter came to the rescue. Johnny Nash was cast alongside Christina Schollin in a Swedish film, a romance called *Love Is Not a Game*.[263] Nash had visions of it being 'potentially as big as *Love Story*', and when he was also commissioned to compose the soundtrack for the film, he turned to Marley for help.

Bob Marley flew to Sweden to take up the offer. Nash had assembled a motley crew of musicians, including John 'Rabbit' Bundrick and Guy Roel, and lodged them in a large, rented house on the outskirts of the capital, Stockholm. 'A songwriting factory' was Bundrick's description of the house. 'As you walked through it you would hear a conglom-eration of different types of music,' a cacophony of mostly competing and sometimes complimentary sounds issuing from each bedroom, 'all fighting for the same ear space'. There were moments of socialising but mostly each of the writers, including Marley, retreated to his room and set to work.

Bundrick and Roel offered conflicting accounts of Marley's state of mind during his Swedish retreat. According to Bundrick, he kept himself apart from the Swedish contingent. The first encounter wasn't encouraging. One of the Swedes had asked him whether he could 'say something in Jamaican'. Marley didn't answer. After that, whenever 'they did approach him he mumbled and stared at them'. Eventually he'd move off to some other part of the house, 'grumbling something that sounded like "Rass-Clatt" or "Blood-Clatt", or something that I'm sure nobody could quite make out.'[264] Bundrick's impression of Marley's mood was backed up by Rita Marley's estranged father, Leroy Anderson, who bumped into his compatriot and son-in-law during this period. Anderson felt Marley had become mentally 'spooked' and was 'seeing things'. This, though, is more likely to have been a consequence of the hallucinogenic properties of the copious amount of marijuana that Marley was smoking, rather than any serious psychosis.

Far from being a sociopath, Roel remembered him regularly holding forth. Even though Marley made little impression on him save for his 'beautiful "Afro" hairstyle' (after all he was a 'nobody' at this time), Roel was struck by the thought that 'Bob seemed more like a preacher-man than a musician.' He couldn't be sure just what kind of religion it was. Only years later would Roel come to realise that, as they sat around Marley, everyone had been listening to the enthralling 'sermons' of a religious faith largely unknown outside of Jamaica: Rastafari.[265]

Everyone was pleased with the progress of the soundtrack's composition, but after several months of intense labour, the musicians were notified that the producers had run out of money, and that their salaries would be stopped. As the musicians began packing their bags, Nash's manager, Danny Sims, suddenly had a brilliant idea about how to 'find' the extra cash. He would summon an expert card sharp from America and they'd seek out and engage Stockholm's best poker player in a night of gaming. The card sharp arrived, magically, with an enormous amount of cash, and the game was on. Marley and Bundrick were confined to the kitchen, so far away so as not to see any of the action (not even the identity of the American card sharp), but close enough to hear the Swede repeatedly 'shuffling money to his side of the table, saying something in Swedish, which probably meant, "Better luck next hand."'

But there was no better luck. The steadily diminishing mountain of cash and subsequent stream of curses from Danny Sims elicited uncontrollable guffaws from Marley and Bundrick. When every last dime was gone, Danny Sims stormed into the kitchen obviously about to vent his frustrations violently. With a vicious blow, Bundrick was knocked to the ground. It was Marley's turn next. Sims was a 'big guy' but Bundrick was amazed to see that Marley remained coolly in his chair. As Sims approached, Marley fixed him with an even stare and said with barely a trace of emotion: 'Yuh rass, yuh nah rass wit I, mon, clatt.' Sims didn't need a translation. He hesitated, thought better of it, turned and left angrily; and Bundrick witnessed a slow grin play across Marley's face. Rastafarians renounced violence but Marley (even though a small and tidily built man) never lost the ability to suggest its imminent arrival.

Love Is Not a Game was not a high point in Swedish cinematic history. Finished in a hurry, it played for the premiere and then disappeared from the nation's screens. The romance was a disaster, critically and financially. And 'there was a general escape' afterwards, remembered Roel, 'All of them ran away without paying the bills.' But even so, Nash was particularly aggrieved that Marley had left before him, taking Nash's guitar in lieu of outstanding fees. 'When I work,' Marley would tell an interviewer many years later, 'I have to get pay.'

Bob Marley seemed to have a knack for being off the island at key moments in its history. He had flown to Europe, leaving Bunny Livingston and Peter Tosh behind (Rita had decamped with the children to the USA to stay with Marley's mother) in the run-up to a tumultuous general election.

One of the many peculiarities of Jamaica is that both main political groupings, the People's National Party (PNP) and the Jamaican Labour Party (JLP), make the claim that they are a workers' party. They have no choice if they want to win. Victory can only be achieved by winning the working-class vote: the electorate is overwhelmingly black and working class.

The JLP would appear to have had a head-start. It grew out of the first major trade union on the island, the Bustamante Trade Union, modestly named after its founder, Alexander 'Busta' Bustamante. A popular leader ('messianic' was the preferred phrase of his critics), Busta's reputation rested on the arguable distinction of being 'for the poor people'. The British considered him volatile. At the height of his popularity, after the 1938 Frome Rebellion, Bustamante was reported in correspondence with the Colonial Office to have 'once advised cutting the throats of all the white population'.[266]

'Busta' had dubbed the rival PNP as the 'brown-man's party'. On first inspection the argument could not be brooked. Founded by the fair-skinned, middle-class lawyer Norman Manley, and fiery intellectuals (all from 'good homes') who initially ploughed their energies into the independence movement, the PNP was assumed to cater politically to the middle-class palate. But then in 1940 the PNP declared itself to be a socialist party – notwithstanding the purge of its radical wing shortly thereafter.

Both parties, by degrees, championed the idea that, after 1962, the post-independence nation had moved into a period commonly known as 'Black Man's Time'. But though they might harangue each other on the election stump or across the floor of the House, out of hours they packed away the rhetoric and passed the cocktail glasses. In the 1970s, after a night of trading insults with each other the two leaders of the political parties would sit down and breakfast together.[267] A more appropriate and shared political slogan might be: 'Government for the (black) people, by the (brown) people.'

It was perhaps the genius of Michael Manley (the successor to his father, Norman, as leader of the PNP) to align himself with black people through cultural artefacts, in a manner which made him unassailable. Manley recognised the importance of reggae and other symbols of working-class identity, and he clothed himself in them. While the JLP clung to the tradition of the European coat and tie, Manley's frontbench was marched off to seamstresses to be fitted out in the 'Kariba' (a two-piece suit with a safari-type jacket), which was more suited to a tropical climate. Michael Manley also courted Rastafarians, convening a meeting with elders who called their particular Rasta order (House) the Judah-Coptic Theocracy Government, and made a much publicised trip to Ethiopia. He claimed to have been given a special rod by Emperor Haile Selassie and brandished it at political rallies. When the people looked up at the platform, they no longer saw a privileged 'brown man' who the generation before might even have 'passed' for white. They held their heads up high and marvelled at how Manley had been transformed into Joshua, with his rod providing correction to his rival, the prime minister, Hugh Shearer, who was cast unwittingly as Pharaoh. Moses had brought the enslaved Jews out of captivity but it was Joshua who led them to the Promised Land; Manley's acceptance of the title was underscored by his rallying cry that 'the New Jerusalem is ours to build, and we will say with John in the Book of Revelation: "And I saw a new heaven and a new earth; for the first heaven and first earth were passed away."'[268]

Rita and Bob Marley had been sufficiently seduced by Michael Manley's rhetoric to sign up for the PNP leader's 'caravan of stars', accompanying him on the campaign trail. The entertainers would serve as Joshua's trumpets to bring down the old regime and free the people. Livingston only agreed to perform once he was assured of a $150 performance fee. 'Joshua' criss-crossed the island in the weeks leading up to the election, heralded by the sound of his adopted campaign song, the hugely popular, 'Better Must Come', which was played by Delroy Wilson (Batman's brother) and his band at several PNP rallies.

The song's opening line: '*I've been trying a long, long time, still can't make it*,' might have applied readily to the Wailers, as well as the scores of hopeful youths who continued to pour into Trench Town. Mostly, they constituted unemployed 'gangling teenagers,' recorded Michael Thomas, who had run away 'from cane fields and five-acre farms, all looking for something faster than chopping cane and humping bananas all their lives. Not sure . . . what they're looking for at all – except they all know about Jimmy Cliff and Desmond Dekker and the rest of them.'[269]

Many of the youths who came from the countryside soon regretted their impetuousness. They found themselves with limited prospects, and could only dream of the stellar success of the leading vocalists, Jimmy Cliff and Desmond Dekker.

Local triumph was gratifying but ambitious reggae acts like Dekker, Cliff and the Wailers yearned for the scale of recognition and rewards that could only come from gaining the attention of much bigger audiences in the U.K. and U.S.A. The Wailer's brief sally into North America at the end of 1971 – trying out at half a dozen venues in New York and Pennsylvania – had passed largely unnoticed by the trade press and public. By 1972, like Cliff and Dekker, Bob Marley was on the fringes of the great London metropolis, where he was joined by the rest of the Wailers in the spring.

Bob Marley's estrangement from Nash and Sims hadn't lasted long, and the Texan singer's anger at the 'borrowing' of his guitar seems to have dissipated by the time of their reunion. The secret to his magnanimity might have been detected in the wide grins of the CBS executives who had signed Nash to their label. The Texan had struck gold with his very first outing for the recording giant with the reggae-inspired album, *I Can See Clearly Now*. As a flattering review in *Rolling Stone* pointed out, up until then the 'irresistible rhythms of Jamaican music' had been overlooked by much of the great British record-buying public. Aside from an early interest in ska expressed by the mods and skin-heads, reggae was 'generally despised rather as rock'n'roll [was] in the 1950s, as performed by and for ignorant people'. But according to the review the 'brilliant pop record' had changed that perception in an instant. Thousands of copies disappeared from the shelves every day. Marley was credited as a 'session musician' on the album but also the author of three songs that had the potential to be hits – 'Stir It Up', 'Comma Comma' and 'Guava Jelly'. Magnanimity was the very least he might expect.[270]

Bob Marley had been signed to CBS along with Johnny Nash, but largely as a favour to Nash and Sims. The African-American duo had brokered that deal to appease a restless Marley and perhaps give truth to the lie that, now that they moved among the 'players' in the recording industry, his goal of recognition beyond the limits of Jamaica was within their power. Actually, Marley was only of marginal interest to CBS. He cut a single called 'Reggae on Broadway' whose banal, sexually sugges-tive lyrics only lacked the sound of the bottom of a barrel being scraped. Possessing neither the wit nor exuberance of Chuck Berry's 'My Ding-a-ling' or Max Romeo's 'Wet Dream', Marley's CBS debut suggested that, in a drive for some kind of commercial success, the compass that had guided him to the creative stable of Lee Perry had gone awry in England. Perhaps mercifully, 'Reggae on Broadway' was poorly promoted. 'Johnny was the big star,' recalled Stuart Slater, a publicist for CBS. Slater arranged a mini tour for Nash and Marley, mostly of schools and Mecca social clubs (on non-bingo nights). He didn't 'remember anyone saying [about Marley], "Watch out for the support act, he's brilliant."'[271]

If Bob Marley was an appendix of Sims and Nash's grand ambi-tion, then the rest of the Wailers were appendices of an appendix. All were waiting for something – anything – to happen. They had hoped Nash's success would have had a knock-on effect, a seamless transfer of kinetic energy akin to the silver-balled executive toys that were becoming fashionable. Suspended from a frame, each ball gently abutted the other to form a cordless necklace. You raised one ball in the air, let it drop, it swung into its stationary cousins in the middle, and miraculously shunted the end ball to a height seemingly equal to the first. In the case of the Wailers, there was little reverberation from Nash's triumph, hardly even a tremor, although Nash was gracious enough to have Marley tag along (as the friend of the star), and to introduce him to potentially useful contacts. But Marley's invitation, for example, to join music-industry revellers on the last commemorative journey of the luxury commuter train the 'Brighton Belle', travelling from London to Brighton, may have been a privilege but was unlikely to lead to anything other than a day out at the seaside.

Paul Merry, another press officer for CBS, recalled the unknown Jamaican sitting quietly in the shadow of Johnny Nash as he gave important interviews to music magazines. The picture would have been complicated had his partners been invited. Livingston and Tosh would have had more trouble refraining from comment. To the effusive rock journalists who touted the Texan pop star as *the* King of Reggae, Tosh and Livingston would have protested: 'You lie! You lie!' And while Nash was pampered by CBS executives and stayed in an elegant Georgian apartment in central London, the Wailers (joined by the Barrett brothers) were decanted to the suburban wilderness of Neasden – though not far from Trojan Records (a label which collaborated with Island Records in distributing Jamaican music). Finally, 'Reggae on Broadway' was not the cocky calling card of a group on the cusp of popular acclaim, nor was there reassurance to be gained from performing as the support act for Johnny Nash at ballrooms in unfancied Dunstable, Northampton or Croydon.

In the Amharic language of the Rastas' beloved Ethiopia, there are seven different types of silence. One morning the Wailers woke to the kind of silence that is accompanied by dread – the horrible silence familiar to sailors whose engine has failed and who are now left becalmed. Livingston, Marley and Tosh woke to the realisation that they could no longer wait for, or rely on, Danny Sims to engineer the next all-important stage in their career. Several competing associates have sought credit for what they did next. No matter the veracity of their claims, one thing is clear: later that cold September morning in 1972 the Wailers boarded a bus and wended their way to Basing Street.

The deconsecrated church at 8–10 Basing Street in Notting Hill served as studio and offices for Island Records, a label run by their countryman, Chris Blackwell. They had never met, but Blackwell's reputation preceded him. Lately the triumph of *The Harder They Come* (Blackwell had released the soundtrack to the film) had been followed by a calamity: the loss of its star, Jimmy Cliff. Blackwell had spent a considerable amount of time grooming Jimmy Cliff as the next big thing. He had loaned him to the film-makers for the duration of the shoot. Critics had been amazed by the depth of the music and by the dramatic background which the movie revealed. Newcomers to reggae who stumbled across the film were struck by the raw and powerful sound that was 'as bone-marrow irresistible as the blues'. Critics lined up and genuflected. Cliff was at the helm of music 'more earthy and real than Johnny Nash's', according to *Phonograph Record*. 'Believe me,' wrote its critic 'you'll wonder how you managed to live so long without it.' The journalists were mostly saying the same thing: 'You've been happy enough with the sizzle, but here is the meat.' On the back of its critical success, the Island boss had exciting ideas about how to build on the rude boy, rebel image that Cliff's character projected in that film. But after the release of *The Harder They Come*, Jimmy Cliff decided he no longer needed Island Records and was snapped up by a bigger record company, EMI. Blackwell was devastated.

If Mortimo Planno had demurred over the film's depiction of Rasta life, then Jimmy Cliff began to feel ambivalent about his association with the problematic image of the badass black man who would cut you if you crossed him; in his own life, Cliff was more choirboy than rude boy. Whatever Chris Blackwell had had in mind, his projection obviously ran counter to Cliff's image of himself. Blackwell, though, was not alone in his sense of the passing of a great opportunity. Perry Henzell, the director of the film, also believed Jimmy Cliff had made a miscalculation: 'Right after the movie [Jimmy] got into a black Muslim thing.' In fact, on the album that he released after *The Harder They Come*, 'he was wearing a suit and tie and carrying a briefcase, and he had sort of close-cropped hair.'[272]

One week after Jimmy Cliff left Island Records, the Wailers breezed through the front door at Basing Street and into the office of Chris Blackwell. Livingston, Marley and Tosh looked like they had just walked off the set of *The Harder They Come*, recalled Blackwell. They possessed an attitude that was both defiant and arrogant, which left some people appalled. Blackwell was thrilled.

If the Island headquarters was not entirely well cool, it was on its way to being so. The progressive independent label took its cue from its founder. Island was relaxed. The one concession to security, noted a regular visitor, was to insist that none of the staff 'smoked dope on the premises during office hours'.[273] Chris Blackwell and Island was surely a company that the fiercely independent Wailers could do business with.

'Soon Come', the Jamaican mañana, was, I had presumed, an attitude adopted by the black man. Growing up in a Jamaican household, my siblings and I, along with all our black friends, simply characterised it as 'Black Man's Time' and an alternative to Greenwich Mean Time. As the decades passed though, with each visit to Jamaica, I came to see it less an expression of a laid-back, laissez-faire attitude and more an act of revenge. After centuries where every hour of the working life of their enslaved forebears had been prescribed, it was time for black people to declare: 'It's we turn now'. Black Man's Time was a facet of Black Power. It explained the surliness of the chef whom I'd heard a few years ago 'talking back' to the waitress as she relayed my complaints about the length of time it took for the food to arrive. The chef had shouted, all the better for me to hear, 'Mek him wait!'

But I had been wrong about one aspect of 'Soon Come'. I had assumed it to be a 'black thing'. If so, then the blonde-haired, green-eyed Blackwell was as black as they come.

Never before had it been suggested to me that I might like to take a swim before conducting an interview. Chris Blackwell was running late (shorthand for he'd gone for a ride on one of his jet-skis). Through her array of communication gadgets, Blackwell's assistant had only determined that he was somewhere in the vicinity of Golden Eye, his exclusive estate, formerly the home of Ian Fleming. Since purchasing the property, Blackwell had added to and transformed Golden Eye into a scattering of discreet and luxurious holiday chalets, complete with a perfect beach overlooking an azure sea. 'No trunks?' said the assistant. 'No problem.' She disappeared and returned shortly with a pair. 'Chris won't mind. He has lots of pairs.'

After the swim, I was escorted down to a hidden alcove where Blackwell was waiting. Despite his fisherman's cap and crumpled tracksuit, and one leg draped over the arm of a wooden chair, his bearing was that of an aristocrat, freed from prevailing standards of convention. Immediately, I was impressed by two things: his Jamaicanness and his charm, which is quiet but radiant.

Blackwell's eyes grew ever more lambent as he recounted the story of his initial involvement with Jamaican music, firstly ska. No, the upper-class son of a plantation-owning family did not feel out of place in that black working-class environment. Even when his would be the solitary white face in the impromptu dancehalls of downtown 1950s Kingston, Blackwell felt at home.

Chris Blackwell ascribed his comfort being amongst black people to a childhood blighted by asthma. He grew up sick and 'isolated from other children, from other English or expat children in Jamaica'. He wasn't involved with the usual upper-crust social set. In fact, the only people he 'interacted with were the staff'. The staff were black. Consequently, said Blackwell, 'at dancehall sound systems I was very at ease because as a child the only people I'd spent time with was the simpler people.' And the impetus for his subsequent involvement in the music industry stemmed from that simple pleasure in 'turning people on to things that you liked'.

Blackwell has a connoisseur's delight in words and storytelling. He spoke deliberately and thoughtfully. In a curious way, though he never used expressions like 'yes man' and 'you dig', you half-expected them at the end of every sentence. 'Evenings at the dancehall were electrifying. You'd just go to a yard, and the sound was pulsating from a huge box. This incredible sound would burst forth. The speakers and amps were put together by Jamaicans which allowed for them to carry a huge amount of bass. Terrific, very, very exciting.' The more Blackwell spoke, the more he conjured up for me the image of Norman Mailer's hip 'White Negro'. Ska had been a substitute for jazz. Like his counterpart in Greenwich Village, Blackwell was an urban adventurer 'who drifted out at night looking for action with a black man's code to fit their facts'. In the bone-quaking excitement of downtown dancehalls, among poor but unfettered revellers, the Jamaican hipster 'had absorbed the existentialist synapses of the Negro, and for practical purposes could be considered a white Negro'.[274] Blackwell didn't recall anyone putting down their drink when the white boy walked into the dancehalls in the 1960s. 'I must have appeared an odd character, but they accepted me. No one troubled me.' And a decade later, when the Wailers walked through the door of his office, Chris Blackwell attempted the same trick of disabusing the black guys of any preconceived notion of him as a representative white Jamaican.[275]

*

In 1972 the British public's excitement about a piece of African-centred exotica peaked, but not with the arrival of the unheralded Wailers. More than a million Britons, enthralled by tales of mummies and ancient Egyptian curses, joined the eight-hour-long queues for a glimpse of the remains of Tutankhamen's tomb, exhibited at the British Museum. That curiosity was not extended to a Jamaican band.

For months, the Wailers had been foraging in the dark, making little progress or impact in England. The jig was almost up: they lacked even the funds to return to Jamaica. But Chris Blackwell believed that it was *his* good fortune to meet them. They announced themselves through their smell: an ever-present, cloying fug of marijuana clung to them. 'They were nobodies, but they were like huge stars in their attitude and the vibe they gave off,' recalled Blackwell. He had been warned that in reality they were much more like the Rhygin character played by Jimmy Cliff in *The Harder They Come*. They were 'trouble', but Blackwell immediately saw their potential. The minute they stepped into the studio, they demonstrated their worth. 'They were ready to work but wanted to do things pretty much on their own terms.' As Jamaicans would say, they would 'eat the fish but spit out the bones'. Chris Blackwell knew instinctively that 'they were the real thing' – elemental and talented musicians, though with an undeniable rude-boy attitude that was yet to be reckoned with.[276]

From the very beginning Blackwell demonstrated an unusual sensitivity towards the Wailers. He certainly wasn't going to 'rough' them. An aesthete at heart, Blackwell was so delighted by the magical first encounter with the trio that there was no contract suggested or signed that day. Talk about money would have sullied the romance of it all.

The gentleman's agreement would be ratified shortly after. Eventually, a figure of £4,000 was agreed as an advance on a future album for Island Records, to be recorded back in Jamaica. The deal though was predicated on being able to extract the Wailers from their contractual obligations to Danny Sims and JAD.

Danny Sims was a reluctant divorcee. John 'Rabbit' Bundrick witnessed the final explosive argument between Marley and the boss of JAD Records in a suite at the Grovesnor House Hotel when Marley tried to break the news to him. Danny Sims hadn't seen it coming. The corollary for Sims's dilemma was to be found in one of the central storylines of *The Harder They Come*. A Kingston pastor had taken in an orphan girl from the country. For years he had attended to her spiritual and material needs. For her part, she had excelled as a member of his church's amen corner, and kept house for him. But the pastor's virtue had masked his lechery for his pre-pubescent charge which, with the arrival of an unworthy suitor, had come to a head. Now that the girl was ripe and ready, the pastor wanted first pick.

The analogy only held up to that point. For when Sims and Blackwell hammered out the generous terms of the separation, Sims insisted on a proviso – his retention of publishing rights to the works of the Wailers – that sweetened the loss.

All sides pronounced themselves content, but Chris Blackwell had perhaps taken the bigger gamble: a £4,000 advance was much more than the Wailers had ever been paid. On one level it was just a risky move by an otherwise shrewd businessman. Though when one considered the shared history of these countrymen, Blackwell's offer could be seen to be not just an act of faith, but also an unstated acknowledgement of the past toxic relations between Jamaica's white and black population.

For almost a decade the group had been at the mercy of parasitic middlemen whose only saving grace was the fact that they were black and not white. Exploitation by your fellow black man had to be judged alongside centuries of ancestral hurt – even if it was never examined or articulated in those terms. All producers were 'pirates', according to Peter Tosh. Nonetheless, the Wailers were astounded by Blackwell's relative largesse. They were not alone: Island Records executives could not fathom their chief's inexplicable decision. Ultimately, Blackwell had acted on a hunch. 'Something about them' convinced him that they wouldn't disappoint.

Chris Blackwell hadn't been so excited about a Jamaican artist since the spectacular success of Millie Small and 'My Boy Lollipop'. His signing of the Wailers was like a homecoming. There was a renewed spring in his step when a few months later he disembarked from the plane bringing him back to Jamaica. Despite the outward appearance of calm, he was riddled with an energetic nervousness. Like the 'birthday boy', Blackwell could barely contain his eagerness to find out what the Wailers had created with the money. Tosh, Marley and Livingston swung by the hotel and picked up Blackwell to take him the studio. The first song they played to him was 'Slave Driver'. And Blackwell confessed the truth that he was so 'excited that they had recorded anything!' Somehow in the intervening months he had managed to keep that doubt from himself. Now he could relax. 'It had this great bass line.' Hearing the line 'catch a fire' in the second song, Blackwell immediately thought of it as a possible title for the album. The next song up was 'Concrete Jungle', which the Island boss considered 'the most complex reggae song' he had ever heard. Miraculously, the Wailers had produced the militant rebel music he'd been hoping for. He could have been forgiven for giving himself a hearty pat on the back. Blackwell's trust in the rebel group had been rewarded: 'I knew enough about music to recognise that every penny of the £4,000 had gone into the album.' The master tapes would be sent to London, where Blackwell planned to smooth over the rough edges of the music, to sweeten it, in order to make the record 'more palatable for the rock audience'.

I pondered just why the unashamed honesty of Chris Blackwell was so disarming, as, when the the interview was over, we climbed up from the alcove to join his lunch guests: an assembly of Jamaica's wealthy elite, whose complexions ranged from apple blossom to ebony. Perhaps the enigma of Blackwell was that as well as the shrewdly calculating businessman, he retained something of the quality of an amateur botanist or lepidopterist who worried over his impact on the ecosystem. This came to mind with Chris Blackwell's reflections on Millie Small. In 1964, after the astonishing worldwide success of 'My Boy Lollipop', Blackwell had accompanied Small as she returned to the island to a spectacular hero's welcome. Thousands lined the roads as her motorcade passed from the airport to the hotel. When they arrived, Blackwell was struck by an odd and unsettling gesture from Millie Small's mother, a simple country woman who had put on her Sunday best to come to town. The fifteen-year-old pop star glided out of the limousine, down the carpet to the atrium to be reunited with her mum. And Blackwell was astonished to observe that, when Millie Small's mother came forward, she curtsied to her daughter.

Ten years on, having listened to the Wailers' extraordinary raft of songs, Chris Blackwell contemplated the impact of his intervention on the future of both the group and Jamaica.

11

VOW OF THE NAZARITES

THROUGHOUT the spring of 1973, the Wailers' tour bus, an old Mercedes, sped along asphalt roads that were a monotonous, gun-metal grey, straight and never-ending, or so they seemed. England was cold and unforgiving. Compared to their life lived in the open in Jamaica, especially in Livingston's estimation, Albion was a locked-up nation, a grey fortress of stone.

Catch a Fire had been reviewed favourably in the UK. In 'The Wailers and the New Reggae', Carl Gayle enthused: 'It would be a sin for me to recommend the rebel music of the Wailers to anyone who had not previously listened to reggae music, because it is too good.' The photo accompanying that newspaper article, showing the group in a studio laying down a track called 'Reincarnated Souls', perhaps explained why the rock pundits were so intrigued: they had never seen anything quite like them before; the Wailers were without precedent. In the middle of the frame, sporting a lumberjack shirt and mini-dreadlocks, Marley sings with unbridled joy; Bunny Livingston, in an oversized, woollen beany hat, fumes quietly on the drums; and in a crocheted bobble hat and sunglasses, a frowning Peter Tosh looks strangely detached. The Wailers gave the impression of simultaneously being idiosyncratic and exquisite in their appearance, as well as not caring a jot.

British journalists, just like their American counterparts, were enthralled by the look and sound of the Wailers, but their enthusiasm had not been matched by punters who, even if they had heard of the Wailers, were largely indifferent. 'They weren't terribly well known,' recalled the tour manager, Benjamin Foot, 'They'd be booked into grotty little clubs,' often as the support act to an equally obscure band. 'There was barely enough room to move on stage, but they were all incredibly professional.'[277]

Each morning the band would pile into the Mercedes on the next leg of its charm offensive. Before anything else of course, even before breakfast, remembered Foot, the serious business of rolling the first spliff of the day would begin. Benjamin Arthur Foot, the son of Sir Hugh Foot, the former governor of Jamaica, had been handpicked by Blackwell to act as minder and tour manager for the group. One of his foremost tasks was to secure a regular supply of marijuana to meet their daily requirements. Foot did not notice any difference between perform-ances with or without ganja because there never was an occasion when they went without. Food was yet another important consideration. The British diet of meat-and-two-vegetables was out of the question, as was the staple fish 'n' chips supper. Foot spent much of his time sourcing Indian restaurants (where they ate almost exclusively) and ringing ahead to remind the chef not to add any salt to the pot. Anxiety over food was later quelled by the arrival of a man named Gilly, when he joined the tour as soulmate and unofficial cook for the Wailers.

Coincident with the emergence of a European philosophy of existen-tialism, Rastafarians had evolved an existential and holistic way of being which had come to be called 'livity'. It encompassed a set of fundamental principles. Healthy living would be ensured only by consuming (v)ital foods (mostly vegetarian); a draw of herb aided mental hygiene, and spiritual contentment might eventually be reached through the adherence to a set of doctrinal teachings centred on the Old Testament. Benjamin Foot was struck by the sincerity of the Wailers' Rastafarian faith. They were 'down-the-line Rastas', and Tosh, in particular, had the bearing of the 'Mountain Rastaman'.

Being on tour in the decadent heart of Babylon would prove problem-atic. Livity was more difficult to achieve in the urban conurbations of Kingston and Montego Bay than in the bush, where you might live off the land – sowing your crops of callaloo, yams and potatoes or catching fish or janga in the streams when the 'river come down'. But over several decades, the Rastafarian lifestyle had adapted to the shape and contours of Jamaica's ghettoes. In any event, the towns were never fully urban; peasant migrants brought the countryside with them and, in part, replicated a rural existence. English cities and towns – London, Bristol, and Milton Keynes – posed much greater challenges to an idea of livity.

Though Benjamin Foot had spent his early years in Jamaica and understood patois, he noticed that, at times, 'the Wailers would launch off into extreme patois, hoping you wouldn't understand'. But stranger than the attempt at exclusion was Foot's realisation that the three burgeoning reggae-rock stars were not conforming to type in arguing about the state of hotel rooms, the order of songs in the set, or gossiping and fighting about girls, girls, girls. Rather, the windscreen would fog up with heated exchanges about the Bible; and though not necessarily theological discussions, their language was always peppered with quotes, biblical metaphors and allusions.

The tensions between the trio and the other band members, the Barrett brothers and Earl 'Wire' Lindo, were of a different character. Though Tosh, Livingston and Marley undisputedly formed the nucleus of the Wailers, the others, especially Aston Barrett, resented the supposition that *they* were merely session musicians for hire. Privately, Barrett maintained that it was only after the Wailers had 'joined forces with the Barrett brothers that they begin to have real success'. The brothers had not been party to the contractual arrangements with Island Records. Only Tosh, Marley and Livingston had been signed, and Aston Barrett harboured an unarticulated resentment that later would be couched in the language of betrayal: 'From we move out of Jamaica, there were five of us. It was like an army, a battalion, and we were all together, so if one man got wounded, then you're not supposed to leave him. You're supposed to pick him up and bring him in.' For now he was keeping such feelings to himself. In any event 'Family Man' believed that they had an oral agreement, and placed his faith in Marley (from whom they received their wages) that he would not skank them.[278]

At times Barrett found all three frighteningly elitist. Livingston, in particular, could be distant and disparaging – barely disguising his feelings that, but for the vagaries and discomforts of touring, he and Barrett had little in common. Clearly they did not belong to the same reading circle. While Livingston snuggled up with a chapter of Revelation, Barrett would be poring over comics. On one occasion he reported how his schoolyard efforts to share his comics were rebuffed. 'The man gets real vex, saying not to touch him and that any man who touches him will get sick.'[279]

Bemused, Barrett suffered occasional bizarre discourtesies and lapses in grace but more often Benjamin Foot found himself the object of their unbridled prickliness.

On the road, the Wailers expected their formidable work ethic to be reciprocated. Difficulties often arose, however, because they were three powerful personalities, and the twenty-one-year-old Ben Foot could not conceive of a unifying and standard approach that would satisfy each of them. 'Bob, Peter and Bunny all had their idiosyncrasies. If something went wrong when dealing with Peter, you'd be exposed to his deep well of anger. You'd be in even more trouble if you'd inadvertently done something to upset Bunny. He was the most scathing. Bob could be counted on usually to remain sanguine and amenable – but not always.' Generally, though, the group was amused by the irony that 'the son of the former governor of Jamaica was at their beck and call, looking after a bunch of Rastas'.

Nevertheless, an undercurrent of tension around race relations was ever present. For instance, 'In personal dealings with Bob, it was always fine,' recalled Foot, 'but if you met him in a group of people and asked him to do something that hadn't been initiated by him, then he could be unbelievably rude,' unleashing a stream of vitriol with the final words 'white boy' attached like the crack of a whip. Then Foot would serve as a proxy for Babylon, responsible for all the present and past transgressions, slights – real and imagined – against the black man.

Like many black people in London at this time, the Wailers felt themselves under scrutiny by the host population, and their antennae were alert to any suggestion of treatment different from that afforded to, or expected of, the native Englishman. They were particularly perplexed when the demands expected of them were *less* than they expected of themselves.

Tosh, Marley and Livingston recognised that they were, in a sense, on trial in the UK, with the prospect too of further scrutiny in the US. The terms of the trial were simple. Island Records would fund them for the duration of the tour. In return, they had three months to generate a following for themselves and to convert the pleasing reviews into respectable record sales. A spot on 'The Old Grey Whistle Test' would help.

With the passage of time, the BBC television programme has assumed an importance of mythic proportions in serving as *the* platform for emerging bands to break through to a mainstream audience. Actually, it was a programme for 'serious rock' aficionados recorded on the kind of shoestring budget which reflected its minority appeal. Nonetheless, its invitation to the Wailers to broadcast two of their songs represented an enormous opportunity. The title of the show was inspired by an old tale about the doormen of the music publishing houses in London's Denmark Street (known as Tin Pan Alley). Back then, so the fable went, the first pressing of a record was always played to the grey-suited doormen, 'the old greys'. The tunes that the doormen could both remember and whistle, having heard just once or twice, were said to have passed the old grey whistle test.

The Wailers prepared for the programme as if 'The Old Grey Whistle Test' was an actual test. Somehow, between the trio, the thought had arisen and taken root that crossing into the bastion of Television Centre they'd be met by facety (facetious) and sceptical BBC men who would doubt not only that the instruments they held belonged to them but also whether they knew how to play them. The BBC was regarded as the custodian of culture, not only in Britain, but beyond its shores and especially in its former colonies. Auntie (as the organisation was affectionately known) held all the cards, offering true validation of everything on offer. On 1 May 1973, Livingston, Tosh, Marley and the rest of the band squeezed into the tiny clapboard studio and began to play; and any vestige of scepticism, if it had ever existed in the minds of the BBC technicians, disappeared. 'Very cool, professional and laid-back,'[280] was the photographer Alan Messer's memory of the session. Almost forty years on, the recording still possesses an eerie quality that is affecting and powerful.

A strangely haunting sound creeps up and rises from the guitar opening of 'Concrete Jungle' into the mesmerising and ethereal harmonies of the three men. It is an extraordinarily unguarded performance, evident in the soaring lyrics but also in the intimations of suffering and flashes of sorrow on Marley's face. At times you feel you shouldn't be watching this narrative of their ghetto lives rendered in song – such is the sense of a private display of a profoundly felt emotion.

At subsequent radio interviews and press calls, Foot noticed that Marley was frequently nudged forward as the front man. Not that he was the leader of the band, just that he seemed most at ease with the media requests. Journalists were seduced by the Wailers' cool, and failed to disguise their thrill in being so close to it. This was not the make-believe, middle-class cool of the Rolling Stones variety; it was cool of another order. One that came naturally, an enigmatic, black, Miles Davis kind of cool – chilled but dangerous. The black brethren who headed up the Wailers exhibited a total coolness that was at once both ancient and modern: a cool as old as the eternal Maasai warrior watching over his herd, or the cheetah stalking a gazelle; and as new as the Black Panther leader, Huey Newton, pictured in an iconic photo enthroned on his African wicker chair, in black leather jacket and beret, with a spear in one hand and a rifle in the other. Music journalists imagined themselves arbiters of cool as they 'hung out' with the band and detailed their Jamaican mojo. Just how cool? Check out the spliffs, brother. Forget the little piddly shared hippie spliffs passed round so often you ended up sucking on air. The Wailers rolled Cuban cigar-sized spliffs; cathedrals of cannabis packed into cigarette papers sculpted into the shape of ice-cream cones. But outside of the gushing, journalistic interest, the rewards from 'The Old Grey Whistle Test' were not immediately apparent.

Inevitably, the length of time spent on the tour was subject to the law of diminishing returns. But if Livingston's perception of what they were being asked to do and how they were treated was increasingly negative, no one was particularly surprised.

Bunny Livingston's antipathy towards touring had been expressed even before boarding the plane for London. In Jamaica, he hadn't showed up for many of the rehearsals, preferring to remain at the shack he'd bought with his earnings at Bull Bay, a simple Rasta settlement. Physically just a dozen miles from the capital, but spiritually light years away, Bull Bay was where you went if you were a town Rasta and wanted to renew your faith; to connect and ground with your brethren, and savour the 'sea and fresh air and inspiration'. The joy of Bull Bay for Livingston was that there were 'no mechanical devices, just tree and birds and butterflies ... Not like the concrete jungle what just destroy the youth.' Bull Bay was littered with temporary shelters now fashioned into more permanent abodes and populated with nomadic brethren who might have attended one of the big Nyabinghi ceremonies there, and had been so seduced by the vibe and the setting that they'd stayed on. It presented you with the kind of life, mused Livingston, 'what everyone should have the opportunity of living'.[281]

Esther Anderson, a twenty-six-year-old model, actress and photographer, had been appointed by Blackwell to assist in managing the Wailers, and along with Tosh she'd been sent to fetch Bunny Livingston from Bull Bay. When Livingston spied her at his gate, said Anderson, 'he started ranting like a madman'. She was not allowed inside, but as 'the shack was full of scorpions running across the floor', Anderson was not especially disappointed. Lunchtime passed. Suppertime came and went. Then, close to midnight, remembered Anderson, 'we heard him start to sing. It was scintillating and beguiling. He sounded just like Jimmy Cliff. I was just knocked out, and Peter turned to me, smiling and said enigmatically, "You see how it go."'[282] Tosh coaxed his compadre back to Kingston. They flew to England the following week. And Anderson was reassured that, despite her irritation, Livingston had been worth the wait. But the roots of his discontent were never unearthed or articulated, and just a few months later, halfway through the tour, Bunny Livingston's doubts started to re-emerge.

Not just Livingston's but all of the group's suspicions were aroused when they were lined up to appear on another 'live' television show. But this time, there was no sound check for the microphones, 'and rather than plug their leads into amps, they were told to put them in their back pockets.' The Wailers 'had a serious problem', recalled their manager, 'with the idea that they were being asked to mime'. It appeared to be some kind of 'joke t'ing' and did not sit comfortably with men who, though still only in their late twenties, were decade-long veterans of the music industry.

Being on tour in a foreign country is dislocating. The skewed experience of the traveller schools him in paranoia: harmless episodes appear sinister; you wander into an area which locals swear is safe but seems more like a danger zone. Esther Anderson recalled one day mustering the courage to ask Peter Tosh why he permanently wore dark glasses. Tosh answered, only partly in jest: 'Me nah want Babylon to see what I am thinking.' But there was no comic relief to be found in Livingston's company; each day his mood darkened further.

He struggled to dismiss the looming impression that venues which had earlier appeared quaint and quirky were actually 'freak shows', frequented by proto-punks who spent most of the evening leaping and spitting into the air, and skinheads 'all in leathers, dangerous-looking guys, with tattoos all over'. Still, no matter their vulgarity and yobbish-ness, at least their testosterone-fuelled actions were familiar; but every Wailer, to some degree, agonised over what they'd signed up for when the clubs began to look suspiciously camp and possibly gay.

On closer inspection by Livingston, even the London house which served as a base for the group was a measure of the disrespect shown to them. According to Anderson, the very worst that might be said of the accommodation, a three-storey house off the King's Road in a fashionable part of the capital, was that it was 'shabby-chic'. But when Livingston pushed open the door all he saw was 'a little dump that was occupied by some artists who hadn't yet moved out . . . [with] a narrow staircase and just one mattress on the ground.'

Livingston's was not a view widely held. But to the suggestion that Marley was content, he might have argued: 'Well, that's because Brother Bob doesn't live here any more.' Marley was more often now to be found around the corner at Esther Anderson's place. Yet the place was not the main attraction. Esther Anderson was a stunning middle-class, light-skinned Jamaican model. In recent years, she had swapped bill-boards for the silver-screen, and was last seen in an amorous embrace with Sidney Poitier in the heartrending love-story *A Warm December*. Miss Anderson had, in the words of the *New York Times*, delivered a 'breathtaking performance' and was 'an actress to watch';[283] she most certainly was not the sort of young lady who was meant to be found in the company of a 'dutty Rasta-boy'. The subtleties of her indiscretion would be lost in London's permissive society, but it was an index of the changes in *Jamaican* society that she embraced the idea of flying back home with Marley once the tour was over, and continuing their romance.

Livingston chalked up her name to the list of ills of Babylon to which they were exposed. His displeasure seemed to be based more on the fact that Marley was taking up with a middle-class woman, rather than his being unfaithful to his wife. The vows of fidelity fell outside of the vows of the Nazarite. Rastafarian livity did not extend to the holistic desirability of monogamous relationships. 'Although Rastafarians argue strongly for the integrity of the nuclear family,' Carole Yawney observed drolly, 'their attitude in this regard is approximate to a double standard. In the area of intersex social relationships, the Rastafarians appear to have maintained traditional West Indian standards.'[284] The Caribbean writer V. S. Naipaul had put it more bluntly: they were 'lethargic except when sexual predators'. As their fame grew, then so too did the propensity of the Wailers to 'scatter their seed', and with the myriad women came additional pickney (children). By the final count, Livingston failed modestly to break into double figures; Tosh took his tally to ten children; Marley soared ahead with thirteen; and the bass player, Aston 'Family Man' Barrett, settled for fifty-two.

When questioned about the women in Marley's life, his friends would answer that 'Bob was a man who just love women.' He was not alone. Judging from my random survey on the island, there was a whole lot of loving going on.

It wasn't long before I worked out that Trevor, the driver who would carry me all over the island, worked to his own rhythm. Luckily, I was staying at the guesthouse which he ran with his wife Yvonne, so he was punctual in the mornings and would always get me to my destination on time. But thereafter his timings became more haphazard. After dropping me off in the morning there would be a long wait for his return. I suspected he was disappearing each time to spend a few hours with a girlfriend. I didn't want to broach the subject because I had grown fond of Yvonne and was nervous about where the conversation would lead.

I stumbled into a potential trap one afternoon when I asked Trevor about the very many ringtones on his phone. Each time his phone rang it seemed to do so with a different tone.

He played them back to me. 'This one I know is Sylvie, this one Nadine, this one Margery,' and so on and so on. 'Anytime the phone ring I know who it is even before I pick it up.'

'Who are all these women?' I asked.

'Friend,' he answered in a way that left no room for a follow-up question.

There was no shame in this married man's admission. 'This is just the way it is,' another Jamaican told me. 'My father is a bad-boy rascal,' Tosh had said, 'him just go around and have a million-and-one children!' Marley's father had been prosecuted for bigamy, and Livingston senior was, according to his son, 'a champion when it comes to getting children'.

In Jamaica there seemed almost to be a pathological emphasis on the urge to procreate. Edith Clarke had noted in her survey of sexual attitudes after the Frome Rebellion that the ability to father a child was taken as validation of a man's virility and proof that the woman wasn't a 'mule' and to be pitied. If anything that attitude had hardened over subsequent decades. The greatest insult you could levy against a man was to suggest that he was a homosexual. In her research on Rastas in Kingston, Carole Yawney recorded that when schisms arose and a group split into factions, the rival elders would come and whisper to her about their new-found nemesis, 'but you know, of course him is a batty man'.

What better way to display your heterosexual credentials than to lay siege to all the women on the island, to take your pick of the fruit as soon as it ripened. As I reasoned with myself, the memory of Professor Hickling's apologia sounded in my ears. We should not forget about slavery and the single-sexed barracks and the men encouraged to 'visit to breed' with the women and produce creolised slave children for the plantation. Thinking on this matter did not seem to have evolved much beyond Bustamante's 1930s fulminations in the *Gleaner*: 'The sin of it lies heavily upon the European who had them in slavery, taught them illegitimacy, and bred it in their minds.'[285] Yes, all was true. Undeniably so, but stripped bare of its historical perspective, Hickling's analysis might be just be construed as a version of 'It's just the way it is.'

Cuthbert's hair was blue-black; he'd evidently had some trouble with the dye. The tips were blacker than the roots, giving an overall impression of two tones. It wasn't immediately apparent why he'd felt the need to disguise the grey strands that would ordinarily have grown: he looked younger than the sixty-five years that he confessed to.

Once the formalities were over, I was allowed to call him Bert. That he'd been married five times seemed both a source of pride and amusement for him. Later on, he corrected himself, modestly scaling down. It was 'four wives actually', because one of the marriages had lasted only a month, 'so that didn't really count'. The other four had produced a dozen children. He started an inventory of their names but struggled to complete the list and, when blocked, would return to the beginning again; each time was less successful than the last.

Bert had agreed to give me a lift to Savanna-la-Mar in Westmoreland where Peter Tosh was raised. That morning we set out early, before sunrise, in his huge, pristine Cherokee pickup (a stepladder was extended to help me climb on board) in a hunt for fresh fish for breakfast. All along the great swathe of coast, wooden and bamboo stalls were set back from the road. Whenever we slowed down men came rushing from huts; each one brandishing a string of fish. With casual elegance Bert pressed a button and the driver-side window slid slowly smoothly down and stopped halfway; he peered sceptically at the fish.

'What you have for me?' Bert asked. 'It fresh?'

'Yes boss, fresh, fresh.'

'How many days?'

'Two.'

'Two?'

'Maybe three.'

The window slid back up and we moved on to the next stall. But at each stop, the morning's offering disappointed and Bert would have me (and the vendors) know that he would rather go without than accept inferior produce.

'You see what we dealing with in this country. This is an island. Man, one thing we suppose to have is fresh fish.'

He was still recalling the incident of the fish in the afternoon when we called on Ken, a friend, who was to accompany us on the drive to Savanna-la-Mar, where they both had some unspecified business to attend to. Bert and Ken, it was soon apparent, were part of a generation of 'nasty-men' with a seemingly unquenchable thirst for sex.

I knew from having made the reverse journey a few days before that the road to Savanna-la-Mar was treacherous: twenty miles of barely interrupted potholes. Some rudimentary attempt had been made to fill in the larger holes with boulders but they only added to the danger. I would not have entertained travelling that route again had it not been for the prospect of comfort and safety offered by Bert's shiny four-wheel drive. It was with some alarm then that I observed Bert parking and locking the Cherokee and gesturing me towards Ken's very ordinary saloon car.

'We're not going in the pickup?' I asked tamely.

'Ken a better driver.'

No further explanation was forthcoming. Bert patiently held the door ajar; and not wanting to offend, I slid across and onto the back seat and left the two plump little sexual athletes to chat away up front. We settled into the drive and almost immediately the rains came. I understood Bert's deference. Ken negotiated the hazards with consummate ease.

We zigzagged towards Savanna-la-Mar. Country people huddling from the rain stepped out as our car approached and flapped their arms but Ken hardly seemed to notice them. Throughout the long journey the two men kept up their conversation: there was only one subject.

On countrygirls, Ken preferred them 'barefoot and pregnant'. A recent difficult decision had to be taken with a real beauty who apparently suffered from vaginal warts. Her beauty was such that she was worth a 'roll of the dice'.

I began to appreciate the intensity of the rain; it at least censored parts of the conversation which was probably being staged for my benefit.

'You never guess what happened to me last night,' said Ken.

'What?' asked Bert.

'These young gal just won't leave me alone. I just finish with Mona and she take off, maybe two, three in the morning. I tired, man, I tired, and the phone ring. It Shelly.'

'Which one she?'

'This is a gal I've been wanting, trying to mount for quite some time.'

'Bad timing.'

'Bad timing is right.'

'So what you do?'

'Me can't put it on hold. No, man she come straight over.'

Ken paused. He was drawing out the drama, until the punchline, delivered with a snap: 'I dealt with it!'

Ken took one hand off the steering wheel and slapped Bert's in a 'high-five'.

We went our separate ways in Savanna-la-Mar, and met up a few hours later. The business meeting had evidently not gone well. Something of their aplomb was missing on the return journey. The bravura and machismo had speedily fallen away like beads cut from a necklace. The mood was sombre. A pained silence fell over the car, and the longer it went on the more difficult it became to break. Eventually an amusing thought must have crept into the head of Ken that he just had to share.

'You still seeing that old girl?'

Bert didn't answer.

Ken chuckled to himself. 'I don't get it.'

'What is there to get?'

'She's what – seventy-five, seventy-six.'

Bert wouldn't be drawn further on the subject. He stared out of the window for a very long time. An hour passed and then just as we approached the outskirts of Montego Bay, Ken tried again. His tone was gentle, almost apologetic.

'I just thought, you know, she's seventy-six. Obviously . . .'

He stopped short and Bert spoke now as if to save him from further embarrassment. 'She's seventy-nine. So obviously nothing's going on there. Not like you mean. I just like lying down with her and listening to her stories, listening to her memories.'

Esther Anderson was also alerted to this disconnection between the Jamaican male's demonstrable machismo and an interior life that was more nuanced and gentler, when she travelled back to Kingston with Marley and he introduced her to his son. The boy's mother, Pat Williams (another of Marley's girlfriends), handed him over, and Anderson was struck by the tenderness with which he cradled and fed his son. It was so at odds with her own perception of her countrymen. In conversation with Esther Anderson, Marley was a little coy about his 'other' family, and appeared to be in denial about his wife. When Anderson eventually discovered that he had fathered four children, she was amazed because 'he seemed just a boy himself, not long out of adolescence'. She was even more shocked to learn that he did not want to stop at four; Bob Marley was adamant that she should 'have a baby for him'. Esther Anderson, however, had no desire for 'an illegitimate child', and took the necessary precautions. Their discussions and arguments over contraception would later be played out in song.

Anderson always maintained that she took a pivotal role in the creation of 'I Shot the Sheriff', and that, in particular, the line '*Every time I plant the seed/ You kill it before it grow*' had its basis in their arguments over birth control. Esther Anderson relied on a contraceptive coil but after being regularly harangued by Marley, she agreed to have it taken out. Marley was delighted, unaware that there was a caveat to her surrender. Far from preparing for motherhood, in her wisdom, Anderson had asked her gynaecologist, once the coil was removed, to provide her with contraceptive pills instead. And Marley was happy in his ignorance, up until the moment he discovered a packet of pills in her flat. By Marley's reckoning every month presented the possibility for celebrating her pregnancy. Without fail, he would ask, 'Where is the baby?' Yet every month he was in mourning, for the contraceptive had killed the seed before the foetus could grow.

In his rejection of birth control, Marley fell in line not just with the sensual or selfish Jamaican male who preferred to take a chance rather than strap on a condom, but also with the orthodox Rasta view. Birth control was an instrument not simply for the regulation of procreation but for the control of the black man. And the rebellious Rastaman would not be dictated to by meddling social engineers, schooled in Europe or North America, doing the white man's bidding to keep down the black population. Men like Mortimo Planno preached that contraception was genocide. In 'I Shot the Sheriff', Esther Anderson's gynaecologist, Dr Henderson, who became the target of Marley's ire, was transformed into Sheriff John Brown, and was shot down.

The beauty of Marley's music, of course, is that it operates on many levels, literal and metaphorical, and alongside Anderson's explanation are myriad other interpretations. Commonly it is suggested that the seed refers to the marijuana seed, crops and fields routinely burnt to the ground after police raids in Jamaica. But the 'reading' most often advanced is that the seed is a metaphor for the growth of Rastafari so feared by the authorities.

Finally, Marley suggested that the writing of 'I Shot the Sheriff' came out of the growing conflicts within the group'. In boarding the return flight, Livingston gave clues to his future movements. 'Peter joked,' remembered Anderson, that 'Bunny had bought out the whole of England', because he was so laden with goods packed into the hold and overhead compartment on the plane. Bunny Livingston plainly had no intention of embarking on another tour.

When Esther Anderson began taking photographs of the band for the cover of the next album, *Burnin*, she was surprised when developing the films in the darkroom to discover that without any direction from her, the group had naturally arranged themselves around Marley. He was in the middle. A subconscious deference to Bob Marley was not something which Peter Tosh would have acknowledged. Although Tosh was vexed by the fact that Marley's songs formed the bulk of the tracks on the album with only a couple coming from his own pen, Livingston seemed not so perturbed. Indeed, he had assigned the credit of his songs to Jean Watt – a shrewd move, designed to circumvent any future claims on publishing rights by Danny Sims, rather than a sign of generosity towards his long-term partner.

But Bunny Livingston's strategic planning also included unfathomable elements of quixotic 'knight's-move thinking'. He refused categorically to join the Wailers on the subsequent tour of the USA. It wasn't just the possibility of having to perform at various other 'freak shows', Bunny Livingston was tired of the 'environment where you are moving up and down, here and there . . . Going on tour every time you record an album, you've got to be jukeboxing yourself.' Furthermore, he worried about the lure of premature adulation at the expense of his development. 'People get taken away in getting themselves to be a star,' said Livingston, 'and that is a different thing from getting yourself to be a good writer, musician, producer and arranger.'[286] Ultimately, he just wanted to get back to the garden, to the Eden of Bull Bay, a place where you could 'plant your own corn, watch it grow and then pick it'.[287]

Bunny Livingston's absence would exacerbate the tensions between Tosh and Marley. Carl Levy of the Cimarons, who lived with the Wailers for six months, believed Livingston played a pivotal role. 'Bunny was the central, perhaps spiritual, force in the group. Because Bunny was so sure of himself, he never needed to push himself to the forefront. He left that to Peter. Sometimes it seemed that Peter was not as sure of himself as he'd like to be – perhaps he didn't feel that his music expressed himself as fully as he'd have liked.'[288]

The wrangling over the authorship of songs on the album was further complicated by a noticeable shift in attention by Chris Blackwell at Island Records away from the group as an indivisible entity and onto the individuality of Marley. Up until then, through various arrangements, the band had settled on the title 'The Wailers'. But now, at least in terms of marketing, the trio, accompanied by the Barrett brothers and Earl Lindo, were increasingly promoted as 'Bob Marley and the Wailers'. Tosh was livid. In his conception, the Wailers were a holy trinity: three had been called, and yet now only one was chosen. The determining factor would be their personalities. Livingston's withdrawal was as much an act of internal migration as it was physical removal; Tosh, glowering behind his dark glasses, was volatile and confrontational; while Marley was often a tight ball of screw-faced seriousness, his overall manner was inviting. 'When Bob smiled,' commented one of the journalists on the Wailers' trail, 'it was like seeing the sun come out.' It was as if the compadres were three calves who had grown together in the open, and were now powerful bulls trapped in a paddock. Perhaps it was necessary for someone to lift the latch. And that someone was Chris Blackwell as far as Tosh was concerned.

As the trend of training the spotlight on Marley continued, Tosh began to cast Chris Blackwell as a Machiavellian manipulator, guilty of embarking on a policy towards him which in employment law would be classed as constructive dismissal. The intrusion of race into human relations was never far from Peter Tosh's mind. His contemptuous attitude towards Blackwell characterised in his renaming of the Island boss as Chris Whiteworst, might be dismissed as a silly and somewhat crude pun, but at the back of it lay a deeper antipathy towards, or at least suspicion of, the white man. Blackwell needed only to put on *Catch a Fire*'s lead song 'Slave Driver' to gain further insight (he already knew) about the black man's desire to right the wrongs of the unsettled past. *Slave Driver/ The table is turned*. The prime minister, Michael Manley, understood this distemper better than most: 'Anyone who has ever opened his ears to the language of the Jamaican people,' wrote Manley, 'is struck by the persistent tendency to describe as "slave driving" any injunction or appeal to work harder, provided the call comes from those in authority.'[289]

Benjamin Foot wandered unwittingly into the dispute between singer and record boss when Blackwell sent him on a delicate errand. Tosh had gone missing in the build-up to recording the next album, and Foot's mission was to find him. Once that, by no means simple task had been accomplished, Foot was to remind Tosh of his contractual obligations and return with the recalcitrant and, by then hopefully humbled, musician to the studio.

Peter Tosh was nowhere to be found in Kingston. Benjamin Foot tracked him down in Negril. Tosh was with a group of men, at work building a house for him. He was on the top rung of a ladder, and not in an overly inviting mood. Benjamin Foot was forced to shout up to him but was careful to ensure that his tone was respectful and without any hint of reproach. When, Foot wanted to know, might the musician be able to return to Kingston to begin the recording? If it was convenient he'd be happy to drive back with him. Tosh erupted into a rage of curses, and scampered down the ladder preceded by a succession of foul and biting words to confront Blackwell's impertinent messenger. It was only then that Benjamin Foot noticed that Peter Tosh had a machete in his hand. As the curses leapt from his lips, the blade flashed in front of him. Suddenly, before he could evade it, the machete swung towards Foot. Whether by design or good fortune, it was only the flat of the blade which caught him with a thwack on the arm. Foot turned and, without being seen to hurry, fled back to his car.

Tosh's rage was restricted to words thereafter. In a swirl of gossip, camps evolved with whispering and briefings of one Wailer against the other, like parakeets squawking unutterable truths as relatives arrive at a social gathering. With the goal of international stardom tantalisingly close, the stakes were suddenly so much greater. Bob Marley imagined a future where he would have to explain to his son, Ziggy, that the Lord had given the Wailers a golden opportunity and they had squandered it. He, Marley, was not going to let that happen. But how to square the Rasta ideals of livity with the comforts and attractions of mainstream commercial success? The arguments grew ever more rancorous. Increasingly, Bunny Livingston retreated to the tranquillity of the Rasta settlement at Bull Bay to feed his chickens and plant his crops. When Peter Tosh showed up for rehearsals he and Marley were daily embroiled in discussions that were less like Rasta reasonings and more like a bad-tempered version of the dozens. The fault-lines which had emerged over the last year could no longer be papered over. Who were the Wailers? What was the group? Recalling that time Marley struggled with a definition: 'The group is, the group is,' he turned over the idea like a man cranking up an engine, before settling on a simple formula: 'The group is whoever gwan play with the Wailers . . . Now if you don't want to deal with me then you don't do it.' Marley would later cite the escalating tensions as the inspiration for 'I Shot the Sheriff'. The earlier truth that Tosh Marley and Livingston had been first among equals could no longer hold. Finally, there could only be one sheriff in town. 'Me have to shoot all sheriff,' lamented Marley. Up until then says Esther Anderson, Marley's approach had been one of appeasement towards Tosh – the feud was a fire that he dealt with by letting it die down quietly of its own accord. Well no more.

If, as Anderson believed, the bitterness that Tosh increasingly expressed had its roots in love, then it was a love which passed for hate – the unforgiving hatred that only 'kith can feel for kin.' Months later, Bob Marley was still attempting to make sense of the venom and the split which now seemed to be unstoppable. 'Plenty little remarks pass, which I as a man, don't especially dig,' Marley said with his trademark understated diplomacy.

Finally, the fissures that had opened up could not be breached. But the bonds that held the three Wailers together were not contracted in ink, and the ugly and acrimonious fallout was perhaps inevitable. The Wailers became an abstraction. 'Now we can't have more than one Wailers,' said Marley. The group would be defined by those who remained and were willing to play, but it would have been more accurate to say that the group was whoever played with Bob Marley.

In the end, Tosh and Livingston really had no choice but to walk away and to begin to forge the solo careers that they had anticipated with the formation of their independent record labels a couple of years previously. Ultimately, Bob Marley was right. After the smoke had cleared, all that was left of their ten years together was a name. But Livingston, for one, was not going to leave empty-handed. Thereafter, he would be known as Bunny Wailer.

When challenged about why he had left the group, Bunny Livingston, who had emerged like a butterfly from its chrysalis into Bunny Wailer, would refer the interlocutor to the weirdness of the 'freak clubs' on the British tour which ran counter to the strictures of livity and his inborn conception of Rasta: 'We were people dealing with a consciousness, and so I said, "I'm not into that kind of thing." . . . Bob and Peter seemed to want to continue in that direction, so I said, "OK, one monkey don't spoil no show, I'll just stay in my corner and do whatever I see fit to be done."'[290]

For his part, Tosh would mumble a sentence or two that included the word bombaclaat and the name Blackwell, before reminding whoever cared to listen that *he* was Marley's teacher: 'Bob Marley was my student from the very first moment he put his finger on the string of a guitar.' The following year, Peter Tosh would offer a more conciliatory assessment: 'Well, was not a break-up . . . Is just going three different ways and sending the music in three different directions.' Tosh even held out the prospect of a reunion when he confessed: 'I am thinking of writing a song that the three of us can sing, and the title of that song would be "Here We Are Together Again."'[291]

It was left to Marley to voice his and many others' sad bewilderment about the 'non' break-up when he concluded: 'Up to now, I still don't know why we is not together.'

Even so, alongside their own work and the unity of the message of the songs, all three men were still advancing the Rasta creed and singing from the same *Sacred Songs and Solos* of Sankey's evangelical hymn sheets. Jah lived, even when he seemed to have died with the passing of the deposed Emperor Haile Selassie in 1975. Eventually, there would be a financial settlement with Island Records. From those proceeds, Marley would treat himself to a brand-new BMW, Tosh would place an order for the biggest, baddest bag of 'goat-shit', and Wailer would scour the island until he found his piece of heaven on earth, over 100 acres of land in the deep, deep Jamaican bush.

Blackwell was relieved to conclude business with the original Wailers. He had found it a maddening experience. Working out how to deal with Tosh and Wailer was akin to a driver determining how to negotiate two sets of faulty traffic lights. One set (Wailer) was permanently off so that the driver knew he would have to proceed without guidance but with caution. Due to a trip in the electrical supply, the other set (Tosh) flickered randomly between red, amber and green – governed by some indecipherable internal logic. In this scenario, the driver stalled and was fearful about whether to proceed at all.

Finally, there were many who suspected (including their first mentor, Joe Higgs) that as well as sweetening the music, Blackwell had always been intent on sweetening the image; that Marley's complexion was also an important factor in his elevation. Bob Marley was the bridge for mainstream listeners to cross over into an edgier but ultimately safe experience. Simply put, once Bunny Wailer had removed his name from the line-up, the choice was between Marley's 'One Love' or Tosh's 'No Peace'. There really was no competition. But still dangers lay ahead in sculpting the right image for Marley. Blackwell confirmed that, early on, he had made a pact with Marley that the two should never appear in the same photograph together. It would have sent the wrong message to have a picture of this strident black rebel holding the hand of his white benefactor.

The newly-crowned King of Reggae walked the line between rebellion and acceptability. Blackwell had found in Robert Nesta Marley a fierce but polite revolutionary.

12

UNDER HEAVY MANNERS

Stepping down onto the tarmac at Montego Bay's airport from the plane which had carried him from Havana, Cuba, the tall, golden-brown man with wavy hair was confronted by a gaggle of newspaper journalists. Michael Manley, a Brahmin-like former trade-union leader, educated at the LSE under the tutelage of Harold Laski, already brandished impeccable left-wing credentials that were further inflated by his recent audience with Fidel Castro. While his advocacy of a third way for the Third World might have endeared him to radical chic circles in Manhattan's Upper East Side or London's Hampstead, the comfortable residents of Russell Heights and the Myrtle Bank crowd in Jamaica were *not* impressed. That a majority of the country's wealth and influence was still concentrated in a few hands might be gleaned from the fact that half of all corporate directors and three-quarters of corporate chairmen were drawn from just twenty-one families.[292] These privileged Jamaicans could have discounted Manley's kissing the hand of Castro, or accepting a cigar from the revolutionary Cuban, *but* for one devastatingly important fact: Michael Manley was now prime minister of Jamaica.

Confronted by sceptical and hostile journalists on his return, Manley outlined his vision of Jamaica as a beacon of democratic socialism – a hard-working nation whose population rolled up its sleeves and forged ahead with his great ambition to fashion a more equitable society. He told supporters who had gathered at the airport that there were elements of the business class 'savagely opposed to ... democratic socialism', and he invited them to note that there were daily flights out of Jamaica to Miami 'where they might feel more comfortable'.[293]

It was a forthright challenge to his critics, not atypical of his style and character – a shot across the bows of the whining upper and middle class Jamaicans, many of whom had second homes or businesses in Miami. Just 500 miles (or an hour's flight) away, Miami had become so popular with Jamaicans that it had earned the sobriquet 'Kingston 21'. In some regard, the part-time residents of 'Kingston 21' shared a common outlook with Rastas: mentally, they were semi-detached from the island, believing that Jamaica was somewhere you put up with. Real life was elsewhere. For Rastas it was Ethiopia; for their upper-crust cousins Zion was Miami.

Michael Manley was a sometimes strident but always eloquent and passionate politician. Ever since taking office three years previously, he'd been under siege from elements within the middle class and their allies in industry, especially the hostile main national newspaper, which feared for the consequences of his socialist policies. In a withering editorial, the *Gleaner* was to christen him 'the most messianic figure in Jamaica's political history'. In previous decades the paper had levelled the same charge at Marcus Garvey. For a newspaper that trembled over his 'fanatical impatience' to achieve the 'myriad goals to myriad new Jerusalems,'[294] and whose editor was a former chairman of the rival party, it was perhaps unsurprising that the *Gleaner* leapt immediately on Manley's airport pronouncement with the hysterical headline the next day:

NO ONE CAN BECOME A MILLIONAIRE IN JAMAICA – PM.[295]

The *Gleaner* went on to 'quote' Manley as saying, 'Anyone who wants to become a millionaire in Jamaica, my advice to them is to remember that planes depart five times daily to Miami.' No matter the misrepresentation, the prime minister came to rue his angry slip when he was forced into damage-limitation mode a few days later. Manley clarified that he'd been referring only to those who were 'motivated by the selfish desire to become a millionaire overnight', and who 'refused to regard themselves as part of Jamaican society, and owing an obligation of service like the rest of us.'[296] But the damage was already done, and the middle classes weren't listening to his qualifications; they were too busy packing their bags.[297]

The middle class wasn't just fleeing because they feared Manley was now beginning to reveal his dark intentions to turn the country into a hardline Communist state; they were escaping from the more immediate fear of violence. Within a year they'd be joined by Bob Marley.

Jamaica seethed like a feuding family that had reached a compromise that no one was happy with. At its root was a fundamental and irresolvable paradox. The excitement and success of reggae which raised the profile of the country also came with an unwelcome side effect, as far as the patrician class was concerned. Reggae had become intertwined with Rasta. It was built on a culture that was deemed to be base, dutty and vulgar; belonging to the nasty naygars in whose company you would have to pinch your nose to stop yourself from retching. The rapid and rampant rise of this dirt music as the most potent symbol of a national culture threatened to turn the old order upside down. More than ever it was imagined that the barbarians were at the gates – but they might still yet be denied.

The uptown set may have looked on with dismay at the hijacking of the idea of Jamaica, especially through the musical expression of Bob Marley, but the former Trench Town youth was now impossible to ignore. Just a couple of years earlier, when Marley returned to the island with Esther Anderson, he'd been embarrassed by his inability to even hail a taxi. To succeed, the singer would have to lurk in the background and push his fragrant middle-class beauty to the front. If the drivers saw the Rasta first they would not stop.

Around about the same time that the empty cabs were flashing past Bob Marley, letter-writers to the *Gleaner* were reaching a pitch of fury over the betrayal of one of their own – an airline pilot, captain Michael Batts, whose university education and fair skin were offset by the dreadlocks which unmistakably marked him as a Rastafarian. Was Air Jamaica right to have sacked him? The reader who thought the dismissal of a professed Rastafarian constituted an infringement of his civil rights was in the minority. Batts caused a schism in liberally minded circles: people were publicly supportive but privately appalled that if someone like Batts could be turned then the barbarians had stormed the gates and were now at the controls. Most were content to lay their distress to one side and enter into the sport of mockery. One correspondent riffed on the possible effects of marijuana on the captain's ability when 4,000 feet in the air, advising that 'a pilot should be no higher than his plane', and that passengers would rather 'walk than be flown by a mystic'. Finally, the argument was settled by his employer's winning 'technical' argument that Batts's unruly beard barred him from the captaincy and flying because he would be unable to put an oxygen mask on properly in the event of an emergency.[298]

Once the guffawing was over it was left to the more soberly inclined to point out the dangers to tourism: Jamaica's image and credibility was at stake, once it became known to 'squares' worldwide that ganja-smoking dreads were at the control of the island's aircraft. After all, this came at a time when distressed Jamaicans exhibited a kind of collective nervous paralysis over their failing economy and the social experiments which seemed to drive the government into negotiations for a loan from the unsympathetic IMF. The wealthy agonised over legislation which, if enacted, could see their overseas investments clawed back to the island in taxes, while the rest of Jamaica's petrified people also voiced their concern that 'the country going down'. The sufferers, though, had in mind the shocking plummet in the standard of living, precipitating a return to the dark days when large sections of the populace confined themselves to eating on Thursdays, Fridays and Saturdays. But the feeling that 'the country mash up' came as well from the heavy sense of dread and the pervasive atmosphere of menace and violence abroad in the land.

Both these features of mid-1970s Jamaica could be charted in the changing fortunes of the teashop that had been a favourite haunt of Mortimo Planno and the Wailers.

The teashop was housed in a two-storey building with a restaurant upstairs and a bar below it. The proprietor was easy-going and his establishment popular. Unfortunately, however, it fell along the border-line between rival gangs. In the first instances of trouble, the proprietor responded by blocking off the back and side ways into the building with solid doors and heavy locks; the customers were thus steered to use the front entrance only. Months passed and there was no lessening of 'incidents', so he decided next 'to cage off the service area with a heavy wire screen'. When even this failed to work, the proprietor 'finally sectioned off the eating and drinking areas'. Now the restaurant more resembled a 'holding pen in a prison' than a teashop. 'Everyone was behind bars!' remembered Carole Yawney.[299]

That restaurant had become a microcosm of Jamaican society in the 1970s. Travelling beyond your neighbourhood was hazardous. Trench

Town folk were trapped in their ghetto constituency. In order to go to Coronation Market, for example, they would need to board a bus whose route took them through opposition territory, exposing them to the bullets of gunmen who lined the roofs of the concrete tower blocks.

A shorthand explanation for the state of unrest was to be found in the graffiti. On the shanty-town walls, Michael Manley, the prime minister, was depicted as Castro's poodle, and the opposition leader, Edward Seaga, was routinely the subject of a pun which could have been drawn from the pen of Peter Tosh: 'CIAga.'

Michael Manley was convinced of a conspiracy to bring down the government. He had no doubt that the timing of a series of brutal killings in Trench Town at the beginning of 1976 'were arranged to take place at the very moment when more than 300 international journalists were in the country covering the IMF conference'.[300] His suspicions appeared to be backed up by a couple of rogue gunmen who appeared in a British television documentary claiming that, before switching their allegiance to the governing party, they'd been put on a retainer by the JLP to carry guns and terrorise their opponents.[301] The otherwise inexplicable surge in the number of guns on the island and their use in politically motivated violence; the sharp increase in US embassy personnel in Kingston, alongside the testimony of a former CIA agent, Philip Agee, that Jamaica was the target of covert action, was evidence enough to fuel the conviction of many at the parish pump, the rum-shop and on the debating floor of Jamaica House that Uncle Sam was bent on destabilising the country.[302] Manley would only allude to a plot, stating again and again that there were 'strange things happening' in the country. His Minister for Foreign Affairs, Senator Dudley Thompson, was not so coy. Thompson speculated that 'there are more CIA agents in Jamaica than there are Rastafarians in New York'. He was pretty sure about the unlikelihood of Rastas settling in Manhattan because, of course, 'they don't eat food that comes out of refrigerators'. On the matter of the CIA, Senator Thompson, a lawyer by profession, circumvented the thorny question of the 'burden of proof' with a verbal wink to his interviewer: 'CIA agents don't wear uniforms.'[303]

Thirty years on it was a subject which continued to exasperate and vex the spirit of citizens such as Frederick Hickling. When I suggested to Professor Hickling that no evidence had ever been found of direct involvement of the US authorities in an anti-Jamaican plot, the psychiatrist glared at me as if I was an irredeemable imbecile. 'Then where did all the guns come from?' he bellowed. 'We don't make guns on the island!'

How *had* the guns entered the island? Locked up in imported fridges was one popular theory; that they'd been stuffed inside teddy bears, dolls and other props of visiting circuses was also widely suspected. Whatever the manner of the guns' arrival or the cause that they served, it is true that in 1976 the number of murders trebled. PNP and JLP enforcers took the battle to each other's doorsteps, and the unfortunate were caught in the crossfire.

Under siege in the latter half of the 1970s, the ghetto 'sufferers' could neither leave their homes nor send their children to school. The gunmen became more brazen. Their weapons barked at night and into the early morning. Neville Graham, now a teenager, developed a new hobby, 'collecting spent shells' every morning just after 5 o'clock. The enforcers were not so concerned with demographics, with guaranteeing the allegiances, but rather with maintaining or enlarging the boundaries of the garrison constituencies. Back then that part of Trench Town was a PNP area, but just a few years earlier Neville Graham had witnessed the JLP's Wilton Hill, sat astride a magnificent white horse and riding along 9th Street and 'everybody coming out and cheering confidently [because] it was a bedrock labourite area'. But then the JLP lost that general election and the rival party 'started a sort of ethnic cleansing', moving their own supporters into the new housing project.[304] In the past, the enforcers used clubs; now it was guns.

On a daily basis, the newspapers catalogued the descent into violence, and carried pitiable accounts of the laments and wails of women accompanying their murdered menfolk to the 'dead house' (mortuary). There were also spates of unexplained arson attacks, and the mystery of myriad fatal car accidents caused by the cynical oiling of roads. No one could seriously account for how things had gotten so out of hand. The Minister of National Security, Eli Matalon, argued that drastic measures needed to be taken, while avoiding the declaration of a state of emergency, which 'might give the undesirable impression that the country was in a state of civil war'.

In place of the imagined cordon sanitaire which separated uptown from downtown Kingston, Matalon ordered barbed-wire roadblocks to be rolled out all over the capital. Government adverts began appearing

on billboards and newspapers warning of penalties of indefinite imprisonment for those caught with a gun for which they had no licence, or, as
Manley put it, the gunmen would be given 'indefinite premature pensions
in a safe place of abode for life'.[305] The government introduced a Gun
Court to fast-track miscreants through the judicial system; those found
guilty would be held in ghoulish, blood-red shacks in an enclosure in
Kingston that resembled a prisoner-of-war camp. 'By the time we finish
with them,' Manley warned, 'Jamaican gunmen will be sorry they ever
heard of a thing called a gun.'[306] But even these draconian measures
had failed to curb the violence that Manley lamented was 'on a scale
unique to [Jamaican] history'. Eleven people perished in the Orange Lane
fires, started after feuding gangs surrounded a tenement yard and set
alight a number of shacks, trapping hundreds of people in the yard. At
the beginning of 1976 several police officers were killed. In one week,
three prominent businessmen were shot, then two lawyers were also
gunned down, and then on 14 June 1976, the Peruvian ambassador,
Fernando Rodriques, was stabbed to death in his home.[307]

Finally, on 19 June, less than a week later, the governor-general issued
a proclamation declaring a State of Emergency. And the next morning,
as Bob Marley was to capture in song, he and his compatriots 'woke up
in a curfew'.[308] The government now believed a state of emergency was
the only means by which the unprecedented violence would be locked
down and the rule of law rigorously restored. Manley was putting the
population on notice that he was, in Jamaican parlance, placing the
country 'under heavy manners'. Those forces determined to undermine
and destabilise the country would remain 'under heavy manners as long
as there is any threat of gunmanship and political violence in Jamaica'.[309]

American television crews arrived on the streets of Kingston and
beamed back into the homes of their compatriots the astonishing scenes
of armoured vehicles and tanks on the streets, with gunmen crouching
behind burnt-out cars, hunkering beside walls and firing off shots in
the general direction of an unseen enemy. The tourists stayed away.

'You're not scared are you?' the driver was asking me, but really I
thought the rhetorical question was not directed at me: it was more
a note to himself – a self-help mantra. *He* was not scared. He hadn't

even demanded a top-up to his usual fee to bring me down here. But then, that wasn't his style. His manner was always to leave further remuneration to my discretion as 'an honourable man'. If I wanted to give him a 'little something extra as danger money' it was entirely up to me. But, in the same breath, he had added that it really wasn't necessary because it 'nah dangerous as such'.

The top end of the street was controlled by one gang; a rival group controlled the bottom end. Recently, there'd been a flash of violence and exchange of gunfire over proprietorial rights to the middle. Looking round now it was apparent that most of the surrounding buildings were scarred from old and new bullet holes, like a pock-marked adolescent face subjected to a recent flare-up of acne. No one controlled the middle ground. But it didn't feel like neutral territory; it was more of a no-man's-land. We were in the middle.

It was only mid-afternoon. The driver said it'd be a safer time to arrive. There was no traffic on the road and barely any pedestrians in the area. But there was the same kind of strange stillness about the place that you encounter when you first walk into a mortuary and open the fridges, to see the dead laid out on metal trays. Something bad had happened here.

The former combatants whom I had arranged to meet were nowhere to be seen. The driver paced about – a tightly controlled bundle of energy – his nervousness all the more apparent for his attempts to assume an attitude of casual indifference.

Presently, the combatants arrived, one after the other. The first man announced straight away that he didn't want to be interviewed. He'd changed his mind. 'What has happened?' I wanted to know.

'Not a t'ing 'appen,' he said, 'jus' now is not the time.'

I wondered then why he'd bothered to turn up. He said he hadn't wanted to appear 'ignorant'. But having said his piece, he did not depart; he lingered like the hotel porter who, having carried your bags to the room, now expects a tip. I worried about the veracity of the 'former' in his stated title, 'former combatant'. It was a relief when the other combatant beckoned me to follow him into a concrete building which served as a makeshift youth club. This retired gunman seemed little more than a youth himself: he was twenty-one, he said, but had 'spent some time in shorts', by which he meant the khaki prison shorts that inmates of the island's penitentiaries were required to wear.

Stretched across the room at head-height was a lattice of cables which took a free feed of electricity from the mains. A series of passport-sized photos of teenage girls adorned the back wall. A solitary lizard darted across it, stopping abruptly and momentarily, it seemed, to inspect them. 'Models,' said the combatant. 'We gwan start up a modelling agency.' He searched my eyes for any scepticism. 'This is not a joke t'ing. These girls *can* be models'. He bid me take a closer look. I imagined in among them the barefoot and pregnant girl so admired by Ken and Bert.

The former combatant had given up the gun. He had no explanation other than he 'didn't take to it'. And he rejected the assumption that sociologists in Jamaica had put to me, that many of the armed youth were irredeemable; that twenty years ago the dons, in their thirties and forties, with a semblance of a socialist sensibility, had held things down, if not together; but now the dons were teenagers and they had multiplied, just as their fiefdoms had shrunk; and socialism had been displaced by nihilism.

The combatant brought me back to the gallery of would-be models, and answered my unspoken doubts: 'The Bible say "without a vision you perish". We have to make a start. I know what I'm doing. But what are *you* doing?' He jabbed my shoulder, and I lowered the microphone. Only when satisfied that he had my full attention did he continue: 'You have a job to do too. Write it down. The people have fi know what a-gwan. You just can' come ina here and it just a here today, gone tomorrow situation.' He had met too many superficially sympathetic journalists – tourists with typewriters, he called them. 'What you write brethren have fi mek a difference. Otherwise what am I doing here? Otherwise, it's just ice cream on the pavement.'

By 1976, all three of the original Wailers had moved out of Trench Town. Yard life was always seen as a stage which you passed through. Those who were determined to shake themselves up progressed from tenement yards to the more respected government yards from where entry to the lower middle class was within striking distance. The goal of social mobility towards 'something better' was strongly rooted in the ghetto psyche. For the respondents in Erna Brodber's field research, the Jamaican dream was 'a detached house of your own, perhaps in the middle of Liguanea Plains,' on the eastern outskirts of the capital, 'where your children can run free'.[310]

For Bunny Wailer that dream would be realised for $25,000. For his settlement from Island Records, Wailer had insisted on cash; he organised the bundle of notes into neat piles and crammed them into a suitcase which never left his side. Within a couple of weeks he would ponder the wisdom of that decision. Shortly after receiving the money, Bunny Wailer had received an uninvited visit from the Jamaican Constabulary. He'd watched nervously as the police ransacked his house looking for drugs, and found the suitcase. 'The cops opened the suitcase,' and their eyes lit up. Whereupon Bunny Wailer declaimed in his most perfect Queen's English that he could account for, and had counted, *every* penny. And after some deliberation – much to his relief – they turned to him, and closing the suitcase said, 'Well, dread, we don't touch nothing.'

Thereafter Bunny Wailer's search for something to spend his money on was not so leisurely. Within a month he'd found a plot of land for sale comprising more than 100 acres. He put on a khaki suit, lowered the suitcase of money into the boot of his car, climbed in, swung by to pick up his 'splendidly attired' partner and hit the road. They were headed for the parish of Portland. The cash in the suitcase was to pay for the property he had found in a neighbouring parish; one that was almost impenetrable, 'pure "bush".' Presented with tens of thousands of dollars, the owners of the property were hesitant at first. 'The owners were anxious,' recalled Wailer, 'and scared that it might be stolen.' But he was determined to leave them the cash as a deposit and, after a few checks, the sale went through.

In one sweet deal, Bunny Wailer had acquired five times the acreage of land that his father had built up over a lifetime. He had, as the song said, found his 'heaven on earth'. There was, in a sense, nowhere else to go. The suggestion from his first solo album, *Blackheart Man*, that his dreamland was Ethiopia, was in fact misleading: dreamland could be found closer to home in Portland, Jamaica.

Bunny Wailer's reputation as a mystic stemmed largely from this period of semi-reclusiveness. His rejection of the glamorous lifestyle that had beckoned with the Wailers' success both bemused and intrigued. 'I'm like a messenger,' Wailer explained. 'Sometimes the messenger gets a message, and he doesn't know what's in the message. And sometimes the person that gets the message doesn't let the messenger know what's going on.' When the interviewers took out their tape recorders and Wailer spoke as lightning flashed and thunder groaned in the background, they were stripped of all cynicism and hung on words that may not have sounded so powerful in a more mundane urban setting. Like a grinning audience in a comedy club who don't actually get the jokes, or 'squares' who were afraid of appearing less than 'hip', the journalists who travelled as pilgrims in search of this Jamaican backwoodsman wrote up their encounters, investing his every utterance with the greatest profundity. 'People do generally regard him with awe,' enthused Vivien Goldman. 'He has an extraordinary facility for simply being natural, being closely attuned to the elemental forces.'[311]

Wailer was also hard-headed. For *Blackheart Man*, he had signed a lucrative deal with Chris Blackwell and Island Records. Blackwell was enormously pleased with the results, describing it as the best reggae album to have come out of Jamaica. Even though he held Blackwell in some regard, Bunny Wailer was extremely protective in his dealings with Island Records, as was evident from the various clauses he insisted on being inserted into the legal paperwork.

The stipulation that, in the event of Chris Blackwell's death, Wailer would be released from his contract was considered most bizarre by Island Records. However, more than paranoia, it suggests an old anxiety – the fear of the slave being sold 'downriver' from a goodly master to a virulent one. Such was the fate of Tom in *Uncle Tom's Cabin* who, by the novel's end, is sold 'downriver', down the Mississippi and finds himself the property of the pathological Simon Legree. Yes, Chris Blackwell could be trusted, but what about the others who might succeed him?

The 'deepest' of the original Wailers' trio, Bunny Wailer took his faith most seriously. 'I preserved myself spiritually under the banner of Rastafari,' he recalled.[312] But though, as Lee Perry had alluded, Bunny Wailer was totally immersed in Rastafarian livity, this devout Rasta had no intention of repatriation to Africa.

Increasingly, there seemed to be little reason to agitate further or to hold out for an idea which seemed chimerical and unachievable, especially so after Emperor Haile Selassie was deposed during a military coup. The new Marxist regime in Addis Ababa reneged on the previous agreement under which several hundred acres of land had been set aside for would-be migrant Rastas and other people of African descent. In any event, despite the fact-finding missions and government-sponsored summits into the potential and progress of repatriation, only a few hundred Rastafarians ever ventured to the Shashamane Settlement in Ethiopia. Added to which, though Rastas continued to remain the butt of casual abuse, there were signs of subtle shifts in the attitude towards them, primarily and ironically through the association with reggae.

The roster of those who had heeded the call of Rasta included young men such as Steven 'Cat' Coore, the son of a government minister and key figure in the line-up of Third World, a populist locksed-up reggae outfit. Coore's brother, Ivan, was a rival to Prophet Gad for the leadership of the Twelve Tribes of Israel. And so popular was this sect of Rastas among musicians that it became known as the Reggae House. As the religion grew, competition between the numerous 'Houses' of Rastafari became ever more acute; it was a coup to have attracted so many prominent musicians as members. The biggest catch of all was Bob Marley who underscored his separation from Mortimo Planno and the Nyabinghi Rastas by joining the Twelve Tribes of Israel brethren – though he would continue to serve as a willing ambassador for the Rastafari movement as a whole.

Marley attracted the most attention; but all three of the original Wailers played significant roles in that altered perception – most lately Bunny Wailer with each and every track on his beguiling *Blackheart Man*, an album which evoked the spirituality and religiosity of Rasta like nothing before – or since. *Blackheart Man* conjured a pastoral Jamaican Eden as old as time itself. In an extraordinary feat, Wailer had produced a complex music that appeared as disarmingly simple as a nursery rhyme: it informed the head and melted the heart.

As a child, Bunny Wailer remembered how he had been taught to fear 'the blackheart man [who] lived beyond the boundaries of civilised life'. The blackheart man was a kind of bogeyman but he was also, actually, an early manifestation of the Rastaman. In common conception the blackheart man was a malign yet eerily seductive force that lured you like the sirens towards danger. A blackheart man 'would try to pull you across the line – he was a criminal who'd cut your throat with little hesitation or remorse'.[313]

'I saw myself in blackheart man ever since I started to realise myself,' reflected Bunny Wailer on his deepening commitment to Rastafari. 'The type of impression that I was leaving on my parents . . . they started to treat me like the blackheart man. They look at you and wonder, like they don't know you, like it's some stranger. We are the people our parents warned us against, all over again.'[314]

If, as now seemed likely, the large-scale repatriation of Rastafarians was never going to happen, then, somehow, the Rastafarian outlook in Jamaica would have to be accommodated. PNP politicians, such as Francis Tulloch, even began to voice the hitherto unthinkable heresy that if Rastas considered smoking ganja a religious sacrament, just as, for example, the taking of wine in Holy Communion was for Catholics, then perhaps the law should be amended 'to make an exception for them'.[315] The suggestion would have gladdened the heart of Peter Tosh. For his first outing as a solo artist, Tosh had devoted his considerable musical ability to the creation of an album whose unashamed and insistent anthem was embodied in its title: *Legalize It*.

The existing legislation on marijuana subjected large swathes of the population to low-grade but continual harassment. Tosh's considerable sympathy was always with the sufferer who, at the mercy of his sympathetic nervous system, was forced to 'cork him batty' every time he just wanted a little draw of herb. This zero tolerance inevitably snared more minnows than sharks. Under the earlier Dangerous Drugs Act, possession of ganja was deemed to be a greater crime than smoking it, so that the street-smart man, who clocked an approaching policeman, took a match, struck pre-emptively and inhaled before being apprehended. Though the government was at pains to assure the law-abiding that they had nothing to fear from the new legislation, at times it appeared that no one had bothered to pass the message on to the Jamaican Constabulary. The state of emergency heralded a turn towards a kind of judicial violence that carried with it dangers of police excess.

Peter Tosh had lost count of the number of times he'd run from, and been caught up with, the law. Most of his broken guitars came from hurried scrambling over walls when alerted to a ganja raid by the security forces. He hadn't always been successful. Too often Tosh had been at the wrong end of a policeman's baton, and the magistrate's or judge's ruling. With time, Peter Tosh came to see himself as a marked man – one who was known to the police. On court and other official documents, he noted that there often appeared stamped beside his name a red 'X'.

It was after yet another encounter with the forces of authority in 1973, when Tosh suffered fractured ribs during his arrest for smoking marijuana, that he channelled the experience into the song 'Mark of

the Beast'. Beaten to the ground during a scuffle by these agents of
Babylon, Tosh had looked up and imagined he saw 'the mark of the
beast in their ugly faces'. Peter Tosh saw himself as an everyman
unworthy of the criminalisation and humiliations that he was regularly
subjected to.

Underneath the news report in the *Gleaner* of the latest stage in the
unstoppable rise of Marley's international career, there appeared an
advert for Peter Tosh's *Legalize It*. But, while Marley's music received
unlimited airplay on Jamaica's radio stations, within weeks *Legalize It*
(whose lyrics had the temerity to suggest that even judges were partial
to a puff of ganja) was banned. And, as a further insult to his pride,
Peter Tosh had cause to reflect on the disparity in the fortunes of the
former Wailers, when he was forced to admit that, 'people think we
have money but I don't even have a home'.[316]

Meanwhile, Bob Marley was ensconced in the strangest location of
all – 56 Hope Road. The former HQ of Island Records in Jamaica was
some four miles from the Rock. Although looking out onto a busy road
and a little down at heel, Marley's home was in an area formerly the
preserve of senior civil servants and other government officials; not the
nouveau 'codfish aristocracy' but solid middle and upper-class Jamaicans.
The original name of the house was 'Odnil', an inversion of 'Lindo', the
maiden name of Chris Blackwell's mother, Blanche. 56 Hope Road was
first purchased by Blanche's great-uncle Cecil Lindo in 1914. Bob Marley
had acquired the property almost as a perk, an addendum to his new
and vastly improved contract, and a peace offering.

A few months earlier, Blackwell had taken exception to Marley's
abuse of his largesse. One of the houses in the grounds had been turned
into a rehearsal room and studio. This was reasonable and appropriate.
But out of office hours, the Island headquarters appeared to have been
'captured' by Marley, assorted friends and brethren who regularly hung
out in the grounds. At one stage Bunny Wailer had occupied one of the
outbuildings, as had Esther Anderson, her mother, and Joe Higgs and
family (after they'd been burnt out of their own home), and a succession
of Rastas from Marley's Trench Town days. In a fit of pique, Blackwell
had sent solicitor's instructions for Bob Marley to quit Island House.

But their difficulties had been patched up and Marley was handed the keys to the former Lindo family property.

The poignancy would not have been lost on Marley. The Lindos' colossal impact on Jamaican society stretched back to the days of slavery. Blackwell's ancestor Alexander Lindo was a Sephardic Jew whose predecessors had escaped the Spanish Inquisition to begin new lives in the Caribbean. In the eighteenth century, Alexander Lindo had acted, without shame or fear of censure, as a broker to establish the best price for the newly transported slaves to the island. In the late nineteenth and early twentieth century, the Lindos had become substantial landowners, cultivating bananas and sugar on their plantations. The Appleton sugar estate was included in their portfolio. They also owned and ran Wray & Nephew rum distillers and myriad other businesses.

Chris Blackwell's mother, Blanche, had even been given a banana and coconut plantation as a wedding gift. And as well as 56 Hope Road, another Lindo (Cecil) had also held the deeds to the stately Devon House just a few blocks away. Devon House boasted a grand lobby, a Southern-style veranda, a Wedgwood ceiling in the grand ballroom and imported European antiques. By the time I visited the house in the 1980s, it had been converted into a swanky cultural centre, complete with a nouvelle-cuisine restaurant and gift shop selling high-end tourist trinkets costing five times what you'd pay to the pavement vendors at their 'Bend Down Plazas'. The waltzes no longer played in the ballroom, and entry to Devon House was barred to no one. Yet I recall a flummoxed-looking youngish black man nursing his drink on the veranda, of the restaurant. Rummaging through his pockets, he seemed to be engaged in a mental mathematical calculation while struggling to convince himself of his entitlement to a seat at Devon House. At length he leant over towards me and whispered nervously, 'Brethren, is how much for the orange juice?'

56 Hope Road did not have the intimidating grandeur of Devon House. Nonetheless, had he been so inclined, Marley would have been forgiven for thinking he had 'arrived'. But Bob Marley was no arriviste. Initially, at 56 Hope Road, he attempted to replicate the spirit of Mortimo Planno's open yard. There were no guards on the gates. Anyone and everyone walked in. Only later, when the tension (which everyone called 'the pressure') rose in the city was it considered prudent to perhaps post a couple of Dreads at the gates and keep them locked. Even so, Marley was determined that there should be no display of

opulence which would question the worth of his brethren. He would argue compellingly, if not convincingly, that nothing much had changed; he was just working on a higher rung on the ladder, but it was still the same ladder. And if reggae was booming then it was in no small part down to his hard work and productivity.

Foreign record producers had certainly seen the light, and were arriving in ever-increasing numbers on the island. These prospectors for reggae gold had a certain template in mind: a rootsy sound, a hint of danger, and dreadlocks, definitely dreadlocks. If you didn't locks up, remembered Vernon Buckley, you could kiss goodbye to your chances of signing with one of the international labels. 'I heard that Virgin never sign us because I never carry a Rasta image,' recalled Buckley. 'Those days we used to sell a lot, but we were never really saying "Rastafari".'[317]

By 1976, the converts to Rastafari (at least as personified by Bob Marley) included the editorial staff of the *Gleaner*. While news of *Catch a Fire*'s critical success barely warranted a mention in a tiny 1-inch-square of the paper in 1973, three years later the *Gleaner* was happy to reproduce a feature from *Playboy* magazine with the simple headline: 'Bob Marley: the Prophet'.

Readers of the magazine could take vicarious pleasure in the correspondent's admiration of the singer's 'classic mode of rock-star skinniness,' as befitting a Dylan or a Jagger, but one who wore 'very highly tailored freedom-fighter fatigues [and] a fine snake-coil mane of Rasta dreadlocks which fly about Medusa-like'.

Journalistic interest in Rasta and reggae mirrored a growing academic and anthropological investigation. But *Playboy* was not yet privy to the scholarship which would later recognise Marley's dreadlocks as 'psychic antennae' or 'mystic magnets' in communication with Jah. When Marley flashed his locks they acted as a lightning conductor for the mystical forces destined to bring down a dread judgement and the destruction of Babylon, with no exemptions for soft pornographic magazines that appreciated reggae.

The seeds of Rastafari planted on the campus of the University of the West Indies were soon evident in the locks that began to sprout from the heads of lecturers and students alike. Reggae proved the medium for the message of Rasta to reach the Mona campus. But in the shanty towns of Kingston, Marley's generation of Rastas had a more direct influence on the youths who came after them. Wise men and educationalists were living on the streets, remembered Anthony 'Knowledge' Doyley. 'They were happy to sit down with you and pass on their wisdom.' 'Knowledge' was a bright Trench Town pupil who left school to take up a job as a salesman for the Jamaica Biscuit Company. He had looked up to singers like Marley, clinging to his shirt tails when the Wailer was still resident in the ghetto. 'Knowledge' was just the kind of boy whom social workers held up as a model of what might be possible; that the prospects for ghetto youths did not have to be curtailed and conform to the usual expectations.

'Knowledge' had a respectable job and a route out of the ghetto. But after a while doubts crept in. He remembered saying to himself: 'You know what? This job is stopping you from sparring with Bob, it's stopping you from smoking, from relaxing.' One day he failed to show up at work, and after that he never went back. 'And I said, "I'm not combing my hair no more, I'm just gonna be me." Then a while later, I sat down one day and all my savings that I had was spent, because I was smoking and cooking and was having an initiation of being a Rasta.'[318]

Evidence of the spread of Rasta beyond the island could be found daily in news from as far away as Guyana. In an article entitled, 'A One-sided Love Affair', a dreadlocked Rasta was reported to have taken the first steps to acclimatise himself for the expected repatriation to Africa by bounding over the wall of the local zoo into the lion's den. The Rasta's belief in a 'kinship between [him] and the lions,' only lasted until the lions made it plain that his presence wasn't welcome. The' injured Rasta had felt the weight of the lion's paw and was dragged out and ferried to hospital.[319]

But whether as espoused in George Town, Guyana, Trench Town in Jamaica or on the university campus, Rastafari seemed to answer a difficult question among brown and black people that had previously been resisted and had hardly ever been articulated before: who do you think you are? And if the ideology undermined but ultimately satisfied a fundamental and urgent enquiry into the nature of self, then the music associated with it often acted as a balm.

In the midst of the murder and mayhem of 1976, Bob Marley dreamt up an idea for an event that would allow Jamaicans to take time out from the intense pressure of their lives. If only for one night, the 'Smile

Jamaica' festival would 'put the smiles back onto people's faces'. The government jumped at the idea of a free concert of music and comedy and, initially, offered the lawns of Jamaica House. In consultation with Marley, the concert was subsequently relocated to the National Heroes Park – a larger venue, and one that was not directly associated with the government.

Newspapers announced that Bob Marley and the Wailers would perform at the 'Smile Jamaica' festival as 'Bob's Christmas gift to the pop enthusiasts of Kingston'.[320] The reggae group Third World would add to the feel-good nature of the concert, as well as the comedian Prince Edward and Richard Ace, an eleven-year-old drumming sensation. Peter Tosh and Bunny Wailer were approached, but both declined to participate.

Three weeks after the free concert was announced, more than 140,000 rapturous supporters of Michael Manley's PNP gathered at Sam Sharpe Square, Montego Bay, to hear their leader declare that the general election would take place on 15 December.

The timing was inauspicious. In the heated atmosphere of Jamaican electioneering, even the dullest political mind could see the danger; that the free concert headed by Bob Marley (and sponsored by the prime minister's office) could be perceived as an endorsement of Michael Manley's party.

Bob Marley's psychic antennae (ministered through his dreadlocks) were perfectly tuned to the firmament, but his political antennae needed tweaking. Just days before the concert, he gave an interview to Vivien Goldman where he spelt out the changes in society that he, as a self-confessed 'common-sense man', could see were necessary.

'So much guys have so much – too much – while so many have nothing at all. We don't feel like that is right, because it don't take a guy a hundred million dollars to keep him satisfied. Everybody have to live. Michael Manley say 'im wan' help poor people . . . They feel something good is gonna happen . . . You have to share. I don't care if it sounds political or whatever it is, but people have to share.' He had been saying as much in song, describing succinctly the disparity between the rich and the poor in lyrics such as: *Dem belly full, but we hungry.*'

Marley's acceptance that his words might be construed as 'political' was a reflection that, though he professed to dip on neither side of the political spectrum, his sympathies, like those of Michael Manley, lay with the common people. It was an almost impossible circle to square, and there had been signs that the non-partisan nature of the concert had not been understood; or rather that some *chose* not to understand it.

When Neville Garrick, the Wailers' artistic director, tried to hand out promotional stickers to some Rasta friends, one of the brethren rejected them, saying, 'Me no put no political label deh pon my vehicle, Rasta.' But apart from the heavy sense of dread which all Jamaicans felt in the run-up to the elections, and the occasional florid and supposedly prophetic dream of Judy Mowatt (the group's resident Cassandra), there were few other signals or warnings picked up at 56 Hope Road about what was to come next.[321]

On 3 December 1976, as Rita Marley was preparing to leave through the gates of Hope Road, she paused to let another car drive in. Almost immediately its occupants started firing shots. They jumped out of the car and proceeded towards the rehearsal room, firing at will. Bob Marley was trapped in the galley kitchen with nowhere to hide; later he described how, when the bullets started to fly, he tried to twist his torso to make himself less of a target. Nonetheless, a bullet whizzed past his chest and slammed into his elbow; Rita Marley was wounded in the forehead; Marley's manager, Don Taylor, was the most seriously injured, as he had inadvertently stepped into the line of fire and taken the bullets meant for Bob Marley, before the gunmen fled.

The wounded were rushed to Kingston's University College Hospital. Thereafter, escorted by police guards, Marley was taken to a safe house high up in the Blue Mountains at Strawberry Hill, Chris Blackwell's plantation estate mansion.

Bob Marley was shocked by the attempt on his life. For two days, he remained brooding at Strawberry Hill, ringed by security forces, unsure about whether to proceed with the 'Smile Jamaica' concert as planned. Rita Marley and a number of friends and band members urged him to abandon the event; the bullish representatives of the prime minister argued against cancellation.

At 7 p.m. on 5 December, two hours after the show was scheduled to begin, there was still no sign of Marley. The compère asked the huge audience of 50,000 gathered at the open-air venue to pray for Marley's arrival. After half an hour, she announced that Marley was making his way down the mountain in a convoy of cars with police outriders. At about 8 p.m., the police ordered journalists to clear the platform and Bob Marley stepped forward bathed in light.

'It was a hugely transformative moment,' remembered Perry Henzell, who was in the crowd filming that night. Marley stood defiantly at the front of the stage and dared the gunmen who had shot him to try again.

Everyone was humbled by the reggae star's bravery, Michael Manley especially. He climbed on stage to thank him, before returning quietly to his seat. Just a few days later, on the last leg of his election campaign, Manley praised him again, telling his audience that the key lesson from Bob Marley's ordeal was that on 15 December, the electorate faced a choice 'between violence and heavy manners'.[322]

But the shooting of the island's most famous son showed that no one was truly safe – an assessment which Manley acknowledged tacitly. Whenever he travelled the short distance from Jamaica House to the airport, he did so in a helicopter.

Bob Marley survived the shooting on 3 December but there was no guarantee that he would be so lucky next time. Two days after the concert, he slipped out of the country, at the start of a self-imposed exile in London that was to last eighteen months.

It was a period of great creativity for Marley, in which he produced the remarkable album *Exodus*. He was arguably more productive abroad than his former compadres were at home. After the critical success of *Blackheart Man*, Bunny Wailer defaulted to a position of splendid isolation. In Marley's absence, Peter Tosh's musical voice became the most prominent in Jamaica; his strident and militant tone – dark and foreboding – matched the deepening gloom on the island. Throughout many of his interviews one phrase cropped up again and again, almost as a mantra: 'These are the last days.'

Peter Tosh had an undeniable talent for self-dramatisation, but it is equally the case that during this time, his homeland deteriorated even further; shelves on the supermarkets remained empty, hordes of unemployed youth remained idle, the local currency was devalued once more and the guns began to bark yet again.

But then at the beginning of 1978, two leaders of rival gangs, professing themselves to be sick of the killings, sat down to parley and came up with a novel idea: a truce. All that was needed was something (other than blood) to seal the truce. The cry was 'unity and one love', and there was one man who, more than any other Jamaican, embodied those principles. The gangsters travelled to London to convince Bob Marley to return home to headline a peace concert.

21 April 1978 was an ink-black night. The kind of night where, in the preceding months, under the cover of darkness, down deserted alleyways, the henchmen of Jamaica's rival parties had traded stabbing for stabbing, gunshot for gunshot, beatings, kidnappings and murder – yet another chapter in the undeclared civil war.

Bob Marley had been caught up in the violence eighteen months previously, but had now received assurances that 'everyt'ing was cool'. Marley was back where he left off, and where he belonged: centre stage, the headline act of a musical evening billed as the 'One Love Peace Concert'. A crowd of more than 30,000 'sufferers', including 'bad men' on each side, party activists and combatants, converged on neutral ground in Kingston.

Bob Marley, his dreadlocks whipping the night air, and sweat freely pouring from him, jigged on stage in a frenzy of exaltation that masked any vestige of fear; he struck that trademark pose: an index finger pointed at his temple – a soulful, screw-faced rapture. As the music crested now, the former 'dutty Rasta boy' drew Jamaica's warring political leaders, Seaga and Manley, onto the platform. Prior to this night, these same politicians, 'Castro's poodle' and Edward 'CIAga', had been united only in their intense loathing of each other. Under Marley's direction, they had no choice but to clasp his and each other's hands and raise them above their heads. Marley was the dynamo, providing the electrical charge which would convert their visceral hatred – even if just for one night – into love. The reggae bassline boomed like a thunderclap: the impossible had happened. And though the politicians studiously averted their gaze, Marley was the perfect picture of ecstasy.

Marley's magnanimous act was memorialised that day. Thereafter, Jamaicans will tell you, he was forever cast as the crucified Christ between the two thieves. Marley's spontaneous gesture was without precedent, but the antics of Peter Tosh who preceded him on stage were, in many respects, even more astonishing.

Peter Tosh had taken to the stage an hour earlier. In front of the two eminent guardians of the state, he lit an enormous spliff and proceeded to blow the smoke in their faces. Departing wildly from the 'One Love' script, Tosh's chosen subject for the night was not peace: it was war. 'Peace,' screamed Tosh, 'is the diploma you get at the cemetery.' He didn't want peace; he wanted justice.

It should have come as no surprise. Three years earlier, Tosh had made his stance clear with the anthemic *Legalize It*. Now, on 21 April 1978, with the spliff dangling from his lips, Tosh taunted the politicians and berated them for more than half an hour for their hypocrisy and for refusing to legalise marijuana.

Had Vere Johns been in the audience that night, he would have witnessed an unimaginable sight: it was Tosh, rather than Marley, who received the bigger cheer from the crowd. Furthermore, Tosh also gave the ruling class a history lesson in Jamaica's never-ending litany of plunder and piracy, from the state-sponsored terrorist, Henry Morgan, to the two esteemed leaders presiding over the current 'shitstem'. Tosh's diatribe was nose-end reasoning worthy of Mortimo Planno, laced with the foulest language, a stream of five-pound words.

Early on, Peter Tosh cajoled the TV cameramen to turn off their cameras, and many have argued that it was his one false move; a great shame and a terrible mistake. 'It could have been as seminal a moment as Martin Luther King's "I have a dream" speech at the Lincoln Memorial,' says the reggae archivist, Roger Steffens. But if it was an unprecedented act of revolution, then the revolution would not be televised. In essence, though, was Tosh's gesture any more than that of a waggish schoolboy letting off a fart during assembly to the delight of his classmates? The authorities certainly thought so. It didn't seem to occur to Peter Tosh – perhaps he didn't care – that there might be unwelcome consequences to his disrespectful provocation.

The most immediate consequence was a contract from Rolling Stones Records; Mick Jagger had been in the audience and a witness to the stupefying intensity and shock of Peter Tosh's brilliant and idiosyncratic performance.

In their responses to the 'Peace Concert', the original Wailers posited three competing approaches to making your mark on the world: Marley advocated peace; Tosh ridiculed the notion at a time when there was a war going on; and Bunny Wailer stayed at home.

Peter Tosh could blow a cloud of ganja smoke into the faces of the two leaders of the country's political parties and bound off the stage with impunity. But a little remnant of a spliff snatched from his fingers at Half-Way Tree, months later, would have far more serious consequences. For a start the man doing the snatching was a humour-less policeman.

13

HOW LONG WILL THEY
KILL OUR PROPHETS?

PETER Tosh should not have survived. When, three years earlier, he clambered from the wreckage of the overturned car, his girlfriend, Yvonne Whittingham, lay dying. The intensive care unit of the University Hospital would claim her for a few weeks, before she eventually expired. Despite his friends' attempts to attach blame to the other driver, despite the general acceptance among Jamaicans that their dangerous roads were mere pathways to heaven, Peter Tosh knew the limits of denial and understood, perhaps more than he was prepared to admit, that he was responsible for his girlfriend's death.

Tosh had been behind the steering wheel of the car on 11 November 1975, when, on an impulse, he'd decided to turn around and head back to 56 Hope Road. He was intent on giving a peace offering of a high-grade bag of herb to Bob Marley, whose name Tosh had cursed on a radio show earlier that day. Peter Tosh was already 'blacked-up and charged' from a draw of weed, and the ganja coursing through his brain had probably tricked him into underestimating the degree of difficulty of the manoeuvre. Even a driver uninfluenced by tetrahydrocannabinol[323] could not have managed to perform a U-turn at Six Miles on the Spanish Town Road, especially not with the accelerator pedal through the floor, on tyres stripped bald from too many hairpin turnings in the roads, and with an engine heavily gunned and ready to snap.

Yvonne Whittingham died but Tosh walked away with a visual reminder of the dreadful night that would remain with him for the rest of his life: the scars that the smashed windscreen bequeathed to his previously exquisite face.

Peter Tosh should not have survived, and now three years later he was locked in a cell with plain-clothes policemen who seemed determined to finish the job. This was it. As the batons rained down and boots kicked at his chest and head, all Tosh could do was to 'play dead'.

At 7.30 a.m. on 19 September 1978, five months after the 'One Love Peace Concert', Peter Tosh had been arrested, bundled into a police car and shoved into a lock-up, on suspicion of smoking a spliff. The arresting officer had tried to 'gun-butt' him, Tosh claimed, but the reggae star and budding martial arts expert neatly evaded the blow which landed instead on the cheek of the policeman's colleague. Back at the station, several officers laid into him, and after they were done, Tosh was left with a broken arm, a plethora of bruises and a nasty seeping gash to his skull. Aspects of the incident appear to have been lost in translation by the time the charge sheet was written up; Tosh was accused of unlawful wounding, resisting arrest, assaulting a policeman and using indecent language.

Just a week before, a profile of Tosh had appeared in a full-length feature in the entertainment pages of the *Gleaner*. Though proudly wearing the badge of Rastafari, he'd confounded readers' expectations by disparaging 'the people [who] rub dirt and dung into their hair and don't bathe, claiming to be Rastas'. Tosh revealed fleetingly something of his complex nature, and for once dropped the rhetoric that threatened to crust over him. Readers learnt that as well as being a keen unicyclist, the militant former Wailer was also a lover of birds; he kept a single blue and white parakeet that was given the freedom of his yard. Tosh's new-found ease stemmed largely from his lucrative contract with the Rolling Stones with whom he'd embarked on an extensive six-week tour in June 1978. He'd sung '(You Got to Walk and) Don't Look Back' live on stage in a duet with Mick Jagger, whose unfettered pleasure in performing with Tosh, ranked on a scale of 1–10, looked like it peaked at 11. But even that was as nothing compared to the ecstasy of the night in Los Angeles when Tosh fidgeted in the audience during a Bob Marley and the Wailers show before jumping out of his seat and bounding onto the stage to join his former bandmate for a nostalgic rendition of 'Get Up, Stand

Up'. As Bunny Wailer had alluded, it would be impossible for any of the trio to wash each other out of their hair.

Back on the tour in Philadelphia, Tosh had performed in front of 120,000 – a vast crowd; a head-turning validation of his worth (not that he'd ever doubted it), and a mark of his emergence from Marley's shadow as an international star in his own right. But accompanying this stellar success was the nagging doubt as to the vehicle by which he'd achieved it: not one of his own compositions but a cover of a Smokey Robinson song. Tosh would rather his break-out hit had not been a rendition of the saccharine 'Don't Look Back' which muddied the clarity of his fierce reputation. The former Wailer was understandably pleased by the news that hundreds of thousands of copies of the song were rolling off the presses and into the teenage bedrooms of middle America. But, at some level, the tune also filled him with resentment. 'It's dealing with love; people don't look for me to sing a song like that,' he winced. It presented an uncomfortable dilemma: 'People dem a sneer, but – pure airplay!'[324]

'Volatile' was the description critics most often used about Peter Tosh, but his volatility was of no greater or lesser voltage than that of any Rastafarian purist unreconciled to living in an impure world. 'One has only to ask a Rasta how he is today,' wrote the researcher Sheila Kitzinger, 'to bring forth an immediate outburst about the vengeance of the Lord, the present victimisation and penalisation, the evils of Sodom and Gomorrah ... and the desolation that awaits.'[325]

Peter Tosh might have taken some comfort from knowing that 'Don't Look Back' was not in the same league as Marley's jolly and inoffensive 'Punky Reggae Party': music that teenage private-school girls in London's fashionable Chelsea district could bop along to; music that would have emptied the dancehalls in Trench Town, causing eyes to roll, teeth to kiss, arms to fold and bottles to fly until the selector had the wisdom to return to the real t'ing, to the music of sweat and dirt and ribaldry and grinding groins.

While Bob Marley was smoothing out lines for 'Punky Reggae Party', Peter Tosh (when not crooning with Mick Jagger) was pushing back the boundaries of vulgarity with songs like 'Oh Bumbo klaat' – a profanity whose origins lay in the colloquialism for the bloodied cloth used by menstruating women.

The promotion of the sanitised over the raw and undiluted had been a drama played out before. But Peter Tosh was supposed to be, and largely was different. Tosh would amble through a routine interview, meandering harmlessly until some unexpected corner was turned in the conversation; then he would snap open like a barber's razor. Did he envisage singing further love songs? No, he wasn't going to sing no 'Baby, baby I love you.' He didn't deal with that. Venom pumped through the carotid arteries in his neck at the abhorrent idea that a man would profess his love for his woman before he honoured his Maker.

Tosh's explosive nature was near impossible to predict. He was convinced that the tardiness of his international recognition owed a great deal to his colour. In an audience cresting with applause, Tosh's ears were tuned to discern the slow handclap. In the depths of his music and psyche lurked an unresolved racial injury that, when triggered, had a tendency to confound and bamboozle, reminiscent of the idiosyncratic John Coltrane. Towards the end of his life, Coltrane was asked about his approach to free jazz. He was, he said, 'trying to play the kind of jazz that the white man couldn't copy'. Peter Tosh offered a variant on that theme. He was experimenting with 'a musical form that would mystify the white man and blow his mind'.[326]

Peter Tosh would not submit himself to the kind of cultural bleaching process that might render his music more acceptable to the American mainstream. In any event, if exported Jamaican music was being smoothed and prettified for a foreign audience, then back home, among the crowds to whom Tosh most wanted to appeal, it was taking on an even harder edge. 'The music tek a turn' towards dancehall, recalled Derrick Morgan, just as the country was taking a turn away from ganja and towards crack cocaine. With dancehall came 'slackness' (vulgarity). Perhaps, musically, it was not so much a turn but a return; it 'wheel and come again', as Jamaicans say, back to its rawer origins (steeped in sex and violence), with not even the slightest offer of the illusion of safety.

Peter Tosh had crossed over to the mainstream but with the understanding that, under the cover of darkness, he would always find his way back. Songs like 'Oh Bumbo Klaat' were musical stinkbombs released with abandon; they were not intended for popular international consumption or for the ignorant and faint-hearted; rather, they were a signal to the local hardcore cognoscenti that here was man of no compromise and no surrender.

The reunion with Marley passed fleetingly, there was no fillip to their stalled friendship; after a while the old antagonisms and veiled carping returned. Perhaps, if he'd known that Marley had only a few years left to live, Tosh's resentments might have been diffused and cast to the winds. But unbeknown to all but a few in Marley's inner circle, the melanoma that had been diagnosed after an inspection of an injured toe was already spreading, metastasising stealthily through Bob Marley's body. Though there would be some remedial treatment (a skin graft over the toe and a piece of bone removed), Marley had rejected the radical amputation which his Western doctors had advised. Such surgery ran counter to Marley's Rastafarian livity. Clinics and orthodox medicine were to be avoided. Every Rastafarian knew this to be the case. According to Kitzinger's Rasta informants, 'illness and death are the result of an unnatural interference with the course of nature'. It was a common Rasta belief that 'any death in the hospital is murder by white medicine'. It was not surprising therefore that 'a Rasta would not normally go into a hospital unless he was unconscious'.

Bob Marley placed himself under the care of a Rasta herbalist called 'Doc' Bagga, who was confident that a healing herb or a preparation comprised of several herbs could restore his health. Marley also sought alternative medical treatment at the clinic of Josef Issel's in Bavaria. But the cancer could not be checked. By 1981, Marley had all but given up hope of a cure. Esther Anderson was unaware of her former lover's condition, but shortly after Marley had played a spectacular concert in Zimbabwe (to mark the end of the civil war), she spent an evening with him, and was disturbed by his fits of vomiting during the night. He was disheartened and refused to talk about his illness, she said. Even an amateur sleuth could detect that there was some serious aberration in Marley's behaviour, especially relative to his Rastafarian beliefs. Anderson noted pitifully that there were signs of leftover meat on a plate; she also learnt that he was no longer disinclined to wave away the crates of champagne that were offered after each concert.

At the close of his life Bob Marley appeared to waver in his certainties. After more than a decade of wrestling with the various branches of Rastafari who sought to claim him as their own, Bob Marley was baptised in the Ethiopian Orthodox Church. Though he never abandoned Rastafari, he finally stepped back from all of those who were determined to co-opt him – politicians, friends, brethren.

Marley had said on more than one occasion that he, like the true Rasta, did not 'believe in death, neither in flesh nor in spirit'.[327] In his thirty-sixth year and on the eve of his premature death, Bob Marley's faith obviously comforted him. He knew that he had lived a commendable life, that he had striven to maintain his vows – to his God, his talent, his family and compadres. Rita Marley would later claim that 'when he was sick and losing gravity with life', he pined for his absent friends, Peter and Bunny. Bob Marley was perplexed and hurt by the fact that 'they couldn't even call him', she alleged. They did reach out to him indirectly in tributes to friends and admirers, 'but by then it was too late'.

On the day of Marley's death, Valerie Cowan, a representative from Island Records, decided to inform Tosh, before breaking the news to the radio stations. When she spoke to him on the phone, she was not entirely surprised by the coldness of his reaction. Cowan smiled faintly as she attempted to explain what happened next, as an embarrassed mother might recounting the latest incident of her Tourette's-suffering child. 'Well, if it so it just so,' Tosh had said about Marley's death. 'At least it leave a little space for all of us to go through now.'

There was the common and irritating misconception, said Cowan, that Jamaican music was a one-man-show, that 'if it wasn't Marley, then it wasn't reggae'.[328] Even so, Tosh's suggestion that Marley's giant stature cast a huge shadow over the island's musicians and that his death opened up opportunities for other reggae artists appeared bewildering and callous. It is possible that his words were those of a man in shock at the news of the passing of his old friend. But even if he hadn't meant to be bilious, in the end Tosh had allowed the years of resentment to speak for him. A far more generous response came from Bunny Wailer. When he reflected on Marley's special talent, Wailer concluded that, through his music, Bob Marley had acted as a conduit between man and God. Marley created and played the music, 'but it wasn't him. It was greater than him.'

'You gwan dead tonight.' That is how it sounded to Santa Davis. The musician was visiting Peter Tosh, and those chilling words came from the gunmen who now stood over the singer and his guests.

Peter Tosh was forced to lie face down on the cold marble floor. The barrel of a pistol was shoved into the side of his head. The safety catch was released. But Jamaicans will tell you, with impressive earnestness, that if an attacker shows the knife, machete or gun then he is not going to use it: the hidden weapon is the one you should fear. The gunman, though, continued to shout, growing ever more strident in his repeated threats that the reggae star should prepare himself for death because he would not survive the night. 'I come for kill you.'

All the while the armed intruder and his accomplices kept up their demands for money, which became increasingly hysterical as it began to dawn on them that they were likely to be disappointed. There was no money to be found at 5 Plymouth Avenue. The grandeur of the residence in Barbican Heights, nestled in an exclusive, upper-class suburb of Kingston (you couldn't get any higher), belied the owner's relatively impoverished state. Despite being owed a tidy sum in royalties from record companies, and an expectation of a handsome remuneration from his time in the original Wailers, notwithstanding the fact that he was 'locked in a feud', according to the *Gleaner*, 'over the million-dollar Marley estate', Peter Tosh was currently financially embarrassed.

But on 11 September 1987, Peter Tosh should have been feeling somewhat relieved. That morning he had negotiated a $100,000 (JA) loan from the bank. (The loan was secured; the collateral was to be provided by the title of another property at Sterling Castle.) And even after authorising a third of that amount to be dispersed, to satisfy a pack of creditors, he would still be left relatively cash rich, able to draw on some $65,000. The brief flush of euphoria familiar to the beneficiaries of new credit, who are more accustomed to the steady drip of debt, had not yet evaporated.

And then the night. At about 7 p.m., as the last of the sun dipped below the horizon, and the crickets sounded the evening's familiar chorus, Tosh's dogs began to yelp. Jamaicans rarely kept dogs as pets. Those attached to families, scrawny, 'mawga' (meagre) dogs with protruding ribcages, mostly fended for themselves. Tosh fed his German Shepherds routinely but kept them hungry enough to bite. These were dogs more in keeping with the warnings pinned to the gates and fences of Kingston's homes: 'Beware of Beasts' and 'Bad Dogs'. Comedy for the most part perhaps; for signs such as these (popular even among those who possessed little worth stealing) screamed too hysterically from battered tin plates clanking on rusting gates throughout the capital. 5 Plymouth Avenue had no need of fakery. Having scaled the whitewashed walls, even the most intrepid burglar would hesitate on imagining what might greet him on the other side.

That night Peter Tosh's guard dogs – half a dozen of them – yelped and barked, not in a distracted way, not howling individually at the moon and the stars, but with collective purpose. Their master eventually roused himself and asked Michael Robinson, one of the regulars in his diminishing retinue, to investigate. One remove from sleep, and made mellow from the marijuana that had been passed around, Robinson eased himself down the stairs. He found three men standing at the door, one of whom he recognised. Dennis 'Leppo' Lobban was a slim-built thirty-three-year-old black man, whom police later described as possessing a 'bulging forehead, husky voice and scar on his left cheek'. He was a higgler and a dub poet, whose talents had, to date, remained stubbornly unrecognised by the world. He was, nevertheless, a regular visitor to Tosh's home. Robinson recalled that the other two men wore smart suits and had the bearing of 'executives'. Lobban's countenance was closer to that of a vagabond.

Men like Dennis Lobban were a reminder to Tosh of his sweat-stained past. He was one of a number of unemployed hangers-on, yard-boys and studio rats whose presence mocked the splendour of Tosh's present dwelling in the airy, rustic hills overlooking the teeming city. Though elevated and rimmed with bougainvillea and orange groves, in reality, Barbican Heights – even after the draconian measures ushered in by the state of emergency from the decade before – was not so far removed from Trench Town. And on 11 September 1987, the past, in the shape of Dennis Lobban, came knocking on Tosh's door. No amount of uptown pretension could disguise the stench, squalor and degradation of Kingston's ghettoes that clung to Lobban; the malodour of one defeat after another, exacerbated by a prison term, was the only life Lobban had known.

No one could recall how he'd originally found his way to Tosh's camp. He was known to the reggae star as one of the hoodlums who regularly hung around during recording sessions, adding to, and partaking of, the vibe. In the preceding year he'd joined the ranks of Tosh's solicitous attendants – yardboys grown to men – whose prospects had not much improved with their maturity and yet still carried some unspecified hope of an upturn in their fortunes; that something might be gained merely by their proximity to a famous reggae singer. Lobban seemed more of a loyal courtier than others. He impressed with his loyalty. Allegedly once, when flagged down at a roadblock, police stopped them and found an unlicensed gun in Tosh's car. Lobban (who was one of the passengers) falsely and valiantly claimed ownership of the weapon, sparing his mentor a spell in custody. Lobban, the willing surrogate for his boss, went on to serve a second term in prison, brief but long enough to qualify (in Lobban's calculation) for a reward.

Dennis 'Leppo' Lobban struck many as a man of remarkable intensity but one who otherwise seemed to have little talent, save for violence. His charge sheet included armed robbery, resulting in a twenty-five-year stretch in the General Penitentiary (he served twelve years) for shooting a policeman in the face.

Though not officially employed by Tosh, Lobban called him 'the boss'. After all he, Lobban, was there to help, to be of service. The unfortunate business over yet another accident involving Tosh's car was a case in point. Peter Tosh had gone abroad on tour, leaving his Volvo behind. Weeks later, Lobban claimed he was informed that the car was being driven by one of the boss's retinue without the owner's knowledge. 'While I was at Skateland at Half-Way Tree, my bredda saw the Volvo and brought my attention.' In his account, Lobban confronted the unauthorised driver, and cursed him: 'Wha'ppen ... as the man [Tosh] back turn, you took away the man Volvo, ups and downs in it.' Jamaica's country roads were scarred with potholes and craters down which a car could disappear – an event that occurred with sickening regularity among men who seemed bent on driving straight to heaven. 'That was the Friday,' recalled Lobban. 'The Sunday, he [the rogue driver] went to Hellshire [beach], with some girls, and on his way coming back, the Volvo turn over, all four wheels up in the air.' When Tosh returned, Lobban hurried to brief him on what had been going on in his absence, saving the juiciest details about the car till last, just as he was ready to leave: 'When we reach at the gate ... at 5 Plymouth Avenue, I told him what had happened and he gave me a money.' In a gesture, underlining the rigour of the report, Lobban had rather helpfully suggested that it might not be prudent to confront the suspect. The boss ignored the advice and, when Lobban came back to Plymouth Avenue some time later, Tosh told him frankly that he didn't believe his version of the circumstances surrounding the car accident. Lobban recalled bitterly how Tosh brought the conversation to an end with the words: 'every lying lip is an abomination to Jah'. The accusation caused 'every vein, every bone, in [my] body to revolt'.

Having calmed the dogs and exchanged pleasantries with Lobban and the two 'executives', Robinson turned and started to climb the stairs. But rather than the creak of the gates closing, he was perplexed to hear the steady slap of shoes, as the men slowly and purposefully followed him. He turned and saw they had pulled out guns. Robinson raised his hands and the four men walked up to the open-plan living area on the next floor.

Tosh and his companions were lounging on ornate sofas more given to decoration than comfort. The television turned up loud masked the entrance of the intruders. When Tosh's party woke to the presence of the armed men in their midst, they were, at first, blinded by what they saw. The hallucinogenic properties of the marijuana being carefully passed around the friends who had gathered at Plymouth Avenue would have further contributed to the surrealism of what was unfolding. The drummer Santa Davis recalled feeling that they were the victims of a hoax; that the weapons the men carried were perhaps the props of an elaborate joke. After all, Tosh was not averse to such mock actions himself.

Peter Tosh was a master of menace. Once his spirit darkened it was only a matter of moments before a kind of intellectual fuse was tripped; then 'Bombaclaats' and other bad words flew from angry lips. And sacrificing the good humour of all that might have gone before, Tosh defaulted destructively to his old ways, as a reformed addict might to the alluring familiarity of his vice. At other times, the menace was predetermined and staged. This theatrical version had provided reams of copy for delighted international music magazines for more than a decade. A shuttle of craven journalists would fly in on the eve of a concert for the briefest, scariest audience; they'd genuflect in front of the idiosyncratic reggae star, and stumble through a list of prepared questions, before scurrying back to their offices with outrageous tales of the murderous, near madness of the former Wailer. Bemused cub reporters developed a twitch, a kind of nystagmus, as their eyes flicked nervously between the reggae star (impossible to read behind his mirrored sunglasses) and the machete he sharpened. A strain perhaps for the *NME* or *Rolling Stone* trainee, but ultimately an entertainment to leaven an otherwise routine assignment. The more forensic reader, though, would glean fairly early on that no direct threat had been made, nor was there ever likely to have been one.

Peter Tosh revelled in the notion that he was the 'steppin-razor' depicted in the song of that title – the dangerous man that you'd be a fool to cross. But Tosh's steppin-razor, tough-man stance was just a front, suggests the DJ Wayne Jobson. By way of example, Jobson recalled an incident with Keith Richards where Tosh revealed his true nature. Peter Tosh had been in disagreement with Jagger, Richards and the Rolling Stones' record label. Richards had bought a house in Jamaica which he rarely used, and Tosh had acquired the keys to the property. At the height of their dispute, Peter Tosh let it be known that he had 'captured' the house in lieu of missing payments; and when the news was passed on to Keith Richards, the guitarist was livid. He boarded the very next flight to Montego Bay and rang his home from the airport. Tosh answered and Richards screamed down the line that Tosh should clear out of the property or else. According to the DJ, Tosh answered with his usual feline languor that Keith Richards should hurry up and come if he thought he was 'bad' because he, Tosh, had a gun and would be waiting for him. A furious Keith Richards answered that he should load the gun and take the safety catch off because he was on his way, and slammed down the phone. By the time Richards arrived Peter Tosh had fled the property.

But by 1987, this kind of gamesmanship was not so apparent even to the most seasoned student of Peter Tosh. Many pointed an accusing finger in the direction of his new girlfriend, Marlene Brown. She not only became his lover, but also his manager and gatekeeper. Brown exerted enormous control over the reggae star, dispatching close friends and ostracising others. The spurned friends alleged that Brown dabbled in Obeah and fed Tosh's paranoia about the influence of malign supernatural forces on his life. Tosh told the few remaining regular friends that their home was full of duppies and he was going to clear Plymouth Avenue of every single one of them.

Over the last few years, Tosh had grown increasingly anxious – 'apprehensive' would be closer to the truth – about the public perception of his success and relative wealth. In an interview recorded in Los Angeles in July 1983, he fizzed with irritation at the suggestion, reported in trade magazines, that with the single 'Johnny B. Goode', Peter Tosh had a hit on his hands. Tosh likened such claims to 'spiritual and verbal assassination', as the dissemination of such views could only lead to trouble: 'When the [people] see it as a hit, you know what is created in their mind: "I have money." People have me down, as they did Bob Marley, as a millionaire, and brand you and have you as a target.' Tosh may have prided himself on creating music that was 'an awakening to the slumbering mentality' of those who had been defeated by the 'shitstem'. But he was also keenly aware of the stirrings of jealousy in compatriots who focused less on his musical achievements than on his imagined financial success.

Tosh compared the public's attitude towards him, at this stage, with that they had held about Marley, but there was a difference. The apocryphal-sounding anecdote of Marley and his BMW contains kernels of truth. With the first flush of money coming his way, Bob Marley bought himself a shiny BMW. He'd drive to the heart of the Trench Town ghetto and leave the BMW unlocked. Such was the reverence for this favoured local hero that no one would have dreamt of troubling Brother Bob's vehicle. Tosh, by contrast, turned his back for a moment, found his Volvo with all four wheels in the air.

Peter Tosh was undoubtedly a folk hero in Jamaica, but he was one who had come at a peculiar time in the nation's history. In an earlier innocent age of modest expectations, the population had revelled in the escapist fable of the working-class hero who emerged from their midst; they had toasted his success as their own. But Dennis Lobban had a different mindset; like the Rhygin character in *The Harder They Come*, he wanted his share, 'here and now'. And on 11 September, he laid that grotesque claim before Peter Tosh. Where was the money? he had demanded. It was, in a sense, a reasonable question. Hadn't Tosh appeared on the wireless saying he was going to sue EMI for millions? Envious ears had tuned to the broadcasts on Jamaican radio, alerting listeners to the big pay day that was due to their compatriot. The complexities of the protracted courtroom battles and the diminished returns were lost on the gunmen. Peter Tosh was compelled to remain prostrate, with his face pushed to the floor, powerless and unable to answer.

After half an hour of arguing and reasoning – with Tosh continuing to protest quietly that he had no money in the house – the gunmen turned their weapons on the musician and his associates, shooting them all in the back of the head, before fleeing the scene.

Alerted by neighbours, the emergency services arrived shortly afterwards. They were confronted with carnage. Peter Tosh and his guests lay injured or dying on the floor. Tosh, along with the popular radio announcer Jeff 'Free I' Dixon and the self-styled herbalist Wilton 'Doc' Brown, were among the most seriously injured. The ambulance carrying the stricken reggae star raced desperately to the hospital, but really it needn't have bothered. Peter Tosh was already dead. He was forty-two.

Of the original Wailers, two were now dead, and the last surviving member, Bunny Wailer, had long since fallen silent. In 1981, Wailer had been comforted by a vision of Bob Marley's celestial ascent (to join the ancestors), guided by a flock of seven white doves. No such spiritual reveries accompanied news of Tosh's departure. It was a macabre and pitiful end, shrouded in the rumour that, for some unexplained and unfathomable reason, the gunmen had actually been sent deliberately to murder the reggae star. Though such a theory has never been substantiated, it's clear that during his life Tosh had made many enemies at both ends of the political spectrum with his outspoken criticism of the hypocrisy of the self-serving politicians at the heart of the 'shitstem' whose arming of the ghetto youth had led to violent partisan rivalries in Kingston – Trench Town and Tivoli Gardens, in particular. By local standards, Peter Tosh was affluent. But though, he lived in an enormous house in a plush suburb on the fringes of the capital, Tosh was still 'of the street', and it was at least one gunman from his old neighbourhood in Trench Town who claimed his life.

Peter Tosh had always been the most fiery and militant of the Wailers. But all three had been surrounded by violence ever since their arrival in the capital as youths; they'd acknowledged it and given voice to it in song. The original Wailers had followed the hopeful trajectory of all of the people who found themselves captive in the capital's shanty towns; they had moved up and out of Kingston. The ascent of three Rasta youths had been most unlikely. That one would be pulled back by the undertow of the violent ghetto in the end was not unexpected.

In his last months, Tosh had been plagued by dreams in which duppies had whispered, 'Bloodshed! Bloodshed! Bloodshed!' His paranoia had earlier propelled him onto a plane bound for Nigeria, in search of a famed medicine-man and a potion that would protect him from bullets. His manager, Copeland Forbes, had been appalled by Tosh's determination to hand over tens of thousands of dollars to the renowned fetisheur. On the evening of 11 September 1987, the magic potion evidently had not worked.

'I wasn't looking for him to die that way,' recalled his mother, on hearing the news. She had foreseen that her son's death would be violent, only the method surprised her: 'I was looking for him to die in a car crash. I know he drive fast.'[329]

While no complications accompanied the unbridled national mourning for the loss of Bob Marley, scattered across the island's newspapers were a few dissenting voices who considered Tosh the author of his own downfall and challenged the wisdom of elevating 'a boorish ... foul-mouthed ganja-smoking man' to an icon of heroic proportions.[330] Such views were drowned out by the reverential tones of those who forgave him his foibles and saluted the decision by local radio stations to play Tosh's most cherished music, especially 'Creation', the day after his murder. 'Creation' had always possessed an elegiac quality; and now, with its timeless, ethereal and pastoral beauty, it served both as an anthem for the doomed Tosh and a bridge between the living and the dead. Peter Tosh would have appreciated the irony of the adjustments that many, typified by James McIntosh, now felt compelled to make. His father, whose parental input had not exceeded the impregnation of Tosh's mother, now came forward to scold her for the inappropriate arrangements for the burial of their beloved offspring. McIntosh claimed to be motivated by a desire to spare his stalwart Rastafarian son the final dishonour of being laid to rest in a plot of land assigned to pigs. The allegation was unfounded.

Peter 'Steppin' Razor' Tosh was a witty, reflective and sensitive soul who, when he posed in front of a mirror, saw a rude boy, sharp and dangerous, reflected back at him. In his polemical and confrontational style, Peter Tosh drew the fire to him; he was always more comfortable with rebellion and his outlook, which chimed with many of his compatriots, was expressed through music which was by turns angry and apocalyptic. 'These are the last days,' Tosh would often repeat almost as a matter of fact.

Death held no dominion over Rastafarians. It, in part, accounted for their anathema to the writing of wills which carried the presumption of mortality. Neither Tosh nor Marley left a will. Marley's spectacular funeral inspired Jamaicans with the lasting sentiments of 'One Love'; Tosh's murder filled them with dread. In the wake of Marley's death the newspapers had regularly posed the question: who shall be next? By which they meant: who would ascend the throne made vacant by Marley's passing and assume the title 'The King of Reggae'? Now the same headline began to appear again but it asked a different question: 'Who shall be next – to be killed?'[331]

Tosh had joined the sad roll call of Jamaican musicians and artists whose lives had been brought to a violent end; they included Slim Smith, Carlton Barrett and Stephen Taylor of the Ethiopians. Everyone knew that the list would not end with Peter Tosh. But in one sense, his murder marked the closing of a chapter. The singers were being usurped spectacularly by the dancehall DJs.

Bunny Wailer, who remained brooding in his tent, seemed even less inclined after Tosh's death to battle for the faltering soul of reggae. The music had taken a turn away from the conscious lyric writing of practitioners such as Tosh, Marley and Wailer. If there were any doubt about the end of roots reggae, then Bunny Wailer's reception at the Sting festival in 1990, when sections of the crowd showered the stage with empty beer bottles and stones, put it beyond question.

Bunny Wailer preferred to remember the good times; to conjure his fallen brothers onto the platform with him. The last time bottles had rained down with such fury was at Vere Johns's 'Opportunity Hour' in response to the Wailers' departure *from* the stage, when they were encouraged to 'wheel and come again' and play once more. Fleeing now, to make way for Shabba Ranks and Ninja Man and, more importantly, to avoid injury, left a taste as bitter as the cud. It would take almost two decades before the ghosts of that miserable and ignominious night were laid to rest. Then in 2007, Bunny Wailer took to the stage once more with Marley and Tosh – with their sons, Damian and Andrew, standing in for their fathers.

And when they asked the last remaining Wailer the oft-repeated question about what it was like to play with Peter and Bob, Bunny Wailer would drop back through time to focus his innermost thoughts on his fellow natural mystics: 'It was like the Children of Israel gathered around the Ark of the Covenant. It doesn't happen every day, but when it does, it's something to write about.'[332]

EPILOGUE:
TIME FOR SUFFERER DRIVE BIG CAR

BUNNY Wailer was a riddle that I had not been able to solve. Jamaica is a small island, yet I'd failed to track him down. 'You cyan jus' walk into the man house,' a fixer had once explained to me about the reclusive Rasta reggae star. 'The man have fi sense you, fi feel you. Is not a ordinary man you a-deal with. Is a mystic-man, you know, dread.' But might Bunny Wailer's mysticism, channelled through ganja, have been the simple projection of those who held him in awe? 'You be a-talk with the man one minute,' the fixer had marvelled. 'But turn round and he gone.'

Perhaps, though, the tales of Wailer's ability to disappear in a thunderclap and claims of his simultaneous reappearance miles away in the spirit world of the Jamaican 'bush' merely acted as cover for his countrymen who revelled in obfuscation and real life Anancy stories.

After several trips to the island, after two years of false starts and false sightings, having chased the last remaining original Wailer around Jamaica following a trail of iron-clad tip-offs, having sat for hours in cars at the appointed hour, as dusk descended at the suggested rendez-vous, suspecting – despite the enthusiastic convictions of handsomely rewarded middlemen – that Bunny Wailer would never materialise; having obtained a cellphone number for him that had rung and rung into the ether without answer, I had returned to England having given up all hope of an audience with the elusive singer.

Then one morning the phone rang from one of the many publicists and handlers who had offered a meeting but had finally led me such a merry, ineffectual dance.

'Would you like to interview Bunny Wailer at 10 a.m. on Friday?' asked the publicist. Her precision, at such variance from the previous dozen vague and languorous phone calls, was oddly disturbing. There had to be a catch, surely.

Well, yes, there were, of course, the familiar, last-minute complications. 'I think it's going to be Gatwick airport, but we don't know which terminal; we won't know till the morning,' warned the publicist. And no, she didn't know the answer to my taxing question about which airline he was flying in on! 'But he does have a couple of hours in transit,' she assured. 'And I'll try to slip you in before he heads off to the concert in the south of France.' The publicist was conspiratorial; she gave the impression that we both knew, didn't we, that there was someone out there who needed to be outfoxed. Confusingly, by the end of our conversation, I believed that person was me.

Bunny Wailer appeared through the arrivals' gate. His dreadlocks (decades in the making) were woven and tied with fine red, green and gold thread, so that he seemed to be wearing a prince's turban or an elaborate and jewelled bird's nest. He was kitted out in a khaki suit which would have served as battle fatigues had the creases not been so sharp. In his left hand, adorned with bulky rings, he carried a 12-inch gold-plated rod with a silver crown – the kind of sceptre that bestowed power on a bishop or, in this case, the Rasta elder that he so obviously was. He appeared indifferent to whether anyone had come to greet him, though you couldn't be sure as thick sunglasses obscured his eyes. Once through the barrier, Bunny Wailer proceeded evenly and with purpose like a royal or a president who no one would dream of outpacing. And so it was. The band members who followed fanned out in a triangle behind him.

The interview was to take place on board the purple 'Galaxy' double-decker tour bus, parked and idling, outside the airport. But the publicist was late and no one, it seemed, had alerted the maestro to the arrangement. Wailer and band members entered the bus. The hydraulic-operated doors closed ominously with a thud, leaving me on the pavement. The trombonist had volunteered to act as a go-between to negotiate with Bunny Wailer. His words must have been persuasive because the door suddenly sprung open like a safe whose code had been cracked.

I was led up the stairs to the top deck, feeling my way slowly, as the Galaxy's tinted windows darkened the interior as well. It took a little while for your vision to adjust, like it might on entering a dimly lit cathedral with its weak shards of light through the stained-glass windows.

At the back of the bus, Bunny Wailer was seated on his own on a crescent-shaped sofa with a round table in front. Despite the darkness, he showed no intention of removing his sunglasses. Wailer was perfectly still, almost sculptural. There was something of the quality of a master yoga practitioner about him, one who had achieved stillness through years of meditation. Nothing could trouble him. And as I approached, for a moment he appeared to recede; I did not seem to be getting any closer. Even when I sat beside him, there was no break in his stillness. I took out my microphone and asked him to say a few words so that I could set the recording levels.

'Bunny Wailer, Bunny Wailer, Bunny Wailer, Bunny Wailer.' He chanted in a low sonorous voice.

I had learnt enough about Bunny Wailer not to expect any answer that might be a literal response to a direct question: he did not disappoint. Almost every reply ended with the punctuation, 'The most Haile I Selassie I, Jah Rastafari.' I may have considered that I was conducting an interview, but he laboured under no such delusion. This was to be a kind of liturgy, an opportunity to confirm and recite some of the tenets of the Rasta faith. For instance, when I asked him how his father, a Revivalist priest, had taken to his son's conversion to Rasta, Bunny Wailer reminded me that the question was poorly framed. After all 'everything start with and end with Rasta. My life was designed by Haile I Selassie I long before I even entered my mother's womb. *He* has willed I to be a vanguard, a shepherd of our people, to hope, to pray and cry for the people.'

Wailer's speech was lawyerly, moderated through clauses and subclauses. He was a delight to listen to: the Rasta reasoning, if anything, enhanced its musicality. I would not have been surprised to learn he'd taken elocution lessons. But I had not expected him to enjoy himself so much. His lips curved into a delicious knowing smile as the words tumbled from them like polished pearls. Even when reflecting on the recent calamity in Jamaica – the state of emergency imposed during the manhunt for the Mafia don Christopher 'Dudus' Coke in which scores of people had been killed – the clarity of Bunny Wailer's observations satisfied him. 'Dudus is just like a germ from the original corruption that has so far taken over this little island. From the 60s the gun seed was planted in the process and it has now borne some ugly and bitter fruit.' But Jah Bunny was not too concerned as Jamaica was 'protected and guided by the most Haile I Selassie I, Jah Rastafari'. It was not a dialogue but a monologue, interrupted by my unnecessary questions which were courteously but briefly entertained and then discarded before picking up the thread of his soliloquy. The performance was reminiscent of the seasoned comedian reciting an old joke whose inherent truth continued to amuse him, no matter the audience's familiarity with it.

One of the band members approached with a suitcase filled with what I imagined was marijuana but Bunny Wailer waved him away: he had more things to say. I'd been warned by some journalists who had fallen out of love with Bunny Wailer to expect a darkly brooding man, a low-toned paranoiac whose gaze was foreshadowed with suspicion; an old warrior primed for insults, real or imagined. But the man before me was at ease and much amused.

The humour ran out when I called on him to reflect on the Sting Festival in Jamaica on 26 December 1990 when some in the crowd had sent bottles and stones flying towards the stage, forcing Bunny Wailer to flee. Some argued that he'd been in retreat ever since.

'Sting is that kind of unpredictable event where anything can happen,' he said with a jauntiness that was a little forced.

'Yes but how did you recover . . .'

'Sometimes out of evil comes good.' A steeliness entered his voice: 'What was planned to take place there that night, my being there dampened that, cramped that. What occurred changed the whole atmosphere. With Ninja Man and Shabba Ranks you had a situation that was moving into a politicality where one artist was seen as a labourite and the other as a (rival) PNP, so with Bunny Wailer being there as a *Rastaman*, it took away that negative plan. So yes, I was glad to be there.'

'Surely not?' I suggested, repeating some of the headlines from reports of that night as a 'gross production in shame'. 'You suffered a terrible onslaught that night . . .'

'No sir, not'ing like dat.' Wailer snapped, his language suddenly reverting to Jamaican patois, before he recovered his composure somewhat. 'I was the only one who prayed for life when there were coffins on stage.' Bunny Wailer recalled the caskets in which the chalk-faced duo Ghost and Culture had arrived at the National Stadium. But he didn't see it as a joke. 'People came out of the coffins, so you know what that meant: Sting was supposed to be death. A lot of people supposed to have died at Sting but Bunny Wailer being there changed that.'

After humiliation comes honour, power, riches, might and eternal blessings – so the Rastas believe. The stars of Ninja Man and Shabba Ranks have faded, and the fortunes of the punany lyricists have fluctuated. And when Bunny Wailer said enigmatically, 'what is sweet to the taste is bitter to the belly', I took him to be referring to a diet of music as much as food, for he continued: 'At sixty-three years of age, I'm still jumping.' Bunny Wailer's longevity has proved a mystery to some, but his courage was not mysterious; it was plain. The last remaining of the original Wailers did not brood for long after 26 December 1990 but embarked on several gruelling tours and made new fans. He didn't need to tour, he said, but believed it his duty to sing the history of reggae. 'Bob Marley and Peter Tosh will be here for posterity as their messages are prolific and eternal. Bob said, "You're gonna tire to see my face," and I get some serious vision of Bob and Peter, of us still walking on stage.'

I left the tour bus and arranged to meet Bunny Wailer and his band the following night at their concert in London's Brixton Academy. Two decades on from the debacle of the Sting Festival, in front of an adoring multitude the compère announced that a 'living legend' was about to take to the stage. He called for 'fire, more fire, more fire', and hundreds of fans took out their cigarette lighters to illuminate the teasing and majestic entry of the 'original don dada' Bunny Wailer: grey-bearded, white-suited and regally cloaked, his voice trembling with passion and conviction. Launching into 'Rasta Man Chant', he invoked the demise of Babylon.

The air was not scarred with improvised projectiles. Nothing interrupted his lilting and exalting voice save the slow rumbling locomotion of applause. The voices from the crowd were those of love.

NOTES

1   Reports of Shabba Ranks's limousine and Ghost and Culture's hearse in 'That's Living' *Gleaner* (*Fair* magazine), 31 December 1990

2   Roger Steffens and Leroy Jodie Pierson, transcript from interviews with Bunny Wailer from the unpublished manuscript *Old Fire Sticks*

3   'Bunny Wailer Sings the Blues', *Gleaner*, 24 January 1991

4   *Gleaner*, 10 January 1991

5   Interview with John Masouri, 17 January 2009

6   'Man Talk', *Flair* magazine, 21 January 1991

7   'Letters to the Editor', *Gleaner*, 3 January 1991

8   Ken Post, *Arise Ye Starvelings: The Jamaican Labour Rebellion of 1938 and its Aftermath*, p. 444

9   *Up You Mighty Race*, BBC Radio 4, August 1987

10 Cited in Betty Laduke, 'Edna Manley: The Mother of Modern Jamaican Art', *Woman's Art Journal*, 1986. See also: Dena Merriam, 'A Merging of Cultures in the Sculpture of Edna Manley'

11 Esther Chapman, 'The Truth About Jamaica', *West Indian Review* 4,10 (June 1938)

12 Alexander Barclay, *A Practical View of the Present State of Slavery in the West Indies*, pp. 212–213

13 Padmore's group, the International African Service Bureau, was one of a collective that wrote to the Colonial Office. See 28, CO 950/30

14 Manley's recollection is cited by V. S. Naipaul in *The Middle Passage*, p. 59

15 Rex Nettleford, 'National culture and the artist', *Manley and the New Jamaica* p. 108

16 *Gleaner*, 31 July 1937

17 W. H. Auden, *Look Stranger*, 1936

18 *Up You Mighty Race*, BBC Radio 4, August 1987

19 Evidence to the Royal Commission, 12 November 1938, CO 950/218.

20 Denham to W. Ormsby Gore, 8 May 1938, 3, 'Disturbances', C.O 137/826, file 68868

21 J. Merle Davis, *The Church in the New Jamaica*, p. 34

22 *Gleaner*, 2 May 1938

23 Author interview with Ethlyn Veronica Adams, 24 November 2008

24 'Parliamentary Debate', House of Lords Official report, 109,70, 2 June 1938

25 Herbert. T. Thomas, *The Story of the West Indian Policeman* (Kingston Gleaner Co. 1927), p. 356

26 Claude McKay writes about this conundrum in the preface to *Constable Ballads*, 1912

27 Herbert T. Thomas, *The Story of the West Indian Policeman*, p. 103

28 Richard Hart, 'Diary of Sunday and Monday' (London University Institute of Commonwealth Studies). Quoted by Ken Post in *Arise Ye Starvelings*, p. 302

29 Cited in Ken Post's *Arise Ye Starvelings*, p. 279

30 Cited in *From We Were Boys*, p. 71. There are many versions of Bustamante's speech, but the overriding sentiment is one of his defiance. Ethlyn Veronica Adams's recollection of Bustamante's words were: 'Don't Shoot My People, shoot me!' Author interview 24 November 2008

31 Helen P. Hyatt-Shortt

32 J. Merle Davis, *The Church in the New Jamaica*, p. 35

33 From the documentary 'Steppin' Razor', Red X

34 J. M. Phillippo, *Jamaica: Its Past and Present State*, p. 218

35 Author interview with Frederick Hickling, 31 October 2005

36 Edward Long, *History of Jamaica*, Vol.2, p. 414

37 From the documentary 'Steppin' Razor', Red X

38 The committee of the 'Mass Marriage Movement' included the activist Amy Bailey and other colleagues from the Jamaica Federation of Women.

39 *Gleaner*, 24 July 1940, 9 December 1944, 4 December 1946

40 George Lamming, *In the Castle of My Skin*, p. 11

41 J. H. Hinton, *Memoir of William Knibb*, p. 99

42 F. Burnett, 'Land Settlement Report', 31 May 1939, 6 CO 137/835,68794, Cited by W. Burn, *Emancipation and Apprenticeship in the British West Indies*, p. 443

43 Glenelg's Circular Dispatch 30 January 1836, CO 140/126. Cited by W. Burn, *Emancipation and Apprenticeship in the British West Indies*, pp. 306–307

44 Morris Cargill (editor), *Ian Fleming Introduces Jamaica*, p. 27

45 Taken from the account of the anonymous author in *Marly or a Planter's Life in Jamaica*, p. 194

46 Timothy White offers an account of the wedding from Cedella Booker's perspective in *Catch-a-Fire*, pp. 57–62

47 Edith Clarke, *My Mother Who Fathered Me*, p. 110

48 Petition for the exclusion of Chinese, 1940 Colonial Office

49 Clarence Senior and Douglas Manley, *A Report on Jamaican Migration to Great Britain*, p. 43

50 Phillippo, *Jamaica: Its Past and Present*, p. 234

51 Bob Marley interview (between the tracks) on *Talking Blues*

52 W. MacMillan, *Warning from the West Indies*, p. 128

53 A. G. S. Coombs, 'Memorandum to the Moyne Commission (n.d) p. 14 in C.O.950/135

54 Quoted in Adrian Boot and Chris Salewicz's *Bob Marley: Songs of Freedom*, p. 43

55 So-called 'Clapping churches' were common in Jamaica, no matter the denomination. So many of the countryboys, like Wailer, Frederick 'Toots' Hibbert and Winston Jarrett, who became reggae musicians drew their initial inspiration from the church. See David Katz's *Solid Foundation*, p. 80

56 From the Red X tapes. See 'Steppin' Razor', Red X

57 Jervis Anderson, 'England in Jamaica' *American Scholar*, 22 March 2000

58 Author interview with Wayne Jobson

59 *Gleaner*, cited by Jackie Ranston in *From We Were Boys* p. 68

60 Herbert G. De Lisser, *Twentieth Century Jamaica* p. 98

61 Jervis Anderson, 'England in Jamaica' *American Scholar*, 22 March 2000

62 Councillor Woodham of Kingston believed it was an occasion for mourning 'for the 300 years we have been sat upon by Englishmen.' *Gleaner* 15 February 1954

63 Ian Fleming, *Dr No*, p. 35

64 Orlando Paterson, *Children of Sisyphus*, p. 24

65 *Gleaner*, 4 April 1922

66 Stephens, p. 169

67 Hélène Lee, *The First Rasta*, p. 94

68 Edith Clarke, *My Mother Who Fathered Me*, p. 94

69 Mary Proudfoot, *Britain and the United States in the Caribbean: A Comparative Study in the Methods of Development*, pp. 76–77

70 Patrick Leigh Fermor, *Traveller's Tree*, p. 241

71 Much of the information for the description of the erection of Trench Town is taken from 'Cultural Heritage Case Study: Trench Town, Kingston' by the architect Christopher Whyms-Stone, University of Technology, Jamaica, International Conference, 3 August 2005

72 Author interview with Helene Lee, 27 January 2009

73 See Hugh Sherlock's letter to the *Gleaner*, 21 April 1961 describing the growth of the slums in West Kingston

74 *Gleaner*, 9 October 1947

75 See Colin Clarke, *Decolonising the Colonial City: Urbanization and Stratification in Kingston, Jamaica*, pp. 185–205

76   Father Sherlock, 'Steady is the Word', *Gleaner*, 21 April 1961

77   CO 137/828/12

78   V. S. Naipaul, *The Middle Passage*, p. 36

79   *The Nation*, 18 March 2007

80   Stephen Davis, *Bob Marley*, p. 21

81   Harriet Beecher-Stowe, *Uncle Tom's Cabin*, p. 59

82   Cited by Rick Coleman in *Blue Monday*, p. 210

83   Author interview 21 January 2009

84   David Katz, *Solid Foundation*, p. 49

85   Don Snowden, *Los Angeles Times*, 14 August 1985

86   'Trench Town Experience: Knowledge' Anthony Doyley interviewed by Peter I (http://www.reggae-vibes.com/)

87   Timothy White, 'The King of Reggae Finds His Zion' *Rolling Stone*, 25 June 1981

88   Author interview

89   *Black Music*, September 1976: Vol.3/Issue 34

90   Barrington Spence interviewed by Peter I on http://www.reggae-vibes.com/concert/bspence/bspence.htm

91   Roger Steffens, *Reggae Scrapbook*, p. 100

92   V. S. Naipaul, *The Middle Passage*, pp. 53–54

93   *Gleaner*, 9 August 1959

94   Nathaniel Murrel, William Spencer and Adrian McFarlane, *Chanting Down Babylon: The Rastafarian Reader*, pp. 245–246

95   *The Year That Changed Jazz*, BBC Radio 4, 1959

96   Author interview, 6 July 2009

97   Michael Diebeert 'Sir Coxsone turns on the Power from Kingston to Brooklyn', *Village Voice*, March 2001

98   Murrel, Spencer and McFarlane, *Chanting Down Babylon*, p. 235

99   Chris Blackwell, author interview, 11 February 2009

100   Cited by David Katz in *Solid Foundation*, pp. 38–39

101   Ibid, p. 43

102   Of the 10,267 Chinese in Jamaica, 2,358 resided in Kingston in 1960, and 4,309 in St Andrew. From the *Statistical Yearbook of Jamaica* 1977, Dept of Statistics, Kingston Table 18, p. 110

103   Letter to the editor from C. L. Henry of Brown's Town, *Gleaner*, 27 January 1940, p. 8

104   *Falmouth Post*, 29 June 1855. See also *Lindo Legacy*

105   David Katz, *Solid Foundation*, p. 158

106   Sir Alexander Cadagon to Ambassador Quo Tai-Chi, 21 July 1938, CO 137/833/11

107   Memo from Governor Sir Arthur Richards, 18 August 1939, CO 137/833/11

108   Katz, *Solid Foundation*, p. 69

109   Editorial from *Gleaner*, 10 June 1913

110 Vera Rubin and Lambros Comitas, *Ganja in Jamaica: A medical anthropological study of chronic marihuana use*, p. 67

111 Ibid, p. 79

112 Steffens and Pierson, interviews for *Old Fire Sticks*

113 Martha Warren Beckwith, *Black Roadways*, p. 98

114 Zora Neale Hurston *Folklore, Memoirs and Other Writings*, p. 312

115 'Steppin' Razor', Red X

116 J. J. Williams, *Psychic Phenomena in Jamaica*, p. 156, 158. See also Orlando Patterson's *The Sociology of Slavery*, p. 203

117 M. G. Smith, 'Social Structure in the British Caribbean' Institute of Social and Economic Research of the University College of the West Indies, Vol.1, No.4 August 1953

118 Rita Marley, *No Woman No Cry*, p. 19

119 Ibid, p. 29

120 Beckwith., *Black Roadways*, p. 119

121 Duncan Stewart's memoir of George William Gordon and the 'Time of the Sixty' was published by the London Missionary Society. It is cited by Ansell Hart's papers, Vol. 4, No.2, June 1960

122 *Gleaner*, 13 August 1913

123 Ibid, 15 May 1904

124 Steffens, *Old Fire Sticks*

125 Skatalites website, www.skatalites.com

126 Ibid

127 *Gleaner*, 27 July 1966

128 Steffens, *Old Fire Sticks*

129 Ibid

130 Author interview, 20 April 2009

131 Cited in David Katz's *Solid Foundation*, p. 88

132 Author interview with Esther Anderson

133 Rebel Music TV Documentary

134 BBC TV Documentary, 'The Story of Jamaican Music'

135 The Jamaica Broadcasting Association's 'Top Ten' tunes programme kept a tally on the most frequently bought records, as well as those specially requested. See also Erna Brodber 'Black Consciousness and Popular Music in the 1960s and 1970s' *New West Indian Guide* 61 (1987), No:3/4, pp. 145–160.

136 Cited by Wayne Chen in *Reggae Routes*, p. 198

137 Erna Brodber, *A Study of Yards in the City of Kingston*, p. 42

138 Steffens, *Old Fire Sticks*

139 *Gleaner*, 17 June 1967

140 Ibid, 10 October 1948

141 Author interview, February 2009. Trevor Rhone died just months later on 15 September 2009

142 *Rolling Stone*, 19 July 1935

143 Noel de Montagnac, *Negro Nobodies*. Black Jamaicans were said to be perennially destined to be hewers of wood and drawers of water

144 Clarke, *My Mother Who Fathered Me*, p. 175

145 Steffens, *Old Fire Sticks*

146 Norman Manley, *Manley and the New Jamaica*, p. 279

147 'Garvey Lies in State', *Gleaner*, 12 November 1964. Garvey's remains were returned on the *Coromantee*.

148 From the lyrics of the song 'So Much Things to Say', I'll never forget how they sold Marcus Garvey for rice. Bob Marley and the Wailers. . .

149 *Gleaner*, 15 November 1964

150 Ibid

151 Garvey concluded an open letter to his followers from jail in Atlanta 1925 with the prophecy that in death his memory would be carried in the angry hearts of those who came after him: 'Look for me in the whirlwind or the storm, look for me all around you . . .'

152 The fuss made over Garvey's realignment contrasts with Rasta thought. Rasta's will endeavour, for example, to sleep from north to south, as the east-to-west alignment is one reserved for the dead when buried. See Jake Homiak, *Ancient of Days* p. 234

153 *Gleaner*, 5 September 1965

154 *Gleaner*, 1 December 1948

155 Martin Luther King Jr. visited Jamaica on 20 June 1965 and delivered a speech entitled 'Facing the Challenge of a New Age'. He addressed a large gathering at the National Stadium the next day, telling the crowd that Jamaicans should be proud of what they had achieved thus far.

156 Quoted in Norman Manley's *Manley and the New Jamaica* p. xlv. See also the pamphlet 'The West Indies – Towards a New Dominion', by H. V. Wiseman, Fabian Colonial Bureau 1946, p. 39

157 Cited by Ansell Hart, *Monthly Comments*, Vol.4. May 1960–July 1962

158 Author interview

159 Naipaul, *The Middle Passage*, p. 78

160 'Glorifying the Jamaican Girl': The 'Ten Types – One People' Beauty Contest, Racialized' Rowe *Radical History Review* 2009, pp. 36–58

161 *Gleaner*, 26 July 1964

162 TV documentary 'Rebel Music'

163 Author interview

164 Author interview, 18 February 2009

165 G. W. Bridges, *Annals of Jamaica*

166 Claude McKay, 'My Native Land, My Home', *Complete Poems*

167 Psalm 68:31

168 *Time* magazine, 3 November 1930

169 Cited in Robert Hill, ed., *Marcus Garvey and the Universal Negro Improve-*

ment Association Papers, Vol. 7: *November 1927–August* 1940 (Berkeley and Los Angeles: University of California Press, 1990), pp. 440–41

170 *The Times*, 3 November 1930

171 'footstools ... nations', Amy Jacques, *The Philosophy and Opinions of Marcus Garvey*, p. 77. According to Leonard Howell in *The Promised Key*, the duke (representing his father) knelt before Rastafari and proclaimed: 'Master, Master, my father is unable to come, buts said he will serve you until the end, Master.' Cited by Hélèn Lee in *The First Rasta*, p. 57

172 Robert Hill, *Marcus Garvey and the Universal Negro Improvement Association Papers*, vol. 7: *November 1927 – August* 1940, p. 441

173 Pinnacle Papers, Jamaica National Archives, Spanish Town

174 *Gleaner*, 23 November 1940

175 *Gleaner*, 14, 15,16 March 1934

176 *Jamaica Times*, 7 December 1935

177 Morris Cargill, *Jamaica Farewell*, pp. 215–216

178 Ibid, p. 19

179 The sociologist, George Eaton Simpson, conducted field work among Rastafarians in the 1950s. The gloomy prognosis for their life in Jamaica is articulated in his paper 'Some Reflections on the Rastafarian Movement in Jamaica, West Kingston in the Early 1950s', *Jamaica Journal* 25/2

180 Cited in the report by Smith, Augier, and Nettleford, *The Rastafari Movement in Kingston, Jamaica*

181 PRO.CO 1031/2768 (9 April, 1959)

182 Hélène Lee interview with Bragga for the book *See Trenchtown and Die*

183 Steffens and Pierson, interviews for *Old Fire Sticks*

184 Ansell Hart's monthly journal vol. 4 No.7, November 1960

185 Mortimo Planno, *The Earth Most Strangest Man, The Rastafarian*. pp. 19, 29

186 Smith, Augier, Nettleford, *Report on the Rastafari Movement in Kingston, Jamaica*. p. 39

187 Steffens and Pierson, interviews for *Old Fire Sticks*

188 http://www.niceup.com/interviews/donald_manning

189 Psalm 2:1–4

190 *Gleaner*, 22 April, 1966

191 Steffens and Pierson, interviews for *Old Fire Sticks*

192 *Gleaner*, 24 April 1966

193 *Gleaner*, 16 October 1993

194 From an interview with Professor Leonard Barrett, cited in Murrrell, Spencer and McFarlane, *Chanting Down Babylon*, p. 423

195 *Gleaner*, 23 April 1966, p. 23

196 Ibid, p. 28

197 Fikisha Cumbo, *Get Up, Stand Up: Diary of a Reggaephile*, p. 103

198 Murrell, Spencer and McFarlane *Chanting Down Babylon*, p. 79

199 Ibid, p.242

200 Frank Jan van Dijk, 'Sociological Means: Colonial Reactions to the Radi-
      calization of Rastafari in Jamaica, 1956–1959', *New West Indian Guide*
      69 (1995), no.1/2, Leiden, pp. 67–101

201 Steffens, *Old Fire Sticks*

202 Ibid

203 Carol Yawney, *Lions in Babylon* (unpublished dissertation), p. 273

204 Ibid, p. 279

205 Jake Homiak, *The Half That's Never Been Told*, International Rastafari
      Archives Project, 1989, p. 7

206 'The Rastafarite Cult' CO 1031/2767

207 Smith, Augier, Nettleford, *Report on the Rastafari Movement in Kingston,
      Jamaica*

208 Matthew Lewis, *Journal of a West Indian Proprietor*, 1816, p. 129

209 Yawney, *Lions in Babylon*, p. 260

210 Danny Sims interviewed by Justine Ketola, www.jahworks.org

211 Liner Notes, *Soul Almighty: the formative years*, vol.1

212 Author interview 7 July 2009

213 Steffens, *Old Fire Sticks*

214 Ibid

215 Joel Fort, 'Pot or Not', *International Journal of Psychiatry*, 9: pp. 517–521.
      See also Vera Rubin and Lambros Comitas, *Ganja in Jamaica: A Medical
      Anthropological Study of Chronic Marihuana Use*, p. 159

216 *Gleaner*, 14 June 1951, p. 6

217 Ibid

218 *Gleaner*, 13 April, 27 August 1963.

219 Morris Cargill, *Jamaica Farewell*, p. 215

220 *Gleaner*, 10 March 1968

221 Cited by Diana Paton in *No Bond But the Law*, p. 8

222 *Falmouth Post*, 4 May 1849

223 Norman Manley, *Manley and the New Jamaica*, p. 279

224 Ibid, p. 26

225 Jahworks website, www.jahworks.org

226 Author Interview

227 Yawney, *Lions in Babylon*. p. 116

228 Ibid p. 157

229 Sheila Kitzinger, 'Protest and Mysticism: the Rastafari Cult of Jamaica',
      Journal of the Scientific Study of Religion, 8:2 (1969)

230 Rubin and Comitas, *Ganja in Jamaica: A Medical Anthropological Study
      of Chronic Marihiuana Use*, p. 159

231 Reports on the assassination attempt, with the headline: 'Gunmen Shoot
      at Manley Party', *Gleaner* 13 February 1967

232 Michael Manley, *Jamaica: Struggle in the Periphery*, p. 169

233 Reverend Webster Edwards interview with Hélène Lee

234 Hélène Lee, *See Trench Town and Die*

235 Peter-I, *Trench Town Experience*

236 Bragga interview with Hélène Lee

237 *Gleaner*, 15 July 1949. For a rigorous account of the early growth of political violence on the island see Amanda Sives, 'The Historical Roots of Violence in Jamaica' in Anthony Harriott (ed.) *Understanding Crime in Jamaica*, pp. 49–61

238 Andy Gill, 'Bob Marley: Change is Gonna Come' *Mojo*, August 2002

239 Author interview, 8 July 2008

240 Peter-I *Trench Town Experience*

241 Chris May, 'Starting from Scratch', *Black Music* vol.4, issue 47, October 1977, p. 13

242 Carly Gayle, 'The Upsetter', *Black Music*, vol.2, Issue 14, January 1975, p. 10

243 Cited by John Masuori in *Wailing Blues*, p. 111

244 *New Musical Express*, 17 November 1984

245 Author interview with Donovan Phillips 01 July 2010. See also chapter 5 of David Katz's *People Funny Boy: The Genius of Lee "Scratch" Perry*

246 Steffens, *Old Fire Sticks*

247 Perry remembers the encounter taking place in the back of the Upsetter record shop. His denial appears in Katz, *People Funny Boy*, p. 131

248 *Gleaner*, 11 November 1968, pp. 1, 18

249 Russell Sackett, 'Plotting A War on Whitey', *Life* magazine, June 1966

250 Peter Tosh, 'Mamma Africa'. The song suggested that it didn't matter where you were from, whether an African at home or abroad, you were still an African. So blacks in the diaspora no matter their complexion were at heart African

251 http://www.guyanacaribbeanpolitics.com/wpa/rodney_bio.html

252 Walter Rodney, *The Groundings with My Brothers*, p. 67

253 *Gleaner*, 18 October 1968

254 Carolyn Cooper, 'Remembering the Rodney Riots', *Gleaner*, 12 October 2008

255 Steffens, *Old Fire Sticks*

256 Yawney, *Lions in Babylon*, pp. 290–291

257 Ibid, p. 18

258 Stefan Krause, 'An Afternoon with Perry Henzell', http://rastastudio.com/Perry/

259 *The Harder They Come* continued to be screened at Orson Welles Theatre near Harvard Square for the next five years.

260 Bob Marley, March 1978. Cited in Kwame Dawes, *Bob Marley: Lyrical Genius*, p. 43

261 Michael Thomas and Adrian Boot, *Babylon on a Thin Wire*

262 BBC TV, 'Arena: Bob Marley'

263 The original title of the film was *Vill sa Garantro* or *Want So Much to Believe*

264 See John 'Rabbit' Bundrick's recollection in the liner notes for *Songs of Freedom*

265 Guy Roel interviewed in www.BobMarleyMagazine.com, 29 July 2003

266 Captain Ernest Platt to Bernard Rickatson-Hatt, 18 April 1941 (extract). C.O. 137/859, file 687 14/1. Cited by K. Post, Strike the Iron, vol.1, p. 173

267 Hugh Shearer and Michael Manley would regularly hold breakfast summits in the 1970s. See *Democratic Socialism in Jamaica*, p. 88

268 *Public Opinion*, 15 October 1971

269 Thomas, *Jamaica: Babylon on a Thin Wire*

270 *Rolling Stone*, 12 October 1972

271 Andy Gill, 'Bob Marley: Change is Gonna Come', *Mojo*, August 2002

272 Jeremy Sigler interview with Perry Henzell, *Index Magazine*, 2001

273 Richard Williams, 'Island Records: Reggae to Riches', *Melody Maker*, 25 November 1972

274 Norman Mailer, 'The White Negro', *Dissent* (Fall, 1957)

275 This account is drawn from the author's interview of Blackwell on 21 February 2009

276 BBC TV, 'Arena: Bob Marley'

277 Author interview with Benjamin Foot, 5 September 2009

278 Quoted in *Wailing Blues*, p.210 and author's background interview with Donovan Phillips, 01 July 2010

279 Cited in *Wailing Blues*, p. 244

280 Alan Messer interview in http://www.bobmarleymagazine.com/archives/232 27 February 2006

281 Carl Gayle interview with Bunny Livingston, *Black Music*, October 1976, vol. 3, issue 35

282 Author interview with Esther Anderson, 4 September 2009

283 'Lovers Face a Fatal Illness in "A Warm December".' *New York Times*

284 Yawney, *Lions in Babylon*, p. 120

285 *Gleaner*, 5 September 1935

286 Donald Snowden, 'Bunny Wailer: Wailers Together Again', *Los Angeles Times*, 20 April 1986

287 BBC TV, 'Bob Marley: Arena'

288 Vivien Goldman 'Reggae: Black Punks On "Erb"', *Sounds*, 16 October 1976

289 Michael Manley, *The Politics of Change*, pp. 46, 47

290 *Flair* magazine, 28 October 1986

291 *High Times* magazine

292 Carol S. Holzberg., 'Race, Ethnicity and the Political Economy of National Entrepreneurial Elites in Jamaica', dissertation, Boston University 1974-75

293 *Gleaner*, 18 July 1975

294 *Gleaner*, 2 January 1976

295 *Gleaner*, 16 July 1975

296 *Gleaner*, 18 July 1975

297 Hector Wynter was editor-in-chief at the *Gleaner*, 1976–85. He served as the Minister in the JLP government from 1967–72 and also acted as JLP chairman 1970–72

298 An overview of the dispute over the sacking of Michael Batts is given by David D'Costa, 'Was Pontius Pilate a Conscious Pilot?' *Gleaner*, 8 August 1977. For the growth of Rastafari among the middle classes in Jamaica see Frank Jan van Dijk, *Jahmaica: Rastafari and Jamaican Society 1930–1990*, pp. 222–290

299 Carol Yawney, *Lions in Babylon*, p. 271

300 Michael Manley, *Jamaica: Struggle in the Periphery*, 'Appendix Destabilisation Diary, pp. 223–237

301 BBC TV, 'Under Heavy Manners'

302 The former CIA agent, Philip Agee, was sent to Jamaica by the Human Rights Council to conduct investigations into his suspicions of CIA involvement in the destabilisation of Jamaica. Agee subsequently produced and published a list of eleven operatives at large in the country. His suspicions are spelt out in his memoir, *On the Run,* pp. 253–256.

303 *Gleaner*, 6 June 1976

304 Neville Graham interviewed by Hélène Lee for *See Kingston and Die*

305 *Gleaner*, 20 March 1974

306 Manley was quoted in the *Virgin Islands Daily News*, 24 May 1974

307 In *Jamaica: Struggle in the Periphery*, Michael Manley cites the killing of the Peruvian Ambassador as the trigger for the declaration of a state of emergency, p. 141

308 'This Morning I woke up in a curfew. . .' the opening lyrics to 'Burnin' and Lootin'

309 Manley's speech was reported in the *Gleaner*, 30 August 1976

310 Erna Brodber 'A Study of Yards in the City of Kingston', Institute of Social and Economic Research, University of the West Indies, Jamaica 1974, p. 34

311 Vivien Goldman, 'Bunny Wailer: Reincarnated Soul Makes Year's Best Album', *Sounds*, 16 October 1976

312 *Mojo*, October 2009

313 Steffens, *Old Fire Sticks*

314 Vivien Goldman, 'Bunny Wailer: Reincarnated Soul Makes Year's Best Album' *Sounds*, 16 October 1976

315 PNP MP Francis Tulloch is cited in *Babylon on a Thin Wire* as making the suggestion of a possible exemption of Rastas from prosecution for smoking marijuana. See also Henderson Dalrymple, *Bob Marley: Music, Myth*, p. 64

316 *Gleaner*, 9 May 1975

317 Katz, *Solid Foundation*, pp. 242–243

318   Peter-I, *Trench Town Experience*

319   *Gleaner*, 21 September 1979 and 23 November 1979

320   *Gleaner*, 3 November 1976. As expectations grew for the concert, it was eventually agreed that it should relocate to a bigger stage at National Heroes Park

321   Judy Mowatt of the I-Threes (backing singers for Bob Marley and the Wailers) claims she had a dream involving a rooster (Marley) and three chickens (the I-Threes). In the dream someone shot the rooster. Garrick is quoted by Vivien Goldman in 'Dread, Beat and Blood', *Observer*, 16 July 2006

322   *Gleaner*, 9 December 1976

323   D9 THC. Tetrahydrocannabinol is the psychoactive component of cannabis

324   Goldman, 'Peter Tosh: The Bush Doctor's Dilemma', *Melody Maker*, 9 December 1978

325   Sheila Kitzinger, 'The Rastafari Cult'

326   Red X tapes

327   Goldman, 'Bob Marley In His Own Backyard', *Melody Maker*, 11 August 1979

328   'Steppin' Razor', Red X

329   'Steppin' Razor', Red X

330   Carl Wint, 'Indiscipline at Large', *Gleaner*, 22 September 1987

331   *Gleaner*, 14 September 1987. In an article titled: 'Who will be Next?' the paper's columnist drew attention to a spate of killing of musicians on the island

332   BBC TV, 'Arena: Caribbean Nights: Bob Marley', 15 June 1986

BIBLIOGRAPHY

Books and Selected Journals

Archer-Straw, Petrine and Robinson, Kim, *Jamaican Art: An Overview – With a Focus on Fifty Artists*. Kingston Publishers Ltd, 1990

Auden, W. H., *Look Stranger*. Faber, 1935

Barclay, Alexander, *A Practical View of the Present State of Slavery in the West Indies*. London: Smith, Elder & Co, 1826

Barrow, Stephen and Dalton, Peter, *The Rough Guide to Reggae: The Definitive Guide to Jamaican Music, from Ska through Roots to Ragga*. Rough Guides, 2001

Beckwith, Martha: *Black Roadways: A Study of Jamaican Folk Life*. Chapel Hill, 1929

Bilby, Kenneth, *True-Born Maroons*. University Press of Florida, 2005

Boot, Adrian and Salewicz, Chris, *Bob Marley: Songs of Freedom*. Bloomsbury, 1995

Bradley, Lloyd, *Bass Culture: When Reggae was King*. Viking, 2000

Brodber, Erna, *A Study of Yards in the City of Kingston, Jamaica*. Institute of Social and Economic Research, University of the West Indies, Jamaica. 1975

Chevannes, Barry, *Jamaican Lower Class Religion, Struggles Against Oppression*. PhD Dissertation. University of the West Indies (Mona), 1971

Chevannes, Barry, *Rastafari: Roots and Ideology*. Syracuse University Press, 1994

Clarke, Edith, *My Mother who Fathered Me: A Study of the Family in three Selected Communities in Jamaica*. Allen & Unwin, 1957

Cumbo, Fikisha, *Get Up, Stand Up: Diary of a Reggaephile*. Cace Intl Inc, 2003

Davis, Stephen, *Bob Marley: Conquering Lion of Reggae*. Plexus, 1994

Davis, Stephen and Simon, Peter, *Reggae Bloodline: In Search of the Music and Culture of Jamaica*. Heinemann Educational Books Ltd, 1977

Davis, Stephen and Simon, Peter, *Reggae International: In Search of the Music and Culture of Jamaica*. Heinemann Educational Books Ltd, 1977

Dawes, Kwame, *Bob Marley: Lyrical Genius*. Bobcat Books, 2002

Dijk Frank Jan van, *Jahmaica: Rastafari and Jamaican Society 1930–1990*. Utrecht: Isor, 1993

Harriott, Anthony (editor), *Understanding Crime in Jamaica: New Challenges for Public Policy*. Kingston: University of the West Indies Press

Hebdige, Dick, *Cut 'n' Mix: Culture, Identity and Caribbean Music*. Comedia, 1987

Henke, James, *Marley Legend: An Illustrated Life of Bob Marley*. Simon & Schuster, 2006

Holzberg, Carol S., *Race, Ethnicity and the Political Economy of National Entrepreneurial Elites in Jamaica*. PhD Dissertation. Boston University 1974–75

Homiak, John Paul, *The 'Ancient of Days' Seated Black: Eldership, Oral Tradition, and Ritual in Rastafari Culture*. PhD Dissertation: Brandeis University, 1985

Iton, Richard, *In Search of the Black Fantastic: Politics and Popular Culture in the Post-Civil Rights Era*. New York: Oxford University Press, 2008

Katz, David, *People Funny Boy: The Genius of Lee Scratch Perry*. Omnibus Press, 2006

Katz, David, *Solid Foundation: An Oral History of Reggae*. Bloomsbury, 2003

Lacey, Terry, *Violence and Politics in Jamaica, 1960–1970: Internal Security in a Developing Country*. Manchester University Press, 1977

Lee, Hélène, *The First Rasta: Leonard Howell and the Rise of Rastafarianism*. Lawrence Hill Books, 2003

Lee, Hélène, *See Trench Town and Die*. Flammarion, 2004

Levy, Horace (comp), *They Cry 'Respect!': Urban Violence and Poverty in Jamaica*. Kingston, Jamaica: Centre for Population, Community and Social Change, Dept. of Sociology and Social Work, University of the West Indies, Mona, 2001

Lewis, Matthew, *Journal of a West Indian Proprietor: kept during a residence in the island of Jamaica*. J.Murray, 1834

Long, Edward, *The History of Jamaica*. London: Frank Cass, 1970

MacMillan, William Miller, *Warning from the West Indies*. London: Faber & Faber, 1936

Mais, Roger, *Brother Man*. MacMillan Caribbean, 2004

Manley, Michael, *Jamaica: Struggle in the Periphery*. Third World Media Ltd in association with Writers and Readers Publishing Co-operative Society, 1982

Manley, Michael, *The Politics of Change: A Jamaican Testament*, André Deutsch, 1974

Marley, Rita and Jones, Hettie, *No Woman, No Cry: My Life with Bob Marley*. Sidgwick & Jackson, 2004

Masouri, John, *Wailing Blues: The Story of Bob Marley's Wailers*. Omnibus Press, 2008

Maxwell, William J. (editor), *Complete Poems, Claude McKay*. Urbana: University of Illinois Press, 2004

Murrell, Nathaniel, Spencer, William and McFarlane, Adrian (editors), *Chanting Down Babylon: The Rastafarian Reader*. Philadelphia: Temple University Press, 1998

Naipaul, V. S., *The Middle Passage*. André Deutsch, 1962

Nettleford, Rex, *Mirror, Mirror: Race and Protest in Jamaica*. Kingston: William Collins & Sangster, 1970

Nettleford, Rex (editor), *Norman Washington Manley and the New Jamaica*. Trinidad: Longman Caribbean, 1971

Patterson, Orlando, *The Sociology of Slavery*. MacGibbon & Kee, 1967

Patterson, Orlando, *The Children of Sisyphus*. Harlow: Longman, 1982, c. 1964

Phillippo, James Mursell, *Jamaica: Its Past and Present State*. [S.I.]: Dawsons, 1969

Post, Ken, *Arise Ye Starvelings: The Jamaican Labour Rebellion of 1938 and its Aftermath*. Martinus Nijhoff, 1978

Ranston, Jackie, *The Lindo Legacy*. Toucan Books, 2000

Ranston, Jackie, *From We Were Boys: The Story of the Magnificent Cousins*. Bustamante Institute of Public and International Affairs, 1989

Rubin, Vera and Comitas, Lambros, *Ganja in Jamaica: A Medical*

Anthropological Study of Chronic Marihuana Use. The Hague, Paris: Mouton & Co, Publisher, 1975

Senior, Olive, *Encyclopaedia of Jamaican Heritage*. Kingston: Twin Guinep Publishers Ltd, 2003

Smith, Michael, Augier, Roy and Nettleford, Rex, *Report on the Rastafari Movement in Kingston, Jamaica*. Institute of Social and Economic Research, 1960

Steffens, Roger and Pierson, Leroy Jodie, *Bob Marley and the Wailers: The Definitive Discography*. LMH Publishing Ltd, 2005:

Steffens, Roger and Pierson, Leroy Jodie, *Old Fire Sticks* – Notes for an unpublished MSS biography of Bunny Wailer

Steffens, Roger and Simon, Peter, *Reggae Scrapbook*. Insight Editions, 2007

Stephens, Evelyne Huber and Stephens, John D., *Democratic Socialism in Jamaica*. MaCMillan, 1986

Thomas, Herbert. T, *The Story of the West Indian Policeman*

Thomas, Michael and Boot, Adrian, *Jamaica: Babylon on a Thin Wire*. Thames and Hudson, 1976

White, Timothy, *Catch a Fire: The Life of Bob Marley*. London: Corgi Books, 1983

Williams, Joseph J, *Psychic Phenomena of Jamaica*. New York, The Dial Press, 1934

Williamson, Karina (editor), *Marly; or, A Planter's Life in Jamaica*. Macmillan Caribbean, 2002

Yawney, Carol, *Lions in Babylon* – Unpublished PhD Dissertation

ACKNOWLEDGEMENTS

Give thanks to Sonia Grant for another great job researching the book, and to her able assistants Ethlyn Grant and Robert Donald. Respect to Jo Alderson for her close reading of all the many versions of the manuscript and her shrewd suggestions for improvements; and to the posse, Jasmine, Maya and Toby, for their love of the subject. Lurane Grant deserves marks for her spirit and cheerleading.

The Natural Mystics could not have been written without the generosity and shared knowledge of Roger Steffens and our groundings in the basement in LA. Other key protagonists in the story of the making of this book include Hélène Lee, Donovan Philips, Jake Homiak, Harald Hammarström, John 'Rabbit' Bundrick, Wayne Jobson, Kevin Conroy Scott and Marika Lysandrou.

Bunny Wailer proved a great inspiration throughout the writing as did the editors Dan Franklin and Tom Mayer. Ellah Allfrey and Vanessa Mobley were early and treasured enthusiasts for *The Natural Mystics*. Tom Avery at Jonathan Cape has been a champion at seeing the book through to publication. Thanks to John Freeman and Ollie Brock for the early shout out at *Granta*.

Arise Viv Adams for his continued provocations; Maggie Gee, Nick Rankin, Judith Stein, Jay Mukoro, Emma Dyer and Dan Shepherd for their reasonings.

Peace and love to Trevor Rhone, Mariamne Samad, Edward Seaga, Chris Blackwell, Esther Anderson, Theodore H. MacDonald and all the musicians, writers, readers and the team at Jonathan Cape who gave me their time and encouraged this work to completion.

LIST OF IMAGES

Trench Town (UrbanImage.tv/Adrian Boot)

Marcus Garvey (UrbanImage.tv/Ron Vester)

Alexander Bustamente (www.jamaicalabourparty.com/base/facts-achieve
ments)

The Mystic Revelation of Rastafari (UrbanImage.tv/Adrian Boot)

Negro Aroused (Copyright © Larry Schwarz)

Livingston, Marley and Tosh as the Teenagers (UrbanImage.tv/Adrian
Boot)

The Teenagers with Rita Marley (UrbanImage.tv/Adrian Boot)

Bob Marley and Coxsone Dodd. Downtown Kingston, Jamaica. Original
colour transparency. 1964. (Esther Anderson, Corbis Images)

Vere Johns presides over the talent contest show 'Opportunity Hour'

Don 'Cosmic Don' Drummond (UrbanImage.tv Collection)

Joe Higgs (UrbanImage.tv/Tim Barrow)

Leslie Kong

Lee 'Scratch' Perry (UrbanImage.tv/Adrian Boot)

Chris Blackwell (UrbanImage.tv/Adrian Boot)

Emperor Haile Selassie and Mortimo Planno (Michael Ochs Archives/
Getty Images)

Mortimo Planno

The Wailers in relaxed mode (UrbanImage.tv/Trax on Wax/Ossie
Hamilton)

The 'Old Grey Whistle Test', 1973 (Copyright © Alan Messer/Rex
Features)

The Wailers (from left to right: Wire Lindo, Aston Barrett, Bob Marley,

Peter Tosh, Carlton Barrett, Bunny Livingston). Chelsea, London. Original black and white negative. 1973. A cropped colourised version of this shot appears on the rear cover of *Catch a Fire* (re-release 1974) and full version on the original release of the 45 rpm single of 'Get up Stand up', 1973.

Peter Tosh goes solo with *Equal Rights* (UrbanImage.tv/Adrian Boot)

Peter Tosh and Mick Jagger (UrbanImage.tv/Adrian Boot)

Bunny Wailer (UrbanImage.tv/Rico D'Rozario)

The gates of Bunny Wailer's property (UrbanImage.tv/Adrian Boot)

Bob Marley and Band members are joined on stage at the One Love Peace Concert in 1978 (Echoes/Redferns Collection/Getty Images)

The Natural Mystics. Bob Marley, Hellshire Beach, Jamaica. Original colour transparency. 1973. Bunny Livingston. Downtown Kingston. Jamaica. 1973.

INDEX

Beckwith, Martha 68

Bedward, Alexander 72–3, 122

Beecher-Stowe, Harriet, *Uncle Tom's Cabin* 45, 237

Bellevue asylum 73, 76, 78, 122

Belmont, Westmoreland parish 19–20, 21

'Bend Down Low' (song) 140

Bennett, Louise 116

Berry, Chuck, 'My Ding-a-ling' 200

Best of the Wailers (album) 190–91

'Better Must Come' (song) 199

Beverly Records 58

Bible 188–9, 209, 210

Big Junior 86, 87

Black Panthers 150, 213

Black Power movement 165, 180–81, 183, 185, 203

Blackheart Man (album) 236, 237, 238, 246

Blackwell, Blanche 240, 241

Blackwell, Chris: background, childhood and education 7, 29–30, 204, 240, 241; beginnings of music career 56–7, 203–4; establishes Island Records in London 58–9, 91, 117; success of 'My Boy Lollipop' 91, 206, 207; signing of the Wailers 201–2, 205–7; increasing focus on Marley 222–4, 226; disputes with Tosh 223–4, 225; and break-up of original Wailers 225–6; solo contract with Bunny Wailer 237; solo contract with Bob Marley 240

Blair, Bishop Herro 173

Blue Beat (record label) 59

Bond, James (fictional character): films 86; novels 34, 36–7, 38, 89

Booker, Cedella *see* Marley, Cedella

Boston 192

Boys Town club, Kingston 44–5

'Bragga' (Trench Town amateur historian) 173

Braithwaite, Junior 62

Bridges, G. W. 71, 117

British Museum 205

Brixton Academy 270

Brodber, Erna 235

Brother D (faith healer) 80–82

Brown, Marlene 261

Brown, Wilton 'Doc' 262

Brubeck, Dave 55

Buckley, Vernon 242

Bull Bay 213–14

Bundrick, John 'Rabbit' 195, 196, 205, 280

'Burial' (song) 153

Burnin (album) 221

'Burnin' and Lootin' (song) 233, 281

Burru people 55–6, 62

Bushay, Clarice 29

'Bust Dem Shut' (song) 168

Bustamante, Sir Alexander 5, 15–16, 116, 173, 197, 217, 272

Buster, Prince 61, 182

Buzzbee 90

calypso 30–31

Campbell, Uriah 19–20, 21

cannabis *see* ganja